Revelation for Today

All Scripture quotations are from the King James Version of the Holy Bible.

Printed in the United States of America

Revelation for Today

Dr. N. W. Hutchings

Table of Contents

Foreword

As I tentatively sit down before my trusty 1952 Royal typewriter, I wonder why on earth I am punishing myself by attempting to write an exposition on the Apocalypse. There are at least a thousand acceptable volumes by qualified authors on this book of the Bible. Dr. John Walvoord, Dr. Tim LaHaye, Dr. M. R. DeHaan, Dr. J. R. Seiss, and Dr. Ed Hindson are just a few I could mention. I have already written some one hundred books and thousands of dissertations. And having passed my eightieth birthday this past Wednesday, I am sure that I would find more pleasure in a fishing excursion on Lake Eufaula or a good eighteen holes at Lincoln East Golf Course.

Verse three of chapter one does promise a blessing to those who read the Revelation, but nothing is said about a blessing to those who try to write a book on the Revelation. So, you really want to know why I am writing this book? Simply, because almost everyone I know says I should. Although I feel like Peter must have felt when he was commanded to eat from the sheet filled with forbidden food (slightly rebellious), with confidence I believe that God will be in this humble effort, and the Holy Spirit will reveal to me some truths about this marvelous book that others have not discovered.

Although some of our pre-Millennial and pre-Tribulation friends may not agree with me, I interpret the judgments of Revelation to be mostly literal. What if you were on the Isle of Patmos two thousand years ago, and you were shown visions of modern warfare: jet planes dropping bombs; nuclear missiles destroying nations; tanks, and men dressed in military garb wearing gas masks using flame throwers; modern artillery bringing devastation to cities. How would you describe such scenes with A.D. 96 technology and knowledge? Assyria brought judgment to Israel with a superior army using swords, spears, war chariots, and other implements of war. When God brought judgment against Judah, the Babylonian army invaded with superior weapons of war. Therefore, it is reasonable to assume that the judgments of the Tribulation are nationally and internationally generated. To relegate all the prophetic signs of coming judgments mentioned in the Old Testament, Matthew 24, and other scripture passages to just the seven-year Tribulation is an eschatology cop-out. In this study of Revelation we will show that:

1. Earthquakes are increasing
2. Wars and rumors of wars are increasing
3. AIDS is the greatest pandemic disease ever
4. The days of Noah are here again
5. The days of Lot are here again
6. The Roman Empire is here again
7. Man now has the power to destroy the earth

We read in the Bible about the keys that will unlock the hidden mysteries of God:

1. The key of the house of David
2. The key to the bottomless pit
3. The key of knowledge
4. The keys to the Kingdom of Heaven
5. The keys of death and hell

Daniel has been a sealed book, because many of the prophetic truths of this book of the Bible have had a historical fulfillment. Likewise, many of the truths of Revelation have been locked in symbolic or allegorical language; only in our time are we able to find the keys to open the literal fulfillment of these prophecies to us. Of course, to open a lock you must have the right key. The problem with many books on the Revelation is that the authors have attempted to open the locks with the wrong keys.

In the foreword, we are going to take the first three keys to open truths concerning what the book is about and why Christians should be joyful in studying the book, even though we are informed that in the future Tribulation, millions are going to die.

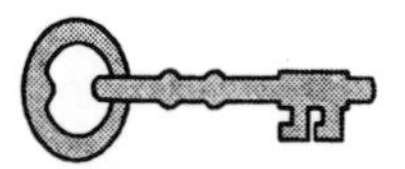

Key #1: The Theme of Revelation

> Behold, he cometh with clouds; and every eye shall see him, and they also which pierced him: and all kindreds of the earth shall wail because of him. Even so, Amen.
>
> —Revelation 1:7

The Revelation is about the Second Coming of Jesus Christ to this earth. The Second Coming was not at Pentecost when 120 of the disciples met after the ascension of Jesus; nor is it when an unsaved person is born again by faith in Him, as some preterists declare. As we are told in the first chapter of Acts, Jesus left from Mount Olivet and He will return to Mount Olivet.

When this happens, as Zechariah foretold, the Mount of Olives will split in the middle. So far, the Mount of Olives has not split in the middle because the literal return of Jesus is still future.

> And the nations were angry, and thy wrath is come, and the time of the dead, that they should be judged, and that thou shouldest give reward unto thy servants the prophets, and to the saints, and them that fear thy name, small and great; **and shouldest destroy them which destroy the earth.**
>
> —Revelation 11:18

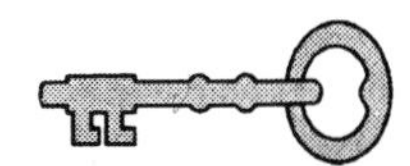

Key #2: God's Purpose for the Second Coming

If Jesus Christ is not coming back to bring in His Kingdom from Heaven, then all the promises made to Israel and the prophets in the Old Testament, as well as the promise of thrones in the Millennium to the apostles, would never be fulfilled. This would make God a liar, which is unthinkable.

Just as importantly in our study of Revelation is that if there were no Tribulation period, which will be terminated with the Second Coming of Jesus, then man himself would destroy the earth. For the first time in the six thousand years of the history of mankind, man has within his power the ability to destroy the earth. This fact in itself proves that the Second Coming of Jesus Christ is near, even at the doors.

The true story of the Revelation is that Jesus Christ is not coming back to destroy the earth, but to save the earth from destruction. He is today that **Blessed Hope** referenced in Titus 2:13, because without the return of Jesus Christ, this world today would have no hope. If the Christian will keep this basic truth in mind while studying the book of Revelation, then we both will be blessed as promised in verse three of the first chapter.

The Prophecies of Revelation

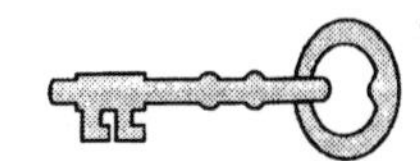

Key #3: Revelation Chronology

Six is the number of man (Rev. 13:18). Man was created on the sixth day of creation (Gen. 1:26). Revelation is the sixty-sixth and last book in the Bible. Revelation is God's message concerning the end of man's day, and the beginning of the Lord's Day.

Iranaeus (A.D. 180), Cyprian (A.D. 250), and other early Christian theologians proposed that God had assigned man six thousand years to prove himself worthy of his own freewill existence; and then God has determined to send Jesus back at the beginning of the seven thousand years, or the seventh day (one day is with the Lord as a thousand years [Ps. 90; 2 Peter 3]), to save the world from man's rebellion.

The theme of Revelation is presented in verse seven of the first chapter: "Behold, he cometh with clouds; and every eye shall see him, and they also which pierced him: and all kindreds of the earth shall wail because of him. Even so, Amen."

As noted previously, the book of Revelation is about the Second Coming of Jesus Christ. The human recorder, the Author, and the reason for the book are revealed in the first three verses:

> The Revelation of Jesus Christ, which God gave unto him, to shew unto his servants things which must shortly come to pass; and he sent and signified it by his angel unto his servant John: Who bare record of the word of God, and of the testimony of Jesus Christ, and of all things that he saw. Blessed is he that readeth, and they that hear the words of this prophecy, and keep those things which are written therein: for the time is at hand.
>
> —Revelation 1:1–3

Author. Jesus Christ is the Author of this book. An angel was the messenger, and the apostle John is the recorder. Preterist theologians (those who contend all Bible prophecy was fulfilled by A.D. 70) say that another John wrote the book, or that its authorship is spurious. This supposed change is to depreciate the divine inspiration of the entire book. They point to the difference in language of grace and love in John's four books in the Bible, to the harsh, judgmental language of Revelation. The difference is that Revelation is not about the dispensation of grace and the Church age, but rather about the "Day of the Lord" which follows the translation of all Christians (1 Thess. 4:13–18). Preterists also contend that the book was written in A.D. 62 instead of A.D. 96. This date would place the prophecies within the time of the destruction of Jerusalem and the temple rather than at the end of the Church age. They also claim that John could not have lived until A.D. 96, yet Jesus indicated that John would live longer than any other of the apostles (John 21:22). Also, Justin Martyr (A.D. 100–165) was executed by Rome at the age of sixty-five. Origen lived to be seventy years of age, and Polycarp lived to be eighty-seven years of age. The apostle John was probably ten years younger than Jesus; therefore, he would have been about eighty-five when he received the Revelation in A.D. 96. It is obvious that men and women in that time lived just as long, or perhaps even longer, than we do today. The claim by some is that the Revelation is so allegorical that no one can understand it, but consider what the early church leaders had to say about this book of the Bible:

Justin Martyr (A.D. 160): "There was a certain man with us, whose name was John, one of the apostles of Christ, who prophesied by a revelation that was made to him."

Iranaeus (A.D. 180): ". . . John in the Apocalypse, indicated to the Lord's disciples what will happen in **the last times. . . .**"

Dionysius (A.D. 262): "I regard it [Apocalypse] as containing a kind of hidden and wonderful intelligence on the various subjects that come under it. Although I cannot comprehend it, I still believe that there is some deeper sense underlying the word. . . . I do not abruptly reject what I do not understand. Rather, I am much more filled with wonder at it."

Eusebius (A.D. 270–340): "With regard to the inspiration of the book [Apocalypse], we deem it unnecessary to add another word. For the blessed Gregory Theologus and Cyril, and even men of still older date—Papias, Iranaeus, Methodius, and Hypolytus—bore entirely satisfactory testimony to it."

Eusebius also wrote that the apostle John returned from Patmos to Ephesus after the death of Emperor Domitian. Domitian killed his nephew Clemens and banished his wife for being Christians. Domitian was assassinated on September 18, 96 A.D. Persecution of Christians eased, and John was released shortly thereafter.

We could reference many other early church ministers and theologians concerning the authorship, date, inspiration, and prophetic chronology of the Revelation.

As we relate in our book, *God: The Master Mathematician,* the Bible is perhaps the most numerically constructed book in the world. In the first forty-three books of the Bible, the Old Testament and the four gospels, a literal messianic Kingdom on earth is presented, and every item or people are numbered, even the soldiers who died in battle. Jesus proclaimed to Israel, "Repent: the kingdom of heaven is at hand."

In the four gospels we find 12 disciples, 70 witnesses, 1,600 furlongs, 153 fish, 6 water pots, 5 porches, etc.

The early church fathers taught that the biblical patterns of numerics—consistently carried through the Kingdom promise books from Genesis to Revelation, by forty writers over a period of sixteen hundred years, even though some did not have preceding books—proved that only a higher intelligence could have directed them. After Israel crucified the Messiah, numbering stopped; however, the Kingdom offer was left open on a conditional or tentative basis—**if Israel will repent and call out to God to send Jesus back, He will come back** (Acts 3:13–21). In this conditional Kingdom promise period under the preaching of Peter, James, and John, there was only approximate numbering—"about an hundred and twenty" (Acts 1:15); "about three thousand souls" (Acts 2:41), etc. In the epistles to the churches, all numbering disappears because only God knows who is really saved by faith in Jesus Christ. However, when we get to Revelation everything is again numbered: seven churches, four beasts, seven vials, seven seals, seven trumpets, 144,000 witnesses, twenty-four elders, and even the exact dimensions of the New Jerusalem are given, etc. This is supporting evidence that the church will not be in that period of desolation that is described in the Bible as the coming "Great Tribulation," the time of judgment prophesied in the Revelation.

The prophet Daniel wrote that at the time God would deliver His people (Israel) and fulfill His covenant promises would be a "time of trouble, such as never was since there was a nation" (Dan. 12:1). Jesus said, "When ye therefore shall see the abomination of desolation, spoken of by Daniel the prophet . . . then shall be great tribulation, such as was not since the beginning of the world to this time, no, nor ever shall be" (Matt. 24:15,21).

The judgments against Israel in the destruction of Jerusalem and the temple was only against this one nation. The judgments of the Great Tribulation will affect every nation. This is what most of this book of prophecy is about.

How long will the Tribulation period be? In the ninth chapter of Daniel we find the prophet praying to God about information concerning the length of time until God would fulfill His covenants to Israel. Daniel was told that it would come at the end of seventy weeks. The weeks were Jewish weeks of years, not days, or a period of 490 years, starting from a decree to rebuild and restore Jerusalem by the Persian king. At the end of the sixty-ninth week, the Messiah would be cut off, but not for Himself. Artaxerxes signed the decree to rebuild and restore Jerusalem in 455 B.C. Four hundred and eighty-three years later (Jewish year was 360 days), Jesus Christ was crucified, not for his own sins, but for the sins of others. When Jesus Christ was crucified, a breach was made between God and Israel, symbolized by the curtain to the Holy of Holies splitting in the temple when Jesus was nailed to the cross (Isa. 30:26; Matt. 27:51). One of the seventy prophetic weeks, or seven years, remains to be fulfilled. According to Daniel 9:27, the clock on the remaining seven years will start when a man who will be the Antichrist signs an agreement guaranteeing the security of Israel. There have already been more than fifty resolutions and treaties relative to the security of Israel since 1948, but **the treaty or agreement** that will start the Tribulation has not been signed as yet. This treaty evidently will permit the rebuilding of the temple on Mount Moriah and the resumption of Jewish sacrificial worship. However, we read that in the middle of the week (after three and one-half years) the Antichrist will stop the sacrifice, declare himself to be God, and two-thirds of the Jews in the land of Israel will be killed; one-third will escape to wait for the Messiah. We believe this place of safety for the Jewish remnant is to be Petra in southern Jordan (Matt. 24:15–21).

According to Daniel 12:7, the Jewish remnant will be scattered for a time, times, and one-half time. A time in Israel was from one Passover to the next, or one year, or a total of three and one-half years, which will be the last half of the Tribulation period. Israel is described in Revelation 12 as a woman with a crown of twelve stars who will be kept by God in the Tribulation for 1,260 days, or three and one-half years, or forty-two Jewish months of thirty days each (Rev. 12:1–8). The time is also given in Revelation 12:14 as a time, times, and one-half time—again three and one-half years. Jesus indicated in Matthew 24:22 that if the Tribulation was longer than seven years, no person on earth would be left alive.

In reference to the end of the age we read in Daniel 9:26, ". . . and the end thereof shall be with a flood, and unto the end of the war desolations are determined."

God promised He would not destroy the world again with water, so the flood in this context means a great rushing of events. The word "shortly" is used a second time in Revelation to mean that when things begin to happen, they will be done quickly (Rev. 22:6). The rapid development of modern science and mechanics fit into the end-time prophetic picture; in just the last one hundred years things like the radio, television, automobile, airplane, nuclear weapons, and biological dangers have appeared.

"I was in the Spirit on the Lord's day, and heard behind me a great voice, as of a trumpet" (Rev. 1:10).

The most common interpretation of this verse is that the apostle John was worshipping on Sunday, the first day of the week. In our opinion, Sunday is no more the Lord's day than a church building is the Lord's house. There was only one physical Lord's house, and that was the temple in Jerusalem. Today, the Christian's body is the Lord's house (1 Cor. 3:16–17). Saturday, the seventh day of the week, represented to Israel the seventh millennium (Heb. 4:1–11), the Lord's Day which was to begin with the Great Tribulation. There are hundreds of scriptures which tell us what the Lord's Day is, and will be. John was transported by the Holy Spirit into the Day of the Lord and was shown what would come to pass in the last days. The trumpet behind him that John heard is probably the trump of God that will call the church (all Christians, dead or alive) out of the world (1 Cor. 15:15–58; 1 Thess. 4:13–18) before the Tribulation begins.

In Revelation 1:7, the apostle John announced, "Behold, he cometh with clouds. . . ." In verses twelve through sixteen, the apostle describes the awesome appearance of Jesus Christ as He will come a second time, not as a lamb to be slain for the sins of the world, but as a conquering Messiah to destroy those who would destroy the world, and then bring in His Kingdom on earth from Heaven.

John, accompanied by James and Peter, had previously seen Jesus Christ as He would come a second time, on the Mount of Transfiguration (Matt. 17:1–13). Peter recounted this miracle in his second epistle, chapter one, verses sixteen through eighteen:

> For we have not followed cunningly devised fables, when we made known unto you the power and coming of our Lord Jesus Christ, but were eye-

> witnesses of his majesty. For he received from God the Father honour and glory, when there came such a voice to him from the excellent glory, This is my beloved Son, in whom I am well pleased. And this voice which came from heaven we heard, when we were with him in the holy mount.

Peter protested the charge that the Second Coming of Jesus Christ was a story which the apostles had made up. Peter knew that Jesus would return to earth as the conquering Messiah because three apostles saw Him change before their eyes into the form He would appear. The heavenly King is the Jesus that John was shown again in chapter one of the Apocalypse.

Peter continued in chapter one of his second epistle to confirm that he actually saw the Lord as He would come again, but he indicated that those who did not believe him could know from the fulfilling of end-time prophetic events according to the "sure word of prophecy" (v. 19).

The message of the Revelation was by Jesus Christ, sent by an angel to John the apostle, to commit to the seven churches of Asia Minor. The seven churches were types of the churches today that are responsible to teach the book of Revelation to their memberships.

We pray that this outline study on the Revelation will help the reader to better understand this book of prophecy and be better prepared for the Lord's coming.

Chapter One

Angels

We notice first that this is a book of "Revelation." Revelation is translated from the Greek *apokalupsis,* which means to reveal or uncover. Jesus said in Matthew 10:26, ". . . there is nothing covered, that shall not be revealed; and hid, that shall not be known."

The book of Revelation fulfills this particular prophecy of Jesus. The revealing of the Antichrist prophesied by Paul in 2 Thessalonians 2:3–6 is presented in Revelation 13. The things that are to be revealed in the "last time" spoken of by Peter in the first chapter of his first epistle are uncovered in the Revelation. We could reference every prophecy relating to the last days and find their uncovering in the Revelation.

This is the Revelation of Jesus Christ, because He is the "spirit of prophecy" (Rev. 19:10). Through a continuing sequence of visions, oral expositions, and angelic promptings, Jesus reveals to John the consummation of the eternal plan and purpose of God. Seven times in the first chapter Jesus is proclaimed to be the Alpha and Omega, the First and the Last, the Ever Living One who knows all things from the beginning to the end. The entire Revelation was signified to John by an angel. Signify in the Greek means to make manifest, or make known thoroughly, or completely. In other words, John was taken by an angelic guide through the events of the seven-year Tribulation.

The things shown to John **must** come shortly. The Greek word for shortly is *en Tachei,* meaning speedily. Seven times this warning is given in Revelation (Rev. 1:1, 2:16, 3:11, 11:14, 22:7, 22:12, and 22:20).

A blessing is promised to those who read the Revelation, or hear it read, with the contingency that the receiver heed, or consider seriously, the intended message. The "blessing" promised also has a chronological contingency—the **time** is at hand. What time? The "time" noted by Daniel: ". . . there shall be a **time** of trouble, such as never was since there was a nation even to that same **time** . . ." (Dan. 12:1). Also the **time** noted by

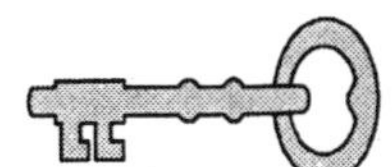

Key #4: Follow the Angels

The Revelation of Jesus Christ, which God gave unto him, to shew unto his servants things which must shortly come to pass; and he sent and signified it by his angel unto his servant John: Who bare record of the word of God, and of the testimony of Jesus Christ, and of all things that he saw.

—Revelation 1:1–2

Blessed is he that readeth, and they that hear the words of this prophecy, and keep those things which are written therein: for the time is at hand.

—Revelation 1:3

Jesus Christ: "For then shall be great tribulation, such as was not since the beginning of the world to this **time,** no, nor ever shall be" (Matt. 24:21).

It is apparent that the blessing is particularly meant for those living in the last days just before the Tribulation breaks upon the world. As Jesus prophesied, today the masses are extremely fearful of those things coming upon the earth, but Christians can be blessed (happy) to know that Jesus will destroy those who have both the means and the will to destroy it (Rev. 11:18).

Again, notice the mathematical perfection of this book as we consider the seven blessings of Revelation:

1. Blessed is he that readeth (Rev. 1:3).
2. Blessed are the dead which die in the Lord (Rev. 14:13).
3. Blessed is he that watcheth (Rev. 16:15).
4. Blessed are they which are called unto the marriage supper (Rev. 19:9).
5. Blessed . . . is he that hath part in the first resurrection (Rev. 20:6).
6. Blessed are they that do his commandments (Rev. 22:14).

John to the seven churches which are in Asia: Grace be unto you, and peace, from him which is, and which was, and which is to come; and from the seven Spirits which are before his throne; And from Jesus Christ, who is the faithful witness, and the first begotten of the dead, and the prince of the kings of the earth. Unto him that loved us, and washed us from our sins in his own blood, And hath made us kings and priests unto God and his Father; to him be glory and dominion for ever and ever. Amen.

—Revelation 1:4–6

The Revelation is from Jesus Christ, signified to John by an angelic guide, and sent by scroll to the seven congregations in Asia Minor. These churches are later identified in verse eleven. I have personally traveled to these seven cities several times. Asia Minor (Turkey) today is 99.8 percent Muslim. Any Christian identity today is only on an individual or visitor-club basis. But the importance of verse four is to emphasize that this book is for the memberships of all churches regardless of national identity or doctrine. At one time, I accepted the traditional explanation that the seven churches represented seven historical church ages. I have now come to believe that these seven church types represent seven churches in these last days.

In verse four we are also confronted with seven spirits before the throne of God. Angels are also referred to as spirits in Scripture, and we read in Revelation 8:2, "And I saw the seven angels which stood before God; and to them were given seven trumpets." It seems to me the seven spirits of Revelation 1:4 and the seven angels of Revelation 8:2 are the same. When the seven angels have sounded all seven trumpets of judgment, then Jesus Christ will have returned and brought in the Kingdom from Heaven on the earth.

In verse four we also notice that John salutes the churches with grace and peace. Grace is unmerited or unearned favor; peace is an experiential relationship with God through the gift of grace. E. W. Bullinger in his book *Number in Scripture* (p. 135), said of grace:

> Grace means favor. But what kind of favor? For favor is of many kinds. Favor shown to the miserable we call mercy; favor shown to the poor we call pity; favor shown to the suffering we call compassion; favor shown to the obstinate we call patience; but favor shown to the unworthy we call GRACE! This is favor indeed; favor which is truly Divine in its source and in its character.

In the Old Testament, the Hebrew word *chen* is interpreted grace thirty-eight times, and most of the scriptures in which it is found refer to grace by rulers, or others, to the poor, the suffering, and the miserable. In the four gospels, the Greek word *charis* is interpreted grace only four times, because the gospel of the Kingdom was in effect as a promise to Israel. In Acts where we see the gospel of the Kingdom offered on a conditional basis to Israel, grace is found in ten scriptures. But when Paul was given the gospel of grace to offer salvation to the Gentiles who were without a covenant, a law, a promise, a Sabbath, a temple, or a sacrifice, we find grace mentioned in his epistles to the churches ninety-six times. This is indeed Good News: unearned, unmerited salvation by faith in Christ's blood that eliminates, eradicates, abolishes every sin. Because Jesus Christ died for all who confess Him as their Savior and Lord, He is now their faithful witness before the throne of God. We, who are members of Christ's true church, will reign with Him in heavenly places forever (Eph. 3:8–10). Christians shall indeed boldly go where no man has gone before, not as paupers or beggars, but as priests and kings.

Jesus Christ ascended to Heaven in a cloud, and He will come back in the clouds. This vision that John was shown is the same as Daniel saw: "I saw in the night visions, and, behold, one like the Son of man came with the clouds of heaven . . ." (Dan. 7:13). Even the verb "behold," describing a scene unfolding before their eyes, is used by both Daniel and John.

Behold, he cometh with clouds; and every eye shall see him, and they also which pierced him: and all kindreds of the earth shall wail because of him. Even so, Amen. I am Alpha and Omega, the beginning and the ending, saith the Lord, which is, and which was, and which is to come, the Almighty.

Revelation 1:7–8

There are words for different types of clouds in the Hebrew used in the Old Testament, just as there are words for different types of clouds in the Greek found in the New Testament. There are Hebrew and Greek words for rain clouds, storm clouds, huge clouds, small clouds, thick clouds, objects in the sky that look clouds, etc. According to *Young's Concordance,* the Greek word for cloud from which Moses and Elijah joined Jesus on the Mount of Transfiguration is *nephele*—a small or thin cloud, the same Greek word for cloud used in Revelation 1:7. Obviously, if Moses and Elijah descended on the mountain in this type of cloud, and Jesus is coming in this kind of cloud, it is a moving cloud, or clouds. Isaiah described the Second Coming of Jesus Christ thusly: "For, behold, the LORD will come with fire, and with his chariots like a whirlwind, to render his anger with fury, and his rebuke with flames of fire" (Isa. 66:15).

Notice that Isaiah used the verb "behold," like Daniel and John, an action of visual observation. Elijah was taken into Heaven by a chariot of fire (2 Kings 2:11). The question often considered by many today is whether there is a connection between UFO reports and the chariots of angels referenced in the Bible. I offer no definitive conclusion myself, but simply submit the information for the readers' consideration.

We should notice that when Jesus comes back to the earth, "every eye shall see him, and they [Israel] also which pierced him." John beheld in a vision the fulfillment of Jesus' prophecy in Matthew 24:30, "And then shall appear the sign of the Son of man in heaven: and then shall all the tribes of the earth mourn, and they shall see the Son of man coming in the clouds of heaven with power and great glory."

It appears to us that the translation of Christians to meet Jesus in the air is a separate event that will occur just before the Tribulation. Nothing is said by Paul in 1 Corinthians 15 or 2 Thessalonians 4 about "every eye seeing Jesus." The translation of Christians, dead or alive at Christ's coming in the air, is not observed by the unsaved world mass. We will consider the two different aspects of the Lord's coming when we get to Revelation 4. We understand that many believe that Christians will endure three and one-half years, or more, of the Tribulation period. My only response is that if some are determined to go through the judgments of this greatest time of trouble the world will ever see, that is okay with me. I personally believe, according to the Bible, if I should live until the Lord comes, I will be out of here before the Tribulation begins.

It is of particular interest that John mentions that Israel will see Jesus as He comes in power and great glory. Jesus said to Israel in Matthew 23:39, ". . . Ye shall not see me henceforth, till ye shall say, Blessed is he that cometh in the name of the Lord."

Peter and John also preached to Israel, "Repent ye therefore, and be converted, that your sins may be blotted out, when the times of refreshing [the Kingdom age] shall come from the presence of the Lord; And he shall send Jesus Christ, which before was preached unto you" (Acts 3:19–20). After the Jews have gone through the Tribulation, and after two-thirds in the land have been killed (Zech. 13:8), "... they shall look upon me whom they have pierced, and they shall mourn for him, as one mourneth for his only son..." (Zech. 12:10).

It will take the Tribulation period to get Christ-rejecting Israel to accept Him as their Messiah. Having been to Israel some forty-five times or more, I can understand why it will take the Tribulation to bring this to pass. For two thousand years the Jews have said, "We will not have this man rule over us."

When will Jesus come back literally to save the world and fulfill God's promise to Israel? When Israel repents of killing their Messiah, accepts Him as their sacrificial Lamb who shed His blood for them, and then cries out to God to send Him back. "And so all Israel shall be saved: as it is written, There shall come out of Sion the Deliverer, and shall turn away ungodliness from Jacob: For this is my covenant unto them, when I shall take away their sins" (Rom. 11:26–27).

John identifies himself with all Christians within the Roman Empire that suffered persecution, even after Nero was expelled and committed suicide in A.D. 68. After Vespasian and Titus, Domitian ruled and he attempted to eliminate Christians who remained alive.

Tertullian (A.D. 197) wrote: "Rome . . . is where the apostle John was first plunged into boiling oil, but was unhurt. He was then banished to his island of exile."

Clement of Alexandria (A.D. 195) wrote: "Listen to a tale, which is not a tale but a narrative, handed down . . . about the apostle John. On the Tyrant's [Domitian] death, John returned to Ephesus from the isle of Patmos . . . there he set in order whole churches. . . ."

Victorinus (A.D. 280) wrote: "When John said these things [the Revelation] he was on the island of Patmos, condemned by Caesar Domitian to labor in the mines. Therefore, it was there that he saw the Apocalypse . . . eventually Domitian was killed and all his judgments were thrown out. . . . John later delivered this same Apocalypse that he had received from God. . . ."

I John, who also am your brother, and companion in tribulation, and in the kingdom and patience of Jesus Christ, was in the isle that is called Patmos, for the word of God, and for the testimony of Jesus Christ. I was in the Spirit on the Lord's day, and heard behind me a great voice, as of a trumpet, Saying, I am Alpha and Omega, the first and the last: and, What thou seest, write in a book, and send it unto the seven churches which are in Asia; unto Ephesus, and unto Smyrna, and unto Pergamos, and unto Thyatira, and unto Sardis, and unto Philadelphia, and unto Laodicea.

—Revelation 1:9–11

From Stephen to Justin Martyr to the present time, Christians have been persecuted and suffered intense periods of tribulation. Our ministry in the 1940s and 1950s maintained mission stations in the Sudan where Christians today are killed and sold into slavery. We have been to Russia and China many times and learned of the millions of Christians killed or imprisoned during the reigns of tyrannical Communist despots. But the greatest era of persecution and tribulation is yet to come—the Great Tribulation, that may be very near, even as we write.

The island of Patmos where John was sentenced to hard labor in the Roman-operated mines is approximately fifty miles due west of Ephesus. We have led Christian Bible tours to Patmos several times. The total surface would be only about ten square miles. It is mountainous; a part of the Greek island chain. A charming Greek village rings the harbor. The one cave on the island is traditionally where John received the Apocalypse. This is doubtful, as probably a Roman army officer or political official would have claimed it.

In verse ten John makes note that he was in the Spirit on the Lord's day. Some of our good pastor brethren like to interpret this to mean that John was in his Sunday-go-to-meeting clothes, sitting on the front row, in church on Sunday morning. But where in the Bible is Sunday, the first day of the week, referred to as the "Lord's day." I would not be surprised if some do not have John giving tithe from his meager slave wages. Christians should support their church, if it is a good church, with their service and offering. But John being in church on Sunday morning has no relationship to the Apocalypse. What is meant by John is that he was transferred by the Holy Spirit into the future, into the Day of the Lord, the Tribulation period, that will rage on earth for seven years. In the Revelation, John records what he sees in the language of A.D. 96.

Dr. John Walvoord in his book on Revelation states,

> There is no solid evidence . . . that the expression used by John was ever intended to refer to the first day of the week. It is rather a reference to the day of the Lord of the Old Testament, an extended period of time in which God deals in judgment and sovereign rule over the earth.

John also notes that as he was found in the Day of the Lord, he heard a great voice behind him that sounded like a trumpet. This voice that John heard is probably the voice calling the church out of the world:

> For the Lord himself shall descend from heaven with a shout, with the voice of the archangel, and with the trump of God: and the dead in Christ shall rise first: Then we which are alive and remain shall be caught up together with them in the clouds, to meet the Lord in the air: and so shall we ever be with the Lord.
>
> —1 Thessalonians 4:16–17

The fact that John heard this great voice behind him would indicate that, in the spirit, the apostle had passed through the Church age (the dispensation of grace), and he was now in the Day of the Lord. As this change occurred, John was commanded to write what he heard and saw and send the script to the seven churches. If, as we believe, the seven churches represent the seven types of churches that would exist just prior to the Day of the Lord, then that would be even more reason for pastors today to teach the Apocalypse to their congregations.

And I turned to see the voice that spake with me. And being turned, I saw seven golden candlesticks; And in the midst of the seven candlesticks one like unto the Son of man, clothed with a garment down to the foot, and girt about the paps with a golden girdle. His head and his hairs were white like wool, as white as snow; and his eyes were as a flame of fire.

—Revelation 1:12–14

When an individual has an experience that has made an impact on their life, they will recount even the smallest detail. The fact that John remembered that he turned his head in the direction where the voice came from adds validity to his story.

The first thing that the apostle saw was the seven candlesticks, which we are informed represented the seven churches of Asia. The church is commissioned to be the light of the world in presenting Jesus Christ to those who walk in darkness.

The person that John saw shining through the candlesticks is described by him as follows:

And his feet like unto fine brass, as if they burned in a furnace; and his voice as the sound of many waters. And he had in his right hand seven stars: and out of his mouth went a sharp two-edged sword: and his countenance was as the sun shineth in his strength. And when I saw him, I fell at his feet as dead. And he laid his right hand upon me, saying unto me, Fear not; I am the first and the last: I am he that liveth, and was dead; and, behold, I am alive for evermore, Amen; and have the keys of hell and of death.
—Revelation 1:15–18

1. Hair like white wool—the ageless I AM.
2. Eyes like flames of fire—nothing is hid from Him.
3. Feet like burned and polished bronze—the Judge of every man or woman.
4. Voice like a great waterfall—calls to all nations to obey the gospel.
5. A high priest's girdle (Exod. 28:8)—the only Mediator between God and man.
6. Sharp sword in His mouth—He is coming back to destroy those who destroy the earth.
7. His face shines like the sun—manifestation of His glory.

The description of the risen Lord as He will come back in all power and glory is also given in Daniel and other books in the Old Testament. John had also seen Jesus as He would come back on the Mount of Transfiguration (Matt. 17:1–3; 2 Pet. 1:16–18).

As occurred on the Mount of Transfiguration, John falls down, hides his face, and doesn't move. In this human body no one can stand before Jesus Christ in His risen glory. All of us, even the so-called best of us, fall short of the glory and righteousness of our Lord Jesus Christ. None of us are worthy to stand in His presence. That Jesus Christ died for us, took our judgment upon Himself, and cleansed our filthy sins in His own blood, magnifies the depth of God's grace.

God informs us that all born of Adam are sinners; the soul that sins will die; and it is appointed to all men to die. As John looks upon the risen and glorified Lord, he realizes that he is worthy of death. However, Jesus in effect says, "Don't you fear John, trust Me. I have the keys to death and hell." "O death, where is thy sting? O grave, where is thy victory? . . . But thanks be to God, which giveth us the victory through our Lord Jesus Christ" (1 Cor. 15:55,57).

Some contend that all the prophecies of Revelation were fulfilled at the destruction of Jerusalem and the temple in A.D. 70. Some contend that Revelation has a historic fulfillment: seventeen chapters have been fulfilled and five chapters are yet future. Therefore, let us consider the instructions that Jesus gave John that resulted in the writing of Revelation, and why we have this book.

Write the things which thou hast seen, and the things which are, and the things which shall be hereafter; The mystery of the seven stars which thou sawest in my right hand, and the seven golden candlesticks. The seven stars are the angels of the seven churches: and the seven candlesticks which thou sawest are the seven churches.
Revelation 1:19–20

The first commandment was to "write the things which thou hast seen." Jesus is not asking John to write about his past. In verse two of chapter one, it is noted that John had already written his gospel. John does not go back and write about the birth of Jesus, or the ministry of Jesus, or His trial, crucifixion, and resurrection. He had already written that. No one can with credibility find anything in Revelation that happened before A.D. 96. We read again from verse three of chapter one: "Blessed is he that readeth, and they that hear the words of this prophecy.... " The entire book is prophecy—future! Even the messages to the churches present their doctrinal and spiritual status at the time of the Rapture.

I once had a good friend, Dr. C. E. McLain, who placed the churches in chapters two and three in the Tribulation. He believed the Rapture would occur before the Tribulation, but he thought there would be a great Christian revival in Turkey after the Rapture. He was close to the truth, but missed it by a few months.

By instructing John to write the things he had seen, the things which are, and the things that would be hereafter, the apostle was simply being told to record the events he had witnessed that applied to the Tribulation, then the thousand-year reign of Christ, the Great White Throne Judgment, and the New Heaven and the New Earth.

The letters to the churches are parenthetical, relating primarily, as we believe, to the period immediately preceding the Rapture depicted in chapter four.

We have no problem with the seven candlesticks representing the seven churches of chapters two and three. However, when we come to the seven stars representing the seven angels of the seven churches, we do have a problem. Most commentaries on Revelation make the seven angels to be pastors of the seven churches, but men or women are never said to be stars. Stars are frequently used to reference angels (Job 38:7; Rev. 12:4–9, etc.).

In the Old Testament, the Hebrew word for messenger is *malak*, which means a messenger. When the text or content indicates the messenger is from God, *malak* is interpreted as "angel." When the text or context indicates the messenger is a man or woman, *malak* is rendered messenger or some other human identification. In the New Testament, the Greek word for messenger is *aggelo*, and the rule for interpreting this word is the same as used in the Old Testament for *malak*.

In the Old Testament there are at least one hundred illustrations of angelic activity and intervention while the promised Kingdom of Heaven on earth was waiting for the coming Messiah. When Jesus Christ the Messiah was born, there was also angelic activity. Even at Jesus' resurrection there was an angel at the tomb. In the book of Acts, angelic activity continued on a limited basis, because through Peter, the apostle to the circumcision, the Kingdom was offered on the conditional basis that Israel repent of killing the Messiah and cry out to God to send Him back (Acts 3:12–21). In Acts 12 we see Peter being freed from prison by angelic intervention, but in Acts 16 Paul is delivered from prison by an earthquake. Paul was advised by an angel in Acts 27 that he would go to Rome, but there was no active angelic intervention.

With the new birth, which places the Christian into a new relationship with God, there is the indwelling of the Holy Spirit. Christians are advised to seek the filling and leading of the Holy Spirit. Nowhere in the epistles to the churches are Christians advised or encouraged to seek help, or even to communicate, with angels. A personal guardian angel is not an entitlement. Of course, in Revelation, angelic activity is multiplied above even that which occurred as recorded in the Gospels. And, as we approach in time the Tribulation period with the "spirit of iniquity" spreading over the earth, angelic activity may increase, especially demonic activity.

As far as the "angels" of the churches in Revelation 2 and 3 are concerned, there remains a question as to whether they are angels of God or pastors. Inasmuch as John was to deliver to each "angel" a script copy of Revelation, we go along with the majority opinion that they are pastors and not angels of God, as we would assume that angels in Heaven would not require a hard copy.

Chapter Two

Letters to the Churches of West Asia

It is assumed that after John was released from exile on Patmos that he returned to Asia Minor (Turkey) with copies of the Revelation to deliver to the seven churches. He would have landed at Ephesus, fifty miles to the northeast of Patmos on the coast. However, Ephesus is no longer on the coast today, as the small river valley has filled up with silt and sand, and the excavations at the location of the old city are now three miles from the coast. I remember on one Bible tour staying overnight at Izmir (Smyrna) with my group. There was a storm during the night, and the next morning in going to the airport to fly to Istanbul, we discovered that a side of a mountain had collapsed burying some one hundred tourists on the highway. Unable to get to the airport, we had to drive all night by bus to get to our next stop. Earthquakes are also common to this area, so the geography of the area has changed considerably since John traveled in this area.

But as John left Patmos with copies of the Revelation for the seven churches, he would have landed at Ephesus, then next to Smyrna thirty miles to the north, then to Pergamos forty miles farther north, then eastward to Thyatira, then southeast to Sardis, then fifteen miles southeast to Philadelphia, then fifty miles still farther southeast to Laodicea. I have traveled this road several times, and observed that John addressed the seven churches in the order he would have come to them. Tourists visiting Turkey for the first time are awed by the beauty of the land—long mountain ranges graced between with lush meadows and fields.

The reader should keep in mind that the Revelation was not addressed to the church at Jerusalem or the churches of Greece and Macedonia. It was in the area of Ephesus to Laodicea that the Gentile church age began. It was also here that the candlestick of each church mentioned in Revelation was removed for reasons given in the letters. If these letters were not meant for churches in these last days, then there would be no reason for them to be in the Apocalypse at all.

Letter to the Church at Ephesus

From the excavations of Ephesus, we know the city was quite large and beautiful. It is estimated the population was one-quarter million. Although in the Roman Empire, Ephesus was granted a free status. The Temple of Diana was located on a high hill about one mile to the north of the city. The temple is noted as being one of the seven wonders of the ancient world.

Paul visited the city in A.D. 55. There was already at least one Christian congregation in the city. Paul created a controversy over the worship of idols, and he later referred to being put into the arena with wild beasts at the theatre. In A.D. 35 when Paul went up to Jerusalem after he returned from Arabia, he saw Peter and James, but nothing is said of John. John may have already gone to Asia. Many of the places in the Ephesus area are named after John. However, Paul does not mention seeing John at Ephesus in his epistles, and neither does Luke mention John being there in Acts. John was to take care of Mary, and according to tradition, John took her to Ephesus. There is a beautiful mountain park to the east of Ephesus where tradition claims Mary lived. I was once also shown a supposed tomb of Mary between Ephesus and the remains of the Church of St. John on the site where the Temple of Diana stood. The church was built in the fourth century by the Byzantines. Some of the walls are still standing, the grave of St. John is marked, and the baptistry in the shape of a cross remains in excellent condition. The sites are maintained for tourism, because as we have noted, Turkey today is 99.8 percent Muslim.

When Paul passed by Ephesus on his way back to Israel in A.D. 58, he met with the elders of the church. He warned them to beware of ravening wolves, enemies from without who would try to destroy the church, and from deceitful and perverse teachers who would try to split the congregation for their own selfish reasons (Acts 20). Thirty-eight years later, Jesus Christ gives John a letter for the church. Let us see how the church had fared since Paul was last there:

Commendations

1. The church remained a working church, faithful in attendance and support.
2. They had heeded Paul's warning against false teachers and apostles.

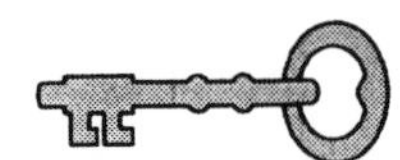

Key #5: The Love-Lost Church

Unto the angel of the church of Ephesus write; These things saith he that holdeth the seven stars in his right hand, who walketh in the midst of the seven golden candlesticks; I know thy works, and thy labour, and thy patience, and how thou canst not bear them which are evil: and thou hast tried them which say they are apostles, and are not, and hast found them liars: And hast borne, and hast patience, and for my name's sake hast laboured, and hast not fainted. Nevertheless I have somewhat against thee, because thou hast left thy first love. Remember therefore from whence thou art fallen, and repent, and do the first works; or else I will come unto thee quickly, and will remove thy candlestick out of his place, except thou repent. But this thou hast, that thou hatest the deeds of the Nicolaitanes, which I also hate. He that hath an ear, let him hear what the Spirit saith unto the churches; To him that overcometh will I give to eat of the tree of life, which is in the midst of the paradise of God.

—Revelation 2:1-7

Good doctrinal foundations were kept.

3. They hated the deed of the Nicolaitanes. According to Iranaeus (A.D. 180), Tertullian (A.D. 197), and Hippolytus (A.D. 225), the Nicolaitanes were followers of the teachings of Nicholas, one of the seven deacons, a Gentile proselyte, chosen by the church at Jerusalem in Acts 6. Nicholas used his church position to engage in gluttony and sex. Others interpret Nicolaitanes to be church bureaucrats, as *nikao* means to conquer and *laos* means the people. There may be no contradiction, as in present segments of the Catholic Church priests and other Catholic officials use their high positions to engage in homosexual and other types of sinful activities. Five hundred years ago Martin Luther tried to get Pope Leo to clean up the clergy and reform the church, but nothing was done. Jesus commended the church at Ephesus for not tolerating deeds like the Nicolaitanes were committing in other churches.

Problems

The church had left its first love. The story is told of John and Mabel Jones driving from their farm to the local county market in their pickup. John was driving and Mabel was sitting across the seat next to the door. As the pickup bumped over the railroad track, Mabel says, "John, do you remember forty years ago when we first drove over this road to our new farm? I was sitting next to you, and you had your right arm around me. But look at us now; it seems we never get that close anymore." John looks at Mabel and replied, "Well, I haven't moved." When the love between man and wife grows cold, although they still may respect each other and maintain a home, one or the other often looks for love elsewhere. The marriage is in serious trouble. Because of cold formality in the major churches, many are trying to find that new love in spiritual experiences: tongues, healings, shakings, laughing, or even worldly activities. As at Ephesus, the church at large has a serious problem. O! to recapture that sweet love for Jesus and the brethren that thrilled our souls when we were first saved. ". . . Thou shalt love the Lord thy God with all thy heart, and with all thy soul, and with all thy mind" (Matt. 22:37).

Warning

Repent, or there will be no church at Ephesus.

Promise

To those who overcome in the church, they will be rewarded with eternal life. "Who is he that overcometh the world, but he that believeth that Jesus is the Son of God?" (1 John 5:5).

Letter to the Church at Smyrna

Smyrna was a city in Asia (Turkey) on the Aegean seacoast fifty miles north of Ephesus. The church was another one of the seven over which John, by tradition, served as bishop. John is thought to have left Jerusalem for Asia between A.D. 40 and 45.

The word for Smyrna in the Greek is often interpreted to mean "bitter," which would be identification with the persecutions of the church in that city. However, smyrna and myrrh are the same thing. The oil of myrrh (ladanum) was used in anointing priests and for the purification of women. It was a pungent perfume from a small tree that was used also in embalming the dead. Ladanum, used extensively to deaden pain before other painkillers were perfected, was offered to Jesus in wine (Mark 15:23). The unrefined myrrh could have had a bitter taste.

Unlike the remains of the Church of St. John at Ephesus, there is no such identification of any former Christian presence in Smyrna. Probably due to the many battles that raged over the city for the past two thousand years, only the walls and a few pillars from an old stadium are in evidence.

After John received the letter from Jesus for the church at Smyrna, persecution did indeed arise. Polycarp was the bishop over the church at Smyrna when the Roman games were held in the city in A.D. 156. Eleven Christians were killed in the stadium to the delight of the crowd. Then Polycarp was arrested and brought into the stadium. The Roman proconsul, Statius Quadratus, attempted to get Polycarp to save his life by denying Jesus Christ as his Lord and Savior. According to Eusebius, Polycarp replied: "Eighty and six years I have served him and He has done me no ill; how then can I blaspheme my King who hath served me?" The crowd screamed for his death, and Polycarp was subsequently burned at the stake in the stadium. The pillars of the stadium where Polycarp was martyred still stand today.

The reference to ten days of coming persecution could have been fulfilled in A.D. 156. It is quite possible that the Roman athletic contests at Smyrna lasted ten days. The anti-Christian mindset of the spectators, and possibly contestants as well, could have increased the frenzy of mob psychology. It is also quite likely this reference may foretell a period of Christian persecution in the future.

Commendation

1. Faithfulness to God and their Christian testimony in spite of extreme persecution and poverty.
2. Not intimidated by the Jews who incited the citizens of the city to kill the members of the church and not give Christians employment.
3. Fearing God more than men.

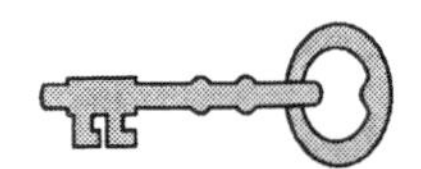

Key #6: Martyrdom

And unto the angel of the church in Smyrna write; These things saith the first and the last, which was dead, and is alive; I know thy works, and tribulation, and poverty, (but thou art rich) and I know the blasphemy of them which say they are Jews, and are not, but are the synagogue of Satan. Fear none of those things which thou shalt suffer: behold, the devil shall cast some of you into prison, that ye may be tried; and ye shall have tribulation ten days: be thou faithful unto death, and I will give thee a crown of life. He that hath an ear, let him hear what the Spirit saith unto the churches; He that overcometh shall not be hurt of the second death.

—Revelation 2:8–11

Problems

All the problems were from outside against the church; no problems within the church.

Warning

Be faithful unto death.

Promises

1. Those in the church at Smyrna who overcome, though they suffer martyrdom, will not be hurt by the second death, eternal separation from God in hell. ". . . In the world ye shall have tribulation: but be of good cheer; **I have overcome the world"** (John 16:33).
2. Those who give their life for their faith in Jesus Christ will receive a special reward, the "crown of life."

There is some confusion about the reference to Jews of the synagogue of Satan. As noted, the instigators of early Christian persecution were often the Jews who rejected Jesus Christ as Savior and Lord. Although today, premillennial Christians support Israel. We keep in mind, of course, that probably no more than one percent of all Israelis today accept Jesus Christ as the Messiah; two-thirds are actually agnostics or atheists. This is what the prophetic Word also says. Two-thirds of the Jews in Israel will die in the Tribulation—not by God but by Israel's enemies. This is not being anti-Jewish, because at least two-thirds of the Gentile world will also die. God, not the government of Israel, determines who is a Jew: "For he is not a Jew, which is one outwardly. . . . But he is a Jew, which is one inwardly . . ." (Rom. 2:28–29). Paul was a Jew; Jesus was a Jew; the first eight thousand Christians were Jews. God has a plan for Israel, and Jesus Christ will yet rule this world from Mount Zion. Every Christian should pray for the peace of Jerusalem, and we know that only Jesus will bring this peace. When we pray for Jerusalem, we are praying for the soon return of our Lord.

The letter to the church at Smyrna has even a greater message for the churches today. For every Christian that was killed at Smyrna, thousands or millions have been martyred in our generation. After 1989 when the Soviet Union imploded, I led missions to Russia. The firsthand accounts of the millions of Christians killed by that nation's atheistic, Communist government between 1917 and 1989 were heartrending. While sailing through the Moscow-Volga Canal, approximately eighty miles long, our guide informed us that eighty thousand Christians died building that canal. I have been to China many times, and every citizen of that country I have talked with had some Christian member of their family killed during the so-called Cultural Revolution by the Red Guard. Owning a Bible or attending a church meant death. Our ministry has assisted mission stations in Sudan, and Christians in Sudan, as well as other Islamic nations, are killed, persecuted, or sold into slavery. We Christians in America have no concept what it means to really suffer for Jesus Christ, but that day may come. If it does, remember the warning and promise of Jesus in this letter: be faithful unto death, and you will receive a crown of life.

The Letter to the Church at Pergamos

Approximately fifty miles north of Smyrna, and also near the coast of the Aegean Sea, was the city of Pergamos. *Aegean* in Greek means "goat." Alexander the Great was nicknamed "the goat," and he is presented as a goat in Daniel 8. In 333 B.C. when Alexander crossed over into Asia in pursuit of his goal to defeat the Persians and conquer the world, he passed by Pergamos without an attempt to conquer the city. Having been to Pergamos I can understand why. The city was built on the top of a high, steep, peaked mountain. Alexander remarked: "I will not waste my army trying to capture that eagle's nest." The marble remains of that once beautiful, mountaintop metropolis are magnificent to behold. After Alexander died, a town was settled on the Selinus River and named Bergama. The old city on top of the mountain was eventually abandoned. One of the historic buildings in Bergama with a church history is the Red Basilica, built in the second century by the Romans. It was at one time used as a church dedicated to St. John. We have already noted that many sites in that part of Turkey continue to have an identity with the apostle John.

One of the landmarks of Pergamos was its theater carved in the side of the steep mountain with seventy-eight rows. During Greek and Roman times, every city of any size had a theater, a sports stadium, and a chariot racetrack. But Pergamos had something else that no other city of that day had: **the first sanitarium for mentally ill citizens!** The hospital (*asklepium*) was at the foot of the mountain where the doctors could avail themselves of water. There were excellent dormitory facilities, but much of the hospital was underground. Patients were also put in underground facilities, joined by tunnels. It was cool and quiet in these subterranean quarters, and water would continually drip down from the ceiling, adding to the patient's tranquility, so the doctors thought. Above, there was a library and a theater where comedy plays would be presented for the patients. Attendants would observe the patients at both the library and the theater to see if they were giving attention or perhaps smiling or laughing. We have walked through the Pergamos hospital, including the underground section, and the traditional medical serpent sign is on pillars that are still standing.

Roman soldiers used the short, two-edged sword. It was more effective

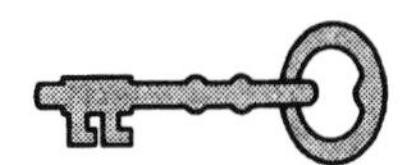

Key #7: Satan's Seat

And to the angel of the church in Pergamos write; These things saith he which hath the sharp sword with two edges; I know thy works, and where thou dwellest, even where Satan's seat is: and thou holdest fast my name, and hast not denied my faith, even in those days wherein Antipas was my faithful martyr, who was slain among you, where Satan dwelleth. But I have a few things against thee, because thou hast there them that hold the doctrine of Balaam, who taught Balac to cast a stumblingblock before the children of Israel, to eat things sacrificed unto idols, and to commit fornication. So hast thou also them that hold the doctrine of the Nicolaitanes, which thing I hate. Repent; or else I will come unto thee quickly, and will fight against them with the sword of my mouth. He that hath an ear, let him hear what the Spirit saith unto the churches; To him that overcometh will I give to eat of the hidden manna, and will give him a white stone, and in the stone a new name written, which no man knoweth saving he that receiveth it.

—Revelation 2:12-17

in close fighting than the longer sword. This weapon was the symbol of Roman power. Pergamos in about 133 B.C. became the center of Roman political and military authority in Asia. In the introduction of the letter to the church at Pergamos, the pastor and membership are reminded that it is Jesus Christ who still maintains the ultimate power over the nations (Dan. 4:17). There are seven scriptures in the New Testament which assure Christians today that Jesus Christ has the two-edged sword of the Spirit that will ultimately decide the future course of human history at Armageddon. No matter how threatening world conditions may be, the future is in His hands. As the Zocor television ad says, "Be there!" Any man or woman can be by receiving Jesus Christ as Lord and Savior.

Commendations

1. The membership of the church at Pergamos evidently maintained some good works. They were also faithful not to deny Jesus Christ as Lord, even though they witnessed and presented a testimony where Satan's seat was. Satan's seat could refer to Roman authority centered at Pergamos, or to the altar of Zeus located near the top of the Pergamos' Acropolis. Zeus is the Greek god that corresponds with Satan in the Bible. He, according to Greek mythology, was the father of all gods. Human sacrifices were offered on the altar of Zeus. The Zeus' altar at Pergamos was taken by the Germans, when Germany was an ally of Turkey in World War I, and moved to the Pergamum Museum in Berlin. Also, in the same museum is the upper structure of the Ishtar Gate of Babylon, along with many other artifacts.
2. Some were faithful until death. Some may have been sacrificed on the altar of Zeus. Of special note is Antipas. Dr. Ed Hindson in his book, *Revelation: Unlocking the Future,* states that according to tradition, Gaius (3 John 1) was the first bishop of the Pergamos church, and Antipas succeeded him. However, this is difficult to correlate from other sources. *Antipas* means "against all," or "standing alone." This references to us the millions of Christian martyrs of these last days in Russia, China, India, Pakistan, Saudi Arabia, and other Islamic nations.

Problems

1. Eating things sacrificed to idols. Paul indicated in his epistles that eating meat sacrificed to idols was really nothing; however, if it was a stumbling block to others, and especially to Jews, Christians should not do it. It would seem that this may have included compromising with keeping idols in the home. Catholic churches today are also guilty of this unscriptural practice—mixing paganism with worship of Jesus Christ.
2. The church allowed Nicolaitanes in the church to commit fornication,

and teach others to do likewise through example. We have noted the practice of these church bureaucrats previously, who follow the sins of Balaam and Balak.

Warning

Get rid of the idols and worldly church teachers and leaders, or Jesus Christ Himself would destroy the church. It is interesting that most of the worldly churches of Europe have only a few present at each service. It is also difficult for many pastors today to preach against sin, because such sins mentioned being prevalent at Pergamos are just as evident today in most churches.

Promise

1. The overcomers in the Pergamos church, as well as all true Christians today who are saved by faith in Jesus Christ in spite of their church, will be fed with hidden manna, the spiritual food of those who inherit eternal life: "They shall hunger no more . . . For the Lamb which is in the midst of the throne shall feed them . . ." (Rev. 7:16–17; see also John 21:16; 1 Pet. 5:2; Acts 20:28).
2. The saved in the Pergamos church will also receive a new name on a white stone. On Mars Hill, near the top of the Acropolis, a court would be held at night when the judges could not even see the faces of the defendant or the witnesses. Only the evidence could be considered. If the one charged was thought guilty, the judges would put a black stone on the table; if not guilty, a white stone would be placed. Like Saul, who changed his name so as not to be identified as a terrible sinner, Christians will receive a new name at the Judgment Seat of Christ. They will be known by a name known only to the Lord.

Letter to the Church at Thyatira

Thyatira, according to historical notes, was probably established as a supply station by Alexander the Great in about 330 B.C. After Alexander died, one of his generals, Seleucus, who had been given one-fourth of the kingdom, saw the potential of the area and, according to Josephus, moved Jews into the village. Seleucus understood that the Jews were good at developing business enterprises.

The town subsequently grew and trade guilds multiplied: coppersmiths, bronze workers, tanners, leather workers, dyers, workers in making clothing, potters, bakers, and even slave traders. Women were granted equal opportunity in the town and some became quite prominent in business, politics, and even theology. Lydia, a sales person from Thyatira, whom Paul baptized in a river near Philippi, was probably a Jewess. Paul explained that the Messiah had come. God opened her heart to the truth, and Lydia was

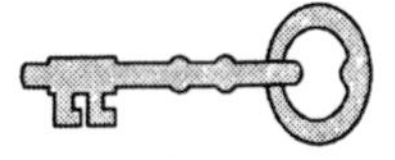

Key #8: Jezebel's Bed

And unto the angel of the church in Thyatira write; These things saith the Son of God, who hath his eyes like unto a flame of fire, and his feet are like fine brass; I know thy works, and charity, and service, and faith, and thy patience, and thy works; and the last to be more than the first. Notwithstanding I have a few things against thee, because thou sufferest that woman Jezebel, which calleth herself a prophetess, to teach and to seduce my servants to commit fornication, and to eat things sacrificed unto idols.

—Revelation 2:18–20

born again a child of God by faith in Jesus Christ. The baptism of Lydia was in a small river near the present ruins of Philippi. A Greek Orthodox church now stands on the spot where the old Roman road crosses this swift stream. It is interesting that much of the finest leather goods sold in America comes from Akhisar, the present name of Thyatira. Expensive Turkish carpets are also made in this area by hand on looms hundreds of years old.

In the introduction in verse eighteen, Jesus Christ is presented to the church as ". . . the Son of God, who hath his eyes like unto a flame of fire, and his feet are like fine brass." Apollo was worshipped by the pagans of the town as the son of Zeus, the chief Grecian deity. Jesus is not the only son of God, He is the only **begotten** Son of God. Fiery eyes and feet of brass speak of judgment.

Commendation

The members of the church were active in service. They gave to the poor; they professed salvation through faith; they did not become discouraged in service; and they had works and they had works (mentioned twice). Works were foremost in their worship.

Problems

1. The members evidently bought meat at the market that had been sacrificed to idols. There were many pagan temples in Thyatira. At the Jerusalem conference in Acts 15, Peter and James instructed Paul that Gentile Christians were not to be associated with idols, commit fornication, or purposely do anything to offend Jewish believers. Paul in Romans, Colossians, and Galatians said that Christians should not be judged for the kind of meat they ate; but he also indicated in 1 Corinthians 8 not to eat meat (pork or meat sacrificed to idols) in the presence of weak brethren should it offend them. If eating meat sacrificed to idols was practiced, some would buy this meat at the temples where temple prostitutes raised money for pagan services, including sacrificial animals. This was forbidden.
2. The pastor, and the membership of the church, allowed a prominent woman in Thyatira, who was also a member, to practice fornication and lead other members to do the same. Some believe that she was the pastor's wife; and if not the pastor's wife, she was probably a heavy contributor to the church. John identifies her as Jezebel, the same name as the wife of King Ahab who enticed and deceived the faithful in Israel to commit both physical and spiritual fornication. We know what physical fornication is; spiritual fornication in Israel was worshipping both God and the golden calf. In Thyatira, it was keeping one foot in the church and one foot in the temple of Diana. We still call deceitful and conniving women "Jezebel."

Warning

1. Jesus warned that all who got in bed with Jezebel would suffer her fate. Not only is Jezebel's sin immorality, but it was also spiritual fornication—worshipping both God and idols. In Vatican II, the Roman Catholic Church stated that Muslims, Buddhists, or adherents to other religions could be saved without knowledge or acceptance of Jesus Christ as Savior and Lord. A large segment of non-Catholics or Protestants got in bed with the Catholic Church on this issue. The Promise Keepers changed their statement of faith to please the Catholic Church, and many pastors and ministers today agree with Rome that it does not make any difference what you believe, or who you believe; as long as the adherent is sincere, he or she will go to Heaven like everyone else. According to Revelation 2:22–23, these professing but unsaved church members will go into the Great Tribulation and there they will be killed and forever lost: "That they all might be damned who believed not the truth, but had pleasure in unrighteousness" (2 Thess. 2:12).
2. Revelation 2:23 warns that the unsaved in these churches will be judged "according to your works" at the Great White Throne Judgment, and it is probable that their judgment in hell will be greater, because they knew the truth but refused to accept it.

Promise

1. The overcomers in Thyatiran churches, those who have been saved in spite of false teachings and doctrines in their churches, are asked to hold fast to their faith until the Lord comes and they will reign with Jesus Christ in His government during the Millennium.
2. To the faithful in the midst of apostasy, Jesus promises the "morning star." The morning star is a special illustration of Jesus Christ as He returns to bring in a new day (2 Pet. 1:19).

It is evident that the Lord's message to the churches represented within the Thyatiran church type is to watch for His coming. Most of the memberships of such churches may be lost and will go into the Great Tribulation to take the mark of the beast. "And of some have compassion, making a difference: And others save with fear, pulling them out of the fire; hating even the garment spotted by the flesh" (Jude 22–23).

And I gave her space to repent of her fornication; and she repented not. Behold, I will cast her into a bed, and them that commit adultery with her into great tribulation, except they repent of their deeds. And I will kill her children with death; and all the churches shall know that I am he which searcheth the reins and hearts: and I will give unto every one of you according to your works. But unto you I say, and unto the rest in Thyatira, as many as have not this doctrine, and which have not known the depths of Satan, as they speak; I will put upon you none other burden. But that which ye have already hold fast till I come. And he that overcometh, and keepeth my works unto the end, to him will I give power over the nations: And he shall rule them with a rod of iron; as the vessels of a potter shall they be broken to shivers: even as I received of my Father. And I will give him the morning star. He that hath an ear, let him hear what the Spirit saith unto the churches.

—Revelation 2:21–29

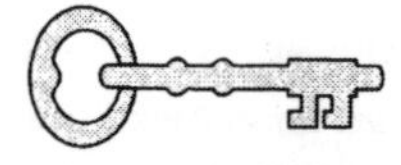

Key #9:
The Walking Dead

And unto the angel of the church in Sardis write; These things saith he that hath the seven Spirits of God, and the seven stars; I know thy works, that thou hast a name that thou livest, and art dead. Be watchful, and strengthen the things which remain, that are ready to die: for I have not found thy works perfect before God. Remember therefore how thou hast received and heard, and hold fast, and repent. If therefore thou shalt not watch, I will come on thee as a thief, and thou shalt not know what hour I will come upon thee. Thou hast a few names even in Sardis which have not defiled their garments; and they shall walk with me in white: for they are worthy. He that overcometh, the same shall be clothed in white raiment; and I will not blot out his name out of the book of life, but I will confess his name before my Father, and before his angels. He that hath an ear, let him hear what the Spirit saith unto the churches.

—Revelation 3:1-6

Chapter Three

Letters to the Churches of East Asia

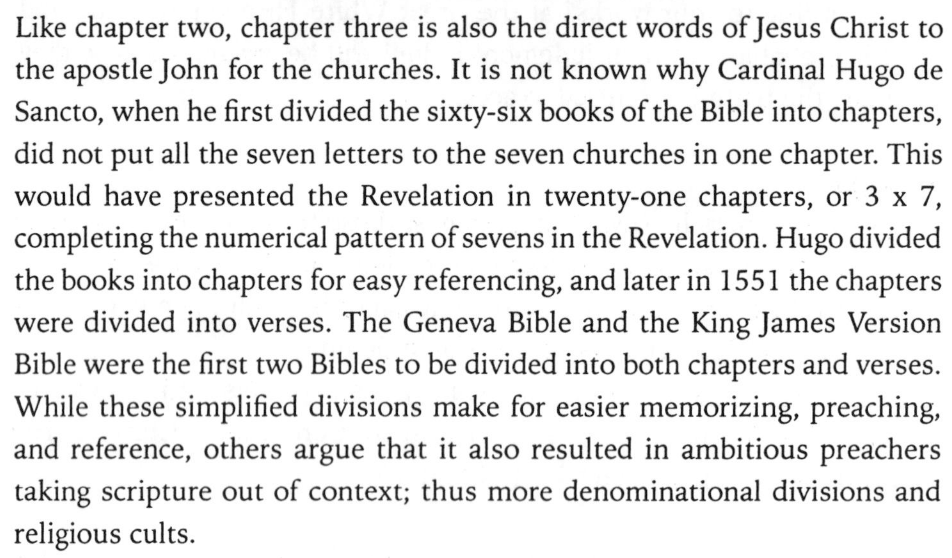

Letter to the Church at Sardis

Like chapter two, chapter three is also the direct words of Jesus Christ to the apostle John for the churches. It is not known why Cardinal Hugo de Sancto, when he first divided the sixty-six books of the Bible into chapters, did not put all the seven letters to the seven churches in one chapter. This would have presented the Revelation in twenty-one chapters, or 3 x 7, completing the numerical pattern of sevens in the Revelation. Hugo divided the books into chapters for easy referencing, and later in 1551 the chapters were divided into verses. The Geneva Bible and the King James Version Bible were the first two Bibles to be divided into both chapters and verses. While these simplified divisions make for easier memorizing, preaching, and reference, others argue that it also resulted in ambitious preachers taking scripture out of context; thus more denominational divisions and religious cults.

Chapter three of Revelation begins abruptly by the risen and glorified Lord Jesus Christ directing John to write to the church at Sardis. This was, of course, one of the seven churches in John's bishopric. Sardis was about forty miles down the highway southeast of Thyatira, and approximately seventy miles from the Mediterranean Sea. In about 1400 B.C. Sardis was one of the more important city-states in the world, the capital of Lydia. This would have been about the time Moses was leading the Israelites out of Egypt. The worship of Cybele, the mother goddess, seems to have originated in Sardis where there was a temple given to this particular brand of paganism and mythology.

Herodotus visited Sardis and wrote about King Croesus of Sardis who seemed to turn everything he touched, businesswise, to gold or silver. Later,

King Croesus became King Midas of the fairy tale. Historical references note that Cyrus of Persia captured Sardis in 546 B.C. However, there appears to be an error of ten years in this reference as Cyrus would not have been on the throne of Persia until 536 B.C. (see Dan. 5). In any event, as Croesus surrendered the city to Cyrus, the Persian soldiers were robbing the palace and the treasury. When Croesus remarked to Cyrus that his soldiers were robbing the treasury, Cyrus proudly replied, "Yes, they are taking your gold and silver." Croesus answered, "No, they are taking away your gold and silver, because everything I had is now yours." Immediately, Cyrus issued orders to his officers to stop the pillage.

While the country of Lydia is referenced several times in the Old Testament, it is not mentioned in the New Testament; Sardis is noted only in the Revelation. The Lydia of Acts 16 was from the old territory of Lydia, and this is possibly where she got the name. The church that was at Sardis was a mission church from Ephesus. We notice in verse one that it was once a living church, preaching the gospel, worshipping the Lord, and winning souls. Then, something happened; it died. The church building was still there, but only the cold embers remained. Few probably attended church; no revival meetings; no souls being saved. Those who did attend only filled the pew and nothing more. It would also appear that most of the members came just "because it was the thing to do," or it was a "family responsibility." Some were saved, but not many.

While the Sardis letters could apply to many churches, or even denominations in the United States and Canada, the primary reference would be to England, Germany, Scandinavia, and the other nations of Europe. While there may be some isolated pockets of life left in the churches of Europe, most of them are dead. The pastors and church workers are paid by the government, so no one worships the Lord with their giving. My Lutheran guide in Finland was typical—attending church only at Christmas, Easter, weddings, or funerals. The great churches of England now often have no more than one or two dozen present on Sunday. Muslim attendance at mosques on Friday now often exceeds Christian attendance in the churches on Sunday.

Jesus addressed Himself to the congregation at Sardis as the One who has the seven spirits of God and the seven stars. As noted before, the stars are the angels (messengers) of the churches and the seven spirits are, we believe, the seven angels of judgment introduced in chapter eight.

Commendations

1. The church had a name for being a light in the community, but anymore the name once earned was not worth much.
2. There were still a few Christians in the congregation that had not been

spiritually corrupted with worldly sins.

Problems

1. The works the church was involved with were not producing faith in the members or winning souls to the Lord.
2. The members were spiritually weak; probably not reading the scriptures, neglecting prayer life, and church attendance.
3. Were not watching for the Lord's return, indicating this letter references such dead and spiritually weak churches in the end of the age.

Warning

1. Repent—return to those church activities within the community that had earned the church a name as a good, soul-winning church.
2. Do as Jesus commanded—teach the prophetic Word and tell others about the return of the Lord. Jesus said, ". . . when ye shall see all these things, know that it is near, even at the doors" (Matt. 24:33). Paul warned Christians, ". . . the day of the Lord so cometh as a thief in the night" (1 Thess. 5:2).
3. Christians in the church should hold on to the faith and not give in to worldly friends.

Promises

1. Those in the church who were not living in a condition of worldliness and sin would enjoy a closer relationship with the Lord. They would walk with the Lord in righteousness.
2. The overcomers, those saved by faith through grace in spite of their church, would **not** have their names taken from the "book of life." Every person born has his or her name written in the "book of life." If a person dies in their sins, their name is blotted out of the book of life. "And the LORD said unto Moses, Whosoever hath sinned against me, him will I blot out of my book" (Exod. 32:33). "And I saw the dead . . . stand before God; and the books were opened . . . and the dead were judged out of those things which were written in the books . . ." (Rev. 20:12). But at the Great White Throne Judgment there was another book (singular), the book of life. The ones named in this book will not be judged (condemned) for their works, because their sins have been covered (washed) in the blood of Jesus Christ on the cross. Christians (the saved) will be judged for their works to get a reward earned by their works (Rom. 14:10; 2 Cor. 5:10). The lost will be judged by their works to determine their punishment in hell.

The letter to the church at Sardis has a special warning for Christians today who belong to a dead church.

The Letter to the Church at Philadelphia

The city of Philadelphia was located twenty-six miles southeast of Sardis. It was founded in about 150 B.C. by King Attalus II. King Attalus was preceded as king of Pergamos by his brother Eumenes, who was evidently an identical twin. He was given the name Philadelphus by Macedonian mercenaries because he loved his brother so very much. In Greek, *phileo* means "friend" or "love," and *adelphos* means "brother." Thus, Philadelphia, the City of Brotherly Love. It may be surprising to some that Philadelphia really has no meaning as far as Christian brotherly love is concerned. Nevertheless, it is evident from our Lord's letter to this church that brotherly love did reign supreme. John may have been using the church at Philadelphia as an example when he wrote in 1 John 4:20, "If a man say, I love God, and hateth his brother, he is a liar: for he that loveth not his brother whom he hath seen, how can he love God whom he hath not seen?" We should not need to remind the reader that the church at Philadelphia was one of the churches in John's ministry responsibility.

The city of Philadelphia, although rather small, was on the Route 66 of that day, the Roman road that ran from Troy through Pergamos, and on through Philadelphia. The saying that "all roads led to Rome" had meaning, because all the roads that travelers could count on led to Rome. The Romans *really* built roads that lasted, even used to this day—roads made of rock slabs about one foot thick. Anyone who molested a Roman citizen on a Roman road would be executed by the Roman government. This is why Paul used his Roman citizenship for safety when traveling.

Philadelphia is also known as "the city of earthquakes." It is in the area where devastating tremors occur consistently. Other cities also within the location of the seven churches have been destroyed by earthquakes, including Ephesus.

If historical accounts and traditional notes have any validity, the first church at Philadelphia was founded by Christians from Pergamos and possibly Sardis. It was a mission church: poor, evangelical, and ministered in fellowship as one, which all churches should do. As in the letter to Smyrna, Jesus offers no criticism of the church at Philadelphia. In the Byzantine era, there were several churches in Philadelphia (present name, Alasehir). Most of the archaeological remains of churches in Turkey have been destroyed by encroaching Muslim authority between A.D. 650 and 1920. Dr. John Walvoord in his excellent book on the Revelation notes that there were a few nominal Christians in Philadelphia until World War I (1914–1918) when they left for Greece to escape persecution. Dr. Walvoord offers no documentation, but this great man's word should be documentation enough.

Jesus introduces Himself to the church at Philadelphia as "He that has the key of David," and the door that He opens, no person will be

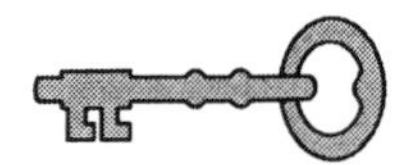

Key #10: Brotherly Love

And to the angel of the church in Philadelphia write; These things saith he that is holy, he that is true, he that hath the key of David, he that openeth, and no man shutteth; and shutteth, and no man openeth; I know thy works: behold, I have set before thee an open door, and no man can shut it: for thou hast a little strength, and hast kept my word, and hast not denied my name. Behold, I will make them of the synagogue of Satan, which say they are Jews, and are not, but do lie; behold, I will make them to come and worship before thy feet, and to know that I have loved thee. Because thou hast kept the word of my patience, I also will keep thee from the hour of temptation, which shall come upon all the world, to try them that dwell upon the earth. Behold, I come quickly: hold that fast which thou hast, that no man take thy crown. Him that overcometh will I make a pillar in the temple of my God, and he shall go no more out: and I will write upon him the name of my God, and the name of the city of my God, which is new Jerusalem, which cometh down out of heaven from my God: and I will write upon him my new name. He that hath an ear, let him hear what the Spirit saith unto the churches.

—Revelation 3:7-13

able to shut again. Eliakim had the key to the palace and treasury, and he was the only one who could open and lock the doors. Eliakim was also in the lineage of David, and through the virgin Mary, would bring forth the Savior. According to the prophecy in Isaiah 22:21–22, the government would be committed to ". . . his hand: and he shall be a father to the inhabitants of Jerusalem, and to the house of Judah. And the key of the house of David will I lay upon his shoulder; so he shall open, and none shall shut; and he shall shut, and none shall open." This complete prophecy by Isaiah was never fulfilled through Eliakim, but it will be in Eliakim's Son, who also is David's Son. ". . . the Lord God shall give unto him the throne of his father David: And he shall reign over the house of Jacob for ever; and of his kingdom there shall be no end" (Luke 1:32–33).

Within the letter to the church at Philadelphia is another reference to those who "say they are Jews, and are not." As noted in our comments on the letter to Smyrna, these are doubtless the Jews who opposed the Christians, because many were engaged in making idols. Jews who also belonged to the church at Jerusalem migrated to both Asia and Galatia, raising serious doctrinal problems by telling the Gentile Christians they were not saved unless they were circumcised and kept the traditions incorporated in the law of Moses. Such Jews thought the Gentiles were still unclean and that God could not love such sinful people. But Jesus Christ in the letter to this church instructed the members that such Jews would in due course worship at their feet and know that God loved them enough to send His only begotten Son to die for them. The Philadelphian believers in these last days, the evangelical Christians, are the best friends in the world that Israel has. While 99 percent of Israel are still unsaved and refute Jesus Christ as God's only begotten Son, or as their Messiah, we know that when the Lord returns all Israel left alive will believe on Him, accept Him as King of Kings, and fulfill God's plan and purpose. I have led Bible tours to Israel over forty times, and some ask me why I go to Israel, because those old Jews will not believe the gospel. I reply that if Israel, nationally, accepted Jesus as the Messiah today, then the Bible would not be true. Only when they see Jesus Christ coming in all His glory, and cry, "Blessed is he that cometh in the name of the Lord," will Israel be saved (see Ps. 118:26; Matt. 23:39; Rom. 11:26).

Commendation

1. The church had a little strength. Just as the church at Philadelphia was rather small in comparison to the other six churches, the evangelical and fundamental churches in these last days are rather small in comparison to Christendom in general. Yet, the evangelical churches of today are

the only ones that have an impact on the cascading immorality that is burying the human race.

2. They kept the "word" of Jesus that there was no other Name under Heaven whereby the lost must be saved. The church was also a missionary church in reaching out as far as possible with the gospel.
3. They did not deny the Name of Jesus Christ under the threat of martyrdom. Christians were given the opportunity to deny Jesus Christ as Savior and Lord to save their lives. Like Christians at Sardis, Christians at Philadelphia suffered death rather than deny Christ. As noted previously, millions of Christians in these last days have also died rather than deny Christ. But today church leadership representing a billion church members or more deny Jesus Christ, who said, "I am the way, the truth and the life: no man cometh unto the Father, but by me" (John 14:6). Nostra Aetate, Declaration on the Relation of the Church to Non-Christian Religions, Second Vatican Council, clearly accepted Allah, the moon god of Islam, as the God of the Bible. Also, under item five of the second article, the Constitution on the Church, Vatican Two of the Catholic Church states: "The non-Christian may not be blamed for his ignorance of Christ and his church; salvation is open to him also, if he seeks God sincerely and if he follows the commands of his conscience, for through this means the Holy Ghost acts upon all men; this divine action is not confined within the limited boundaries of the visible church." In other words, Muslims, Buddhists, Hindus, or Jews do not have to believe in Jesus Christ to be saved. The majority of Protestant and non-Catholic churches in the world today follow this doctrine of universal salvation. This is just as evil, or worse, than the denial of Christ's Name in the first centuries by those who did so to save their lives.

Warning

1. Jesus warns that when the things written in Revelation are in view, He will come "quickly." The word in the Greek, *tachu*, is used twelve times in the New Testament and seven times in Revelation alone. It always means immediately, or hurriedly: "... go quickly, and tell his disciples ..." (Matt. 28:7). This means that faithful Christians are to watch for His coming, because He could come at any time.
2. Keep the faith in Jesus Christ in spite of persecution or ecclesiastical pressure, else Christians may lose their rewards: "And, behold, I come quickly; and my reward is with me, to give every man according as his work shall be" (Rev. 22:12). (Also read Rom. 14:10; 2 Cor. 5:10.)

Promise

1. Because of their faith and service, Jesus Christ promised the members of the church at Philadelphia they would not endure even one minute

of the hour of temptation that would try the entire population left on the earth. This, without doubt, is the Great Tribulation. This is also another clue that the letters to the seven churches are primarily meant for Christians living just before the Great Tribulation, the "last generation," which we believe is today. The members of the Thyatiran church were warned that they would be cast into "Great Tribulation."

2. Evidently, the vast majority of the members of the Philadelphian church, past and present, are overcomers by faith in the blood of Jesus Christ that was shed for their sins. These will be pillars in the temple of God in the New Jerusalem that will descend from Heaven. It is a mark of honor to be pillars in one's community; but how much greater the honor to be a pillar citizen of the New Jerusalem. My passport says that I am an American and have a right to live permanently in the United States. Philadelphia overcomers will be granted an eternal passport to live in the New Jerusalem, never having to leave.
3. A Philadelphia overcomer will also have the "new name" of Jesus Christ. There are dozens of names ascribed to Jesus Christ in the Bible: Wonderful, Mighty God; Creator; Savior; Lord, etc. But there is one name for Jesus that is not in the Bible. We don't know what that name is, but it will be a special reward given to Christians who are especially faithful.

Key #11: Who Knocks At My Door?

And unto the angel of the church of the Laodiceans write; These things saith the Amen, the faithful and true witness, the beginning of the creation of God; I know thy works, that thou art neither cold nor hot: I would thou wert cold or hot. So then because thou art lukewarm, and neither cold nor hot, I will spue thee out of my mouth. Because thou sayest, I am rich, and increased with goods, and have need of nothing; and knowest not that thou art wretched, and miserable, and poor, and blind, and naked.

—Revelation 3:14–17

Letter to the Church at Laodicea

As our tour bus stopped at the ruins of Laodicea on my first visit to the site, I was amazed at the desolation. The sloping hillside, possibly one hundred acres, was covered with broken blocks from buildings that had long ago been destroyed in an earthquake. The tallest buildings that stood in the city were crumpled into layers of concrete like a deck of cards, much like the result after tremors today in the large cities. No other landmarks were in evidence with the exception of the chariot racetrack that ran the length of the city on one side.

The history of Laodicea begins in about 350 B.C. In about 270 B.C. the original name of the city was changed. After the breakup of the Grecian Empire with the death of Alexander, Syria was ruled by thirteen kings with the title of Antiochus. In about 270 B.C., the second Antiochus changed the name to that of his wife, Laodicea. Evidently the rock formations in the area contained a chemical that helped to cure both ear and eye infections. So tablets of stone, or tablets that appeared to be stone, were sold throughout the Roman Empire.

Where did the pharmacy merchants at Laodicea get these tablets? They obtained them from Hierapolis (today Parmukkale), about ten miles distance to the east of the city. In approaching Parmukkale from a distance, it appears to be a snow-capped mountain. Upon approaching the mountain on an ascending road, the tourist will pass acres of iron burial vaults. The appearance of "snow," or mineral deposits, is caused by hot mineral springs flowing down the side of the mountain. Those who were sick of various ailments and diseases would go to Hierapolis to bathe in the mineral springs. The burial vaults stand as evidence that not all of them were healed, and the local funeral firm made a handsome profit selling caskets.

Enterprising merchants at Laodicea would travel to Hierapolis and package the rocks that had been soaked in precious mineral water for hundreds of years. The small tablets of rock would be ground up into a powder, and possibly put into a salve solution. It is quite possible that the resulting salve would relieve both ear and eye infections. We have checked several books on the Revelation, and we have found no one other than us who have solved the mystery of the eye salve of Laodicea.

When we went back to Hierapolis a couple of years ago, a UNESCO biosphere sign was at the entrance. The mountain had been cleared off, and the tourist sites were gone. The same sign appears at Petra now, and at forty-seven areas in the United States alone. To name just a few: Virgin Islands, Yellowstone National Park, Golden Gate, Everglades, Mammoth Cave, etc. These are signs posted as indicators of the coming world order of Antichrist prophesied in Revelation 13. To verify, visit the following Internet site: *www.unesco.org*.

The mineral springs on the mountain at Hierapolis formed a fairly large stream at the base. The stream would wind its way to Laodicea, but by the time it got to the city, the water was no longer hot. It was lukewarm. The stream still flows by the deserted site of Laodicea today.

The *Barclay Commentary* (p. 113), gives the following comment:

> The tephra Phrygia, the eye-powder of Laodicea, was world-famous. It was exported in tablet form; and the tablets were ground down and applied to the eye. This Phrygian powder was held to be a sovereign remedy for weak and ailing eyes.

Jesus addressed Himself to the membership at Laodicea as the "faithful and true witness, the beginning of the creation of God." The church was neither faithful nor true to their calling. The Greek word for church means a group of people, whether two or more, who are separated by God from the world. Israel was separated from Egypt and referred to as "the church in the wilderness." The church members at Laodicea had not separated themselves from the world. They loved the world and all the world had to offer, especially riches. Jesus Christ, the Creator, in the beginning created all things; thus, even the riches the Laodiceans had belonged to the Lord.

I counsel thee to buy of me gold tried in the fire, that thou mayest be rich; and white raiment, that thou mayest be clothed, and that the shame of thy nakedness do not appear; and anoint thine eyes with eye-salve, that thou mayest see. As many as I love, I rebuke and chasten: be zealous therefore, and repent. Behold, I stand at the door, and knock: if any man hear my voice, and open the door, I will come in to him, and will sup with him, and he with me. To him that overcometh will I grant to sit with me in my throne, even as I also overcame, and am set down with my Father in his throne. He that hath an ear, let him hear what the Spirit saith unto the churches.

—Revelation 3:18–22

Commendations

None.

Problems

1. Jesus found the members of the church at Laodicea to be "lukewarm" according to faith and service. We either want our coffee to be hot or cold. Just so, there is something about a lukewarm church member that is an abomination to God. The Laodicean church members were self-sufficient. They had plenty of money, a good church building, a good pastor who never ruffled any feathers. In today's America, this would have been considered the ideal church to join. We wouldn't criticize such a church today, because it fits the mold of most churches in our nation. This church, though, was going nowhere. The Greek word for lukewarm, *chliaros,* is not a transition word. It denotes a permanent state. The sun is always hot; ice is always cold; the Laodicean church members were always lukewarm.
2. It seems evident that only the rich and well dressed were welcome in this church. Jesus was accused by the self-righteous scribes and Pharisees of being a ". . . friend of publicans and sinners. . . ." Jesus was indeed sinner-friendly, because He came to save sinners. He ate with publicans (Matthew, Zacchaeus, and others). Sinners commit sin, but Laodicean church members today don't want to witness to sinners who commit sin; they want to witness to their rich peers who don't "commit sin," or at least only commit "acceptable sin." That is why our prisons are overflowing today.

Warnings

The members of this church were warned to "repent." They, like a growing number of congregations today, accepted material blessings as a sign of God's approval. Jesus said, "not so; you are really spiritually wretched, poor and blind." "Try some of your own eye salve so that you might see." The church members that are truly rich, Jesus said, are those who are clothed in His righteousness. ". . . Be found in him, not having mine own righteousness, which is of the law, but that which is through the faith of Christ, the righteousness which is of God by faith" (Phil. 3:9).

Promises

1. "As many as I love, I rebuke and chasten. . . ." Evidently there were some in the church at Laodicea, as there are in these types of churches today, who had gotten saved in spite of their church: "For whom the Lord loveth he chasteneth, and scourgeth every son whom he receiveth. . . . But if ye be without chastisement... then are ye bastards, and not sons" (Heb.

12:6,8). In considering the massive, rich congregations of today that appear to have no problems, we must conclude that such churches are filled with unsaved people pretending to be Christians. Those belonging to such churches today and still have tribulation, consider it is from a loving God who is leading you to come out from among them.

2. "I stand at the door, and knock. . . ." Jesus reminded the self-righteous church members at Laodicea that He was knocking at their door; and He also pleaded with the unsaved in the church that if they would open their doors, He would come in and dine with them. He dined with Matthew, Zacchaeus, and others who were the most hated sinners in Israel. He even offered traitorous Judas the bread of reconciliation at the Passover. And, He is standing at the doors of the Laodicean churches of this last generation. Open the doors . . . tomorrow may be too late.
3. Even in this lukewarm church, a congregation that failed to gain even one commendation, Jesus would still reward those who repented of their selfish and egotistical pride with a seat with Him on His throne. He could not even promise James and John such a seat of honor. Each Christian should strive to overcome the world, the flesh, and the devil to be rewarded with a personal relationship with Jesus in His eternal Kingdom.

Conclusions About the Seven Letters

1. These were literal churches in Asia when John received the Revelation on Patmos.
2. The letters reveal the spiritual conditions in the churches at that time, some good, some bad.
3. Some of the members of these churches were saved, some were only professing Christians. Some were an honor to the Lord, and some were bringing shame on the Lord's name.
4. The candlesticks in all seven churches were removed after A.D. 500. John was the bishop over the seven churches, but Paul also helped to establish and minister to some of the churches, including the church at Ephesus and the church at Laodicea. Paul mentions the brethren at Laodicea four times in his letter to the church at Colosse.
5. Paul warned the church at Ephesus about deceitful and false brethren, and in his last epistle to Timothy written from prison in A.D. 67 he wrote, ". . . all they which are in Asia be turned away from me . . ." (2 Tim. 1:15). While enemies from without have always attacked Christians, collectively and individually, the greatest destroyers of the Christian faith are those who rise up in positions of authority within the churches.
6. Inasmuch as the seven churches of Revelation ceased to exist even hundreds of years before the Reformation, it is evident the letters are

primarily intended for Christendom, and churches included, existing at the end of the age, which we believe is today.

7. There are several references in the letters to the coming Great Tribulation, another clue the letters have a special message for Christians today. It is also evident that the unsaved church members will probably be included in the harlot church of Antichrist and take his mark and number.

Chapter Four

The Rapture of the Church

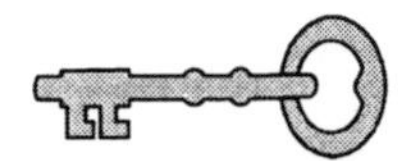

Key #12: The Rapture

After this I looked, and, behold, a door was opened in heaven: and the first voice which I heard was as it were of a trumpet talking with me; which said, Come up hither, and I will shew thee things which must be hereafter.

—Revelation 4:1

Chapter four begins with the apostle John being caught up in the spirit, passing through a door into Heaven. That the church, those who have placed their faith in Jesus Christ as the Son of God who died for their sins, will be taken out of this world in a resurrected body, or a changed body for those Christians alive at the time, is not a subject of doctrinal controversy. At least, it should not be. This event is the translation of the church from earth to Heaven. The disagreement between Christians, or churches, over this event is when will it occur. Will it take place before the Tribulation, sometime during the Tribulation, at the end of the Tribulation, or at the Great White Throne Judgment?

The Greek word for door in Revelation 4:1 is *thura,* which is used in thirty-seven other places in the New Testament, and literally means a door. In this verse, John is referenced in the singular, but the majority of commentaries on Revelation interpret him to be representative of the entire church, those saved during the dispensation of grace, dead or alive, at the time this event takes place.

As noted in our study of the letters to the churches, Jesus Christ warns that the professing church members, the unsaved, will end up in the Tribulation period. Therefore, the chronological order of events would indicate that at the end of the Church age the translation, or Rapture will occur. Some may protest that the word "rapture" is not found in the Bible, but neither is the word "Bible" found in the Bible. The word is from the Latin Vulgate, *rapere,* meaning taken away in a state of joy. If others choose not to use this word for this great event, that is fine with me. And, if some Christians want to go through the Tribulation, that is all right with me also.

But why do we believe that the church will be taken out of the world before the Tribulation begins?

1. Without the slightest doubt, the Tribulation period is the seventieth week of Daniel. The church has no place in the seventieth week of Daniel. Paul said the "church" was a mystery, hidden from the understanding of all men in previous ages (Eph. 3:1–8). Even Daniel had no knowledge of the time gap between the destruction of Jerusalem and the temple and the Great Tribulation.
2. The apostles agreed that ". . . God at the first did visit the Gentiles, to take out of them a people for his name. . . . After this I will return, and will build again the tabernacle of David, which is fallen down . . ." (Acts 15:14,16). The taking out of the Gentiles a people for Christ's name (the church) will end before Christ returns to restore Israel for the Millennium. Israel is the center of Tribulation prophecy; it is unreasonable that the church will be in the world in the Tribulation.
3. Paul in 1 Thessalonians 5:1–3 wrote to the church that the unsaved would not "escape" the Tribulation. If the unsaved are not going to escape, then someone must escape. Who is going to escape? Paul has already informed us in the preceding chapter, the church (1 Thess. 4:13–18).
4. The second epistle of Peter is about the Second Coming of Jesus Christ. In this epistle Peter references the letters of Paul. Within this context, it seems evident he was referencing Paul's prophecy, by the Word of the Lord, about the translation of the church. He indicated that some disputed Paul's revelation, but Peter stressed that God delivered Noah from the flood and Lot from Sodom; therefore, "The Lord knoweth how to deliver the godly out of temptations..." (2 Pet. 2:9). The word for temptation in the Greek used here is *peirasmas,* which also means trial, and the same word used in Revelation 3:10, "...I also will keep thee from the hour of temptation, which shall come upon all the world, to try them that dwell upon the earth." It is apparent the members of Christ's church will not "dwell upon the earth" during the Tribulation.
5. The word "church" is not mentioned after Revelation 3:22 until Revelation 22:16, which is after the Tribulation, after the Millennium, after the creation of a New Heaven and a New Earth. During the Tribulation, Israel is in the world; the unsaved are in the world, the nations are in the world, the Antichrist and the False Prophet are in the world, but no church. It appears evident that the church has been taken out of the time of Tribulation that will test all who have been left behind.

Differences Between the Rapture and the Literal Return to the Earth

Rapture	Glorious Appearing
1. Jesus meets Christians in the air	1. Jesus returns with the church and His angels.
2. Christians are caught up.	2. No one is caught up.
3. No mention of race.	3. Jews are gathered out of the nations.
4. Only Christians see Jesus.	4. Every eye will behold Him.
5. No mention of Armageddon.	5. Returns at Armageddon.
6. Seven years of Tribulation begins.	6. One thousand years of peace begins.
7. Comes to save the righteous.	7. Comes to destroy armies of Antichrist.

Conclusion

The Tribulation is the day of wrath. The present age is the day of grace. The only four verses in the four gospels where grace is mentioned, the reference is to Jesus coming to bring God's grace to the world. Grace is referenced ten times in Acts—God's grace upon all who receive Jesus Christ as Savior; but at the same time, the Kingdom is still being offered to Israel.

Grace is referenced 120 times to the church in the epistles—those who are saved entirely by faith through grace. But grace is found only two times in the Revelation—1:4 and 22:21. God's offer of grace is removed at the taking out of the world the church. If the church of the dispensation of grace is to be in the world during the Tribulation, then the message of grace would still be offered. It isn't there. Even in the Millennium, the Kingdom law will be enforced; sinners will be cut off without mercy.

Is the entrance of John through heaven's door a symbolism of the Rapture? We think so.

Our First View of Heaven

There is a story about a man from Texas who was exceedingly proud of his state's history, as most Texans are. In due course, it came time for this man to depart this life, and so he died, something that will happen to all of us unless the Lord comes first.

This particular Texan came to himself in another realm. A spirit guide at his side instructed this man that this would be where he would spend eternity. As the spirit guide showed this former Texan around his new home the man became more and more excited, and finally shouted in boundless jubilation, "I JUST KNEW HEAVEN WOULD BE LIKE TEXAS."

Key #13: Heaven's First Sight

And immediately I was in the spirit: and, behold, a throne was set in heaven, and one sat on the throne. And he that sat was to look upon like a jasper and a sardine stone: and there was a rainbow round about the throne, in sight like unto an emerald.

—Revelation 4:2-3

The spirit guide looked at the man in amazement and responded, "Sir, this isn't Heaven!"

Being an Oklahoman who has suffered through sixty or more OU-Texas football games, I trust our dear friends down in Texas will forgive me for this pun.

But have you ever thought what your reaction will be to your first glimpse of Heaven? That is, if the reader is certain that he or she has placed their faith in Jesus Christ to get them to Heaven. Otherwise, the reader may join our Texas friend.

We note first that when John hears the voice that sounds like a trumpet giving the command "come up hither," he is "immediately" in Heaven. Paul proposed that at the Rapture when the dead in Christ are raised, they will be changed into a glorified body ". . . in the twinkling of an eye. . . ." And the One behind the voice did not say, "Hey, John, would you like to come up and sit a spell?" It was a command; John was not given an option. This is the way the Rapture will be: "For the Lord himself shall descend from heaven with a shout, with the voice of the archangel, and with the trump of God: and the dead in Christ shall rise first" (1 Thess. 4:16). If the reader is a Christian, and the Lord calls you today in the Rapture, ready or not, you will go to Heaven.

The apostle Paul was taken up to Heaven, but he did not know whether he was taken up in the flesh or in the spirit (2 Cor. 12:1–5). This heavenly trip was for Paul's own edification, because he was forbidden to write about what he saw or heard. The apostle John was commanded to write what he saw and heard, and what greeted him must have been a scene comparable to a thousand sunrises. He saw the Triune God first, with the appearance of a jasper stone (diamond) mingled with the brilliance of a sardine stone (ruby), seated upon a throne with an emerald (green) rainbow over it. The only way we can even imagine such a scene is if John had taken a video camera with him.

However, the colors of the stones identified God with His covenants and promises to Israel. The first stone on the high priest's breastplate was the jasper (diamond) stone for the firstborn of Jacob, Reuben, which means in Hebrew "behold a son." The sardine stone is the last stone on the breastplate, representing Benjamin, which means "son of my right hand." The prophet Isaiah wrote of the coming Messiah, "To us a son is given"; and, after His resurrection Jesus sat down at the "right hand of God." The rainbow around the throne of God symbolizes God's covenant with mankind that the world would not again be destroyed with water (Gen. 9:11–16). The emerald rainbow around the throne of God is also a symbol that Jesus Christ, our Creator, will not allow man himself to ultimately destroy the earth with fire (Rev. 11:18).

The colors that John referred to as the brilliance of God, the first and last colors on the breastplate of the high priest, also signifies that Jesus Christ is the Alpha and Omega, the first and the last, because He is **I AM,** the God of eternity.

There are many mysteries about the Universal Kingdom of God that are difficult for our finite minds to grasp. There is no way we can understand completely how God created this seemingly infinite universe, nor how He keeps it under His control. However, in the fourth chapter of Revelation the curtain of mystery is opened just a crack, and the apostle John presents us with a teasing glance of God's omnipotent government. Keep in mind that the Kingdom of God is indeed a kingdom, complete with a supreme ruler, and angelic subjects of different orders, obeying specific laws.

As John enters the door to the throne of God he sees twenty-four elders. The word for elder in the Greek is *presbuteros,* meaning aged person (old men or old women). Terry Alexander, in his book *Characters of Revelation,* presents twelve things we need to know about these twenty-four elders:

1. Where did they come from?
2. Are there twenty-four elders mentioned in the Old Testament scriptures?
3. Are they men or angels, some have asked?
4. If they are men, why twenty-four? If they are men, why does God wait until Revelation 4:4 to announce to the whole world, "Here they are"? It would seem strange that, if they were only elders in ancient Israel, as some authors have suggested, our God would wait until this heavenly view is unfolding to reveal them.
5. Are they only twenty-four, or do they represent a larger and more comprehensive group of saints?
6. Why are they robed in white raiment?
7. Why are they wearing crowns of gold?
8. Why are they sitting on seats *in God's throne* in Heaven?
9. Why are these twenty-four elders falling down before Jesus Christ and His Father, worshipping and casting their crowns before the throne, declaring that He is worthy to receive glory, honor, and power?
10. Why do these twenty-four elders sing a new song, specifically, the *song of redemption?*
11. What has happened to these twenty-four elders that has let them know that Christ Jesus is the only One worthy?
12. Why are these twenty-four elders mentioned twelve times from Revelation 4:4 to Revelation 19:4 (Rev. 4:4,10; 5:5–6,8,11,14; 7:11,13; 11:16; 14:3; 19:4)?

While we can shed some light on the questions that Pastor Alexander has

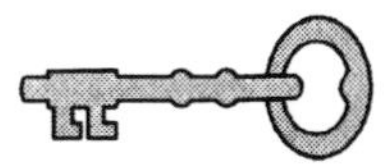

Key #14: Why 24 Elders?

And round about the throne were four and twenty seats: and upon the seats I saw four and twenty elders sitting, clothed in white raiment; and they had on their heads crowns of gold. And out of the throne proceeded lightnings and thunderings and voices: and there were seven lamps of fire burning before the throne, which are the seven Spirits of God.

—Revelation 4:4–5

posed, we cannot say with certainty that we know the complete answer to every question. *Characters of Revelation* may be ordered at a local book store (ISBN #1-57558-090-X), or call Southwest Radio Church Ministries (1-800-652-1144).

Some believe the twenty-four elders are the sons of the high priests of Israel through which the priesthood was divided in twenty-four courses of temple service (1 Chron. 24:1–18). This would, of course, make the elders Israelis, but we read in Revelation 5:10 that the elders are redeemed out of every race, language, and nation. However, this verse alone does not eliminate the possibility that they are Jews, because when Jesus returns, the Jews in every nation will be regathered into the land of Israel. However, the fact that they already wear crowns of gold and occupy seats (or thrones) would indicate they had already received their rewards. This would probably show, as Dr. John Walvoord believes, that they would be either members or representatives of the church, because Old Testament saints will not receive rewards or thrones until the Millennium. The word for crowns upon the heads of the elders is not *atarah* or *diadema,* crowns of earthly kings, but *stephanods,* the crown of a victor, or overcomer, like Stephen. This is the crown also promised to the overcomers in the letters to the churches, who will reign with Jesus Christ. The Olympic athletes of Greece earned a crown of leaves that would last only a few days, but the elders of Revelation 4 earned crowns of gold that would last forever.

John tells us that the elders are sitting on seats, not because they were old or tired, but because the seat in a biblical or political sense means representative authority. Our senators and congressmen run for a seat in Congress. Considering what evidence we have, and for lack of a better answer, it would seem that the elders are singularly or collectively representing the church. They appear in John's vision twelve times, because twelve is the number of government in God's Kingdom: twelve apostles; twelve tribes; twelve gates, etc.

As we continue our study in Revelation we will run into the twenty-four elders again, and perhaps we can shed further light on just what role they play in the Tribulation.

And before the throne there was a sea of glass like unto crystal: and in the midst of the throne, and round about the throne, were four beasts full of eyes before and behind. And the first beast was like a lion, and the second beast like a calf, and the third beast had a face as a man, and the fourth beast was like a flying eagle. And the four beasts had each of them six wings about him; and they were full of eyes within: and they rest not day and night, saying, Holy, holy, holy, Lord God Almighty, which was, and is, and is to come.

—Revelation 4:6–8

If the reader has not read the adjoining scripture, Revelation 4:6–8, please read it now. Now go back and read it again.

What if you actually witnessed this scene that John describes? You would probably think you shouldn't have eaten that last piece of pizza before going to bed.

It would seem that John expects us to rely on preceding revelations by prophets whom God spoke through to understand what he saw. We go back and consider what happened when God decided to humble Nebuchadnezzar: "This matter is by the decree of the watchers, and the demand by the word of the holy ones: to the intent that the living may know that the most High ruleth in the kingdom of men, and giveth it to whomsoever he will, and setteth up over it the basest of men" (Daniel 4:17).

If the "holy ones" of Daniel 4:17 are the same twenty-four elders of Revelation 4:4, then we have a problem, because they could not represent the church. They would be a heavenly judicial body without relationship to Israel or the church. We don't know this to be true, but it is something to consider. In any event, the watcher of Daniel 4:17 would appear to be one of the four "beasts" of Revelation 4:6.

You ask why? Because the beasts of Revelation 4 are evidently watchers over the four basic divisions of living creation on earth: fowl, wild beasts, domesticated beasts, and man. You say, what about the insects, snakes, and marine creatures? We read in Habakkuk 1:14: "And makest men as the fishes of the sea, as the creeping things, that have no ruler over them?"

There is nothing in Scripture that indicates common, everyday angels have wings. Cherubim, God's warrior guardian angels, may have four wings or six wings; seraphim, the highest order, priestly angels, have six wings. *Seraphim* in the Greek means burning, illumine, or in some references, noble (*Young's*). From seraphim we also get serpent (serpentine), which means fearful or creep. If sin, evil, and poison were not associated with snakes, we might think them to be the most beautiful of all God creatures. Satan was in the Garden of Eden when he evidently appeared to Eve in this form. Satan may have been a watcher over this part of creation, even the lizard-like dinosaurs. When Satan fell, maybe the dinosaurs fell and the rest of the creeping and serpentine forms of life were left without a watcher. Scripture and verse? No, but it is interesting anyway.

The Greek word for the beasts of Revelation 4 is *zoon*. We take the "n" off, and we have "zoo," a collection of beasts or animals. The fact that the four beasts are full of eyes, continually turning, never resting or sleeping, tells me that they are watching over the creation. Why are they watching? Somebody has to watch! If the common housefly was uncontrolled in procreation, in a few months at most the United States, from ocean to ocean, would be covered with flies six feet deep. Think what would happen if ants, bees, snakes, cockroaches, or even the birds, began exponentially increasing. There are at least one million forms of bacteria, and thousands upon thousands of forms of viruses. Less than one percent of microscopic life has even been identified. Somebody must be watching over the microscopic world or we would all be dead.

Even so, ". . . we know that the whole creation groaneth and travaileth in pain together until now. And not only they, but ourselves also, which have the firstfruits of the Spirit, even we ourselves groan within ourselves, waiting for the adoption, to wit, the redemption of our body" (Rom. 8:22–23).

As with the case of Nebuchadnezzar, the watchers direct the displeasure of creation (nature) against the sin within the human heart. Even as sin abounds increasingly in our day, we have fire ants; killer bees; 36 million dead of AIDS and another 100 million dying; earthquakes increasing; wars and world terrorism; etc.

As we continue in our study of Revelation, we will find that in the Tribulation, which may be just around the corner, that the animals will turn against men; new kinds of stinging insects increase; new kinds of dreadful diseases will appear. The four watchers over the creation will probably be very busy indeed as the "spirit of iniquity" spreads over the world and God's creation rises up in rebellion.

And when those beasts give glory and honour and thanks to him that sat on the throne, who liveth for ever and ever, The four and twenty elders fall down before him that sat on the throne, and worship him that liveth for ever and ever, and cast their crowns before the throne, saying, Thou art worthy, O Lord, to receive glory and honour and power: for thou hast created all things, and for thy pleasure they are and were created.

—Revelation 4:9–11

As John watches the unfolding scene around the throne of God, the twenty-four elders rise from their seats and fall prostrate before the Lord who was still seated on the throne. With the same movement, they remove their golden crowns and cast them at the feet of the Creator of the universe, worshipping Him with all that they had, including their total being.

The One who sat on the throne was that tiny baby born in Bethlehem, the incarnate only begotten Son of God. He is the same One whom the Magi came from the East and worshipped with gold, frankincense, and myrrh. There is no need for frankincense in Revelation 4 because Jesus has already risen from the grave, and there is no need for bitter myrrh, because He has already suffered the cross for the sins of the world. Only the golden crowns were in order for a gift, the symbol of eternal worth and value. But when the Magi worshipped the baby in Bethlehem, they knew that He was the King of Israel, the Ruler and Creator of the Universe. The word for worship in the Greek text in Matthew 2:2 is the same as the word in Revelation 4:10, *proskun*, which means to "kiss the hand" or the hem of one's garment, thus humbling the worshipper while at the same time exalting the one who is worthy of worship. Notice the ultimate attitude of worship in Psalm 2:12, "Kiss the Son, lest he be angry. . . ."

Recalling the Great Depression days, my father had lost everything. There was simply no money, at least none where we lived in far southeast Oklahoma. Once a month he would hitch up the team to the wagon and drive to Hugo, the county seat, to buy the absolute necessities. At that time, us kids would work at anything that was available: chopping cotton; hoeing cotton; picking cotton; plowing; cutting wood; etc. Most of the money we earned was required to buy clothes or schoolbooks, and we never usually made over fifty cents a day. But how good it made us feel to take what money we had left, if no more than a dollar, to give to our father to help buy the needed food staples.

This example perhaps illustrates in some way the meaning of the elders casting their crowns of gold at the feet of Jesus. The crowns are the rewards they have earned, and how wonderful it is that they give them to the Lord. I think many Christians will be embarrassed when they stand at the Judgment Seat of Christ and have nothing to give Him (1 Cor. 3:11–15).

As declared throughout the Bible, we read in verse eleven that Jesus Christ created everything in Heaven and earth for His pleasure. There are fourteen words in the Hebrew and Greek texts interpreted "pleasure." Each of the fourteen words mean something different. Here it is *thelema* and means will, wish, or plan. It does not mean having fun as the Greeks imagined of their gods in ruling their subjects. If you plan to build a house, and it becomes a reality, then you should have pleasure in living in a house that you planned yourself. In the conclusion of God's plan, He will have a perfect, holy universe inhabited by subjects to worship and serve Him, not because they have to, but because they choose to of their own free will.

Conclusion

In this particular vision in chapter four, the catching up of John into Heaven seems to reference the Rapture of the church. In the vision, the curtain of mystery that hides to some extent the governance of God is parted just a little. The role of the watchers in the Kingdom of God seems more evident than the role of the elders. Nevertheless, the elders assure us that the mansions that Jesus is preparing for the Christians will be completed.

Chapter Five

The Lion and the Lamb

Key #15: The Book

And I saw in the right hand of him that sat on the throne a book written within and on the backside, sealed with seven seals. And I saw a strong angel proclaiming with a loud voice, Who is worthy to open the book, and to loose the seals thereof? And no man in heaven, nor in earth, neither under the earth, was able to open the book, neither to look thereon. And I wept much, because no man was found worthy to open and to read the book, neither to look thereon.

—Revelation 5:1–4

As noted previously, the Bible was not divided into chapters until the thirteenth century and into verses until the sixteenth century. Chapters four, five, and six of Revelation could have been included in one chapter, as all three chapters reveal what John saw around the throne of God when he entered Heaven. This vision sets the stage for the rest of the book.

As John evidently stands in awe of the glory of the Creator on His throne, with an angelic host and men redeemed by the blood of Jesus Christ bowing before Him, he sees the One on the throne is holding a seven-sealed book in His right hand. The fact that the book is in the Creator's right hand indicates that it is a good book. Jesus sat down on the right hand of the Father, because the Father God said, "This is my beloved Son, in whom I am well pleased." (Matt. 3:17). The nations on God's right hand will be welcomed into the Kingdom; those on the left hand will be rejected (Matt. 25).

In the Roman Empire it was customary for wills to be sealed. As others have noted, emperors Augustus and Vespasian sealed their wills with seven seals. There has been much conjecture and opinions as to the nature of the book and what it contained. In A.D. 96 there was no such thing as a bound book. Books were parchments rolled together. It appears obvious that the book was composed of seven parchments, as we read later the seals will be broken and what is written on each individual parchment will be read and acted upon. The seventh parchment would be rolled and sealed, the sixth would be rolled around it and sealed. As each seal is broken, judgments and events take place. When the seventh seal is broken, seven angelic trumpeters appear. When the seventh trumpet sounds, seven bowls of God's wrath are poured out, and when the seventh bowl of wrath is emptied, the world will be saved from those who would destroy it; the armies of the nations will be destroyed; Israel will be saved by believing on Jesus Christ as Savior and Messiah; and Jesus Christ will establish His Kingdom and reign on David's throne for a thousand years. Without the opening of the seals, nothing happens: the world will be destroyed; the Antichrist, who will be Satan incarnate, will win; there will be no Kingdom age.

And one of the elders saith unto me, Weep not: behold, the Lion of the tribe of Juda, the Root of David, hath prevailed to open the book, and to loose the seven seals thereof. And I beheld, and, lo, in the midst of the throne and of the four beasts, and in the midst of the elders, stood a Lamb as it had been slain, having seven horns and seven eyes, which are the seven Spirits of God sent forth into all the earth. And he came and took the book out of the right hand of him that sat upon the throne.

—Revelation 5:5–7

As John continues watching the book, a strong angel appears and announces in a loud voice that any man in Heaven or on earth to step forward who is able to open the seals and perform what is demanded on each of the seven parchments. No man steps forward, and John begins to weep because the devil seems to have won. Man, to this time, has been given six thousand years to eliminate sin; to eliminate the consequences of sin like war and murder; to eliminate diseases that destroy life; to create the perfect government and society. In spite of an exponential increase in knowledge and science, as Jesus said, "Men's hearts failing them for fear, and for looking after those things which are coming on the earth . . ." (Luke 21:26). And as Paul prophesied, "This know also, that in the last days perilous times shall come… evil men and seducers shall wax worse and worse, deceiving, and being deceived" (2 Tim. 3:1,13).

The "strong angel" who asked for a volunteer to open the seals is not identified by name. We assume it is Gabriel, as his name in the Hebrew and Greek means "strong with God." Gabriel also gave Daniel the prophecy of the seventy weeks and the coming Great Tribulation, and he instructed Daniel to seal up his book until the time of the end. Gabriel also informed Mary that Jesus would sit upon David's throne.

As John continues to weep, one of the twenty-four elders informs the apostle that he should cease crying, because there is someone who is able to open the seals of the book and perform what is written inside. The One who is worthy, or able to do this, is the Root of David, the Lion of Judah. But as John looks, he does not see a lion, but a lamb.

We read in Genesis 49:9–11: "Judah is a lion's whelp. . . . The scepter shall not depart from Judah, nor a lawgiver from between his feet, until Shiloh come; and unto him shall the gathering of the people be. Binding his foal unto the vine, and his ass's colt unto the choice vine; he washed his garments in wine, and his clothes in the blood of grapes."

In these three verses we understand that the Messiah would come out of Judah; His law would be enforced in the Kingdom; He would be called the vine; He would ride on the colt of an ass; His garments would be stained with blood. Jesus came from Judah; He was born in Bethlehem; He rode into Jerusalem to present His claim to be the Messiah on a young donkey; and when He comes again, His garments will be stained with blood as though He had treaded in the winepress. He was crucified as a lamb for our sins, but He will come again as the Lion of Judah. Jesus is also referred to as

Shiloh because it was at Shiloh that all the tribes of Israel assembled after the conquest of Canaan. It was the first capital of the Israeli theocracy, and when He comes again, all twelve tribes will once more be together under His government.

The word "lamb" is found twenty-eight times (4x7) in Revelation. Twenty-seven times it refers to Jesus Christ, one time to the False Prophet, or as some believe, the Antichrist, a false christ.

From the Exodus to the present time (approximately thirty-five hundred years), Israelis have offered a lamb at Passover as a symbol of the Messiah who would come and take away their sins. John the Baptist introduced Jesus to Israel with the announcement: ". . . Behold the Lamb of God, which taketh away the sin of the world" (John 1:29).

Since Jesus Christ was crucified for the sin of the world, every time the Jews have continued to offer up a lamb at a Passover, they have committed blasphemy. Israel was given forty years to repent of rejecting their Messiah, and cry out to God to send Him back, but they did not repent. Josephus wrote of the time of the Passover when the Roman army closed the gates to the city:

> Cestius, who being desirous of informing Nero of the power of the city, who otherwise was disposed to condemn that nation, entreated the high priests, if the thing were possible, to take the number of their whole multitude. So these high priests, upon the coming of their feast which is called the Passover, when they slay their sacrifices, from the ninth hour to the eleventh, but so that a company not less than ten belong to every sacrifice, (for it is not lawful for them to feast singly by themselves,) and many of us are twenty in a company, found the number of sacrifices was two hundred and fifty-six thousand five hundred; which, upon the allowance of no more than ten that feast together, amounts to two million seven hundred thousand and two hundred persons that were pure and holy; for as to those that have the leprosy, or the gonorrhoea, or women that have their monthly courses, or such as are otherwise polluted, it is not lawful for them to be partakers of this sacrifice; nor indeed for any foreigners neither, who come hither to worship.
>
> —Josephus, *Wars of the Jews*, book 6, chapter 9

The minimum number at a Passover meal was ten; the maximum number was twenty. If we take fifteen as an average, then there could have been 5 million in Jerusalem (considering Gentiles and the unclean) when the gates were closed by the Romans. It is no wonder that when the forty years of probation were expired, God allowed the ultimate judgment to come upon the city of Jerusalem, the temple, and the nation.

It is also significant that the One who is able to open the seals to the book is of the "Root of David," not the "Seed of David." The olive tree, a symbol of spiritual Israel, can reproduce through seed or the roots. In fact, the roots of an olive tree never die. Some of the olive trees in the Garden of Gethsemane in Jerusalem are over two thousand years old.

The Messiah was to come through King David, and then through his son Solomon. Although Solomon had seven hundred wives and three hundred concubines, he evidently had only one son—Rehoboam (1 Chron. 3:1–10). The Davidic line passed through King Jeconiah, but his line was cut off, and his son, King Zedekiah, was killed along with his sons by Babylon. Also, Isaiah prophesied that the males within the royal line, if any be left, would be taken to Babylon and made eunuchs (Isa. 39:7). Daniel and his three companions were of the royal line, and they were taken to Babylon and made eunuchs (Dan. 1). Quoting from *King Messiah* by John McTernan and Louis Ruggiero:

> The messianic line runs from David to Solomon to Rehoboam to Jeconiah to Zerubbabel to the Messiah. There is no place in the Bible which shows the curse on the kingly line has been lifted. Because of the curse, anyone born of a human father and claiming to be the Messiah will have the curse of Jeconiah to block such a claim. The Messiah of Israel cannot have a human father.

The genealogy of Mary, the mother of Jesus, is given in Luke 3:23–38, showing that she was the family of David. Thus, Jesus was born of the Root of David, but also as prophesied, of the seed of woman, conceived by the Holy Spirit, the very Son of God (Gen. 3:15; Luke 1:30–35).

Therefore, the identity of Jesus Christ in Revelation 5 as the Lion of Judah, the Root of David, the Lamb of God, is proven from Scripture.

As John witnesses the Lord Jesus Christ—exemplified as both the Lamb of God and the Lion of Judah—come forth to take the book, the elders fall down before Him. The elders are no longer wearing gold crowns, because they have been cast at the Lord's feet. One item the elders do have with them is harps. We would assume that they play the harps, as there would be no other reason for them. One denomination does not use instrumental music in the church, because they say no instruments are mentioned as being used in church. If musical instruments are wrong in church, then it would seem they would also be wrong in Heaven.

Another item the elders have with them is vials of odors which are symbolic of the prayers of saints. We are not told if these are prayers that have been answered, or prayers that have yet to be presented to the Lord for His intercession. The altar of incense in the temple was lit and perfumed

And when he had taken the book, the four beasts and four and twenty elders fell down before the Lamb, having every one of them harps, and golden vials full of odours, which are the prayers of saints. And they sung a new song, saying, Thou art worthy to take the book, and to open the seals thereof: for thou wast slain, and hast redeemed us to God by thy blood out of every kindred, and tongue, and people, and nation; And hast made us unto our God kings and priests: and we shall reign on the earth.

—Revelation 5:8–10

smoke filled the building while prayers were being offered. But Christians are told that they do not need to go to a temple, or even their church, to pray. We are assured in Scripture that God hears the prayer of every Christian offered in the Name of Jesus Christ whether in their closet, in a car on the way to work, or walking in the park. A good spiritual exercise is to take a concordance and read the scriptures relating to intercessory prayer. That the elders are presenting the prayers to the Lord is an indication that every prayer in His Name is before Him.

We have commented in some detail as to the identity of the twenty-four elders in chapter four, and here we notice they sing a song about redemption to God in the blood of the Lamb. This also would indicate they are redeemed men and women who praise the Lamb in song for taking them from the penalty of sin to a status of kings and priests in the eternal Kingdom of God. Angels are never described as singing in the Bible. We read in Job 3 and 7 that angels shouted for joy at the beginning of creation, but there was no singing.

We remember the songs we once sang in church from the hymnal:

Redeemed—how I love to proclaim it!
Redeemed by the blood of the Lamb;
Redeemed thro' His infinite mercy, His child,
and forever I am.
Redeemed . . . redeemed, redeemed by the
Blood of the Lamb.
Redeemed . . . redeemed,
His child, and forever I am.

It is indeed regrettable that in many of the church hymnals today songs about the blood of Jesus Christ have been removed . . . or, 7-11 lyrics are shown on the screen. The church song leader will lead the congregation singing seven words eleven times, but nothing about the blood.

The song of the twenty-four elders before the throne of God tells us that we will have the riches of kings in Heaven. Everything we need, God will provide. "But my God shall supply all your need according to his riches in glory by Christ Jesus" (Phil. 4:19).

After the elders conclude their song of redemption, then all the angels join in with the elders and the four beasts in declaring that Jesus Christ is worthy to receive seven things:

1. Power
2. Riches
3. Wisdom

And I beheld, and I heard the voice of many angels round about the throne and the beasts and the elders: and the number of them was ten thousand times ten thousand, and thousands of thousands; Saying with a loud voice, Worthy is the Lamb that was slain to receive power, and riches, and wisdom, and strength, and honour, and glory, and blessing.
—Revelation 5:11-12

4. Strength
5. Honor
6. Glory
7. Blessing

Ten thousand times ten thousand would be 100 million, but then John saw besides these, thousands of thousands. The total number could easily run into the billions of both angels and the redeemed. There is no way we can know the total number of angels in Heaven or the number of saved men and women who will be in Heaven. We know that the Bible speaks of the "fullness of the Gentiles" in reference to the church (Rom. 11:25). Fullness means reaching a specific number or date. I agree with some who believe there is a definite number who will be saved. Some believe that it will be the number of angels who followed Satan and fell from their created order.

After the worship and exultation of Jesus by the angelic host and the redeemed from mankind, they are joined by every other creature in Heaven and on earth. In the Greek and Hebrew there are three separate words for "creature." Sometimes creature means lesser animal life, and sometimes it means men and women, or at least includes men and women. We read that if any man be in Christ he or she is a new creature, and that we are to go and preach the gospel to every creature. Creature in its general meaning refers to any living thing created by God—sometimes human and sometimes living things other than humans.

The concluding question of chapter five is why Jesus Christ needs justification as King of Kings and Lord of Lords by the angelic hosts and the redeemed from the human race. Why must the angels and the members of the church declare Jesus Christ to be worthy? Man must be justified before God; but why must Jesus Christ be justified before angels and men? Satan in the Garden of Eden told Eve that God was not justified in withholding the fruit from the tree of the knowledge of good and evil. But after the Great White Throne Judgment, no creature of God will ever again question the righteousness and holiness of God as the Supreme Creator and Ruler of the Universe, or His only begotten Son, the Lord Jesus Christ.

> Wherefore God also hath highly exalted him, and given him a name which is above every name: That at the name of Jesus every knee should bow, of things in heaven, and things in earth, and things under the earth; And that every tongue should confess that Jesus Christ is Lord, to the glory of God the Father.
>
> —Philippians 2:9–11

And every creature which is in heaven, and on the earth, and under the earth, and such as are in the sea, and all that are in them, heard I saying, Blessing, and honour, and glory, and power, be unto him that sitteth upon the throne, and unto the Lamb for ever and ever. And the four beasts said, Amen. And the four and twenty elders fell down and worshipped him that liveth for ever and ever.

—Revelation 5:13–14

Chapter Six

Judgments of the First Six Seals

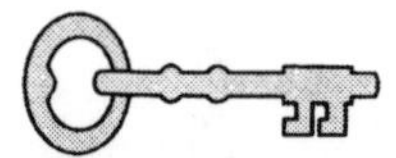

Key #16: Tribulation Overview

And I saw when the Lamb opened one of the seals, and I heard, as it were the noise of thunder, one of the four beasts saying, Come and see. And I saw, and behold a white horse: and he that sat on him had a bow; and a crown was given unto him: and he went forth conquering, and to conquer.

—Revelation 6:1–2

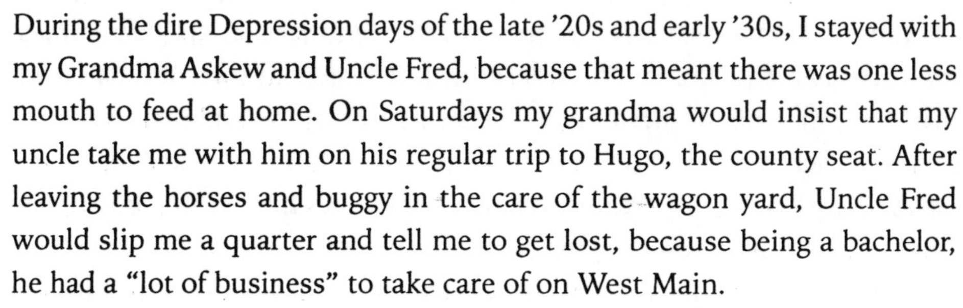

During the dire Depression days of the late '20s and early '30s, I stayed with my Grandma Askew and Uncle Fred, because that meant there was one less mouth to feed at home. On Saturdays my grandma would insist that my uncle take me with him on his regular trip to Hugo, the county seat. After leaving the horses and buggy in the care of the wagon yard, Uncle Fred would slip me a quarter and tell me to get lost, because being a bachelor, he had a "lot of business" to take care of on West Main.

With the quarter, I would first stop by a restaurant (no McDonald's then) and get me a big hamburger for ten cents and a Pepsi cola (twelve full ounces, was a lot), leaving me ten cents for the cowboy shoot-em-up. Even before talkies, I learned that the good guys wore the white hats and the bad guys wore the black hats. It just always seemed to come out that way, except when one of those no-good, rustling polecats would put on a white hat and pretend to be one of the good guys in order to steal the cattle.

In Bible study, it is not so much what color hat the rider wears, but the color of his horse. In this chapter of Revelation we read about a white horse, a red horse, a black horse, and a pale horse. In Zechariah 6 we read also about white, red, black, and bay (pale) horses: "And the angel answered and said unto me, These are the four spirits of the heavens, which go forth from standing before the Lord of all the earth" (Zech. 6:5).

It therefore seems obvious that the four horsemen of Revelation 6 are spirits of God in Heaven, which John saw, that will be sent into the world to bring about events that will fulfill the judgments of the trumpets and vials. It certainly appears evident that the seven seals are forewarnings of things determined in Heaven that will be unleashed upon the earth, or at least judgments that man will bring upon himself according to the foreknowledge of God.

Seal #1

As the introductory scene of Revelation 6 opens, John is in Heaven, evidently watching intently as the first seal is broken. John is suddenly alerted by a loud, rolling peal of thunder. Thunder in Scripture is used symbolically of judgment—past, present, or future. No thunder is mentioned in association with the opening of the remaining six seals; therefore, it can be concluded that all seven seals signify judgment upon the earth.

In checking various commentaries on Revelation, I found that preterists and historic eschatologists have presented the "rider on the white horse" as various personalities like Nero, pagan Rome, Pope Pious, Charlemagne, Martin Luther, Napoleon, Jesus Christ, the Antichrist, etc. I was somewhat relieved to find that no one thought this person to be Mickey Mouse or Hopalong Cassidy. It is my understanding that the entire revelation to John is yet future. The person riding the white horse has not yet appeared, although we may now hear hoofbeats sounding in the distance.

Traditionally and biblically, white is the color of peace or righteousness. When military representatives negotiate for peace, or surrender, they certainly do not use a red or black flag in approaching the enemy. Jesus is coming back to bring in an era of one thousand years of peace on earth. At Jesus' birth the heavenly host announced, "Glory to God in the highest, and on earth peace, good will toward men" (Luke 2:14). Jesus will come back riding on a white horse on a "righteous" mission (Rev. 19:11), to save the world from those who would destroy it. Jesus was born "King of Kings," and He is coming back wielding a great sword (Rev. 19:15–16).

The rider on the white horse of Revelation 6 appears immediately after John is taken to Heaven, a type of the Rapture of the church. This rider is "given" a crown, and he comes with a bow that evidently has no arrows, which is also given him. Although the color of this character's horse indicates that the rider is on a mission of peace, other identifiers indicate he is up to no good. Chronology wise, there is no way this imposter can be Jesus Christ.

Jesus said that, "wars and rumours of wars . . . nation shall rise against nation, and kingdom against kingdom . . ." (Matt. 24:6–7) would be signs of His coming, not peace between nations and kingdoms. Jesus also said there would be false christs and false prophets abounding when He returned (Matt. 24:24).

Immediately after the apostle Paul revealed details about the translation (Rapture) of the church, he wrote: "For when they [the unsaved world] shall say, Peace and safety; then sudden destruction cometh upon them [the unsaved world], as travail upon a woman with child; and they [the unsaved world] shall not escape" (1 Thess. 5:3).

We read also of the Antichrist in Daniel 8:25, "...he shall magnify himself in his heart, and by peace shall destroy many: he shall also stand up against the Prince of princes; but he shall be broken without hand."

Jesus said that in the last days many deceivers would claim to be the Christ (Messiah). Deception is an identifying character of the coming Antichrist (2 John 7). If the readers will check a complete concordance, they will be amazed as to how many times in the Bible that deceiver, deceive, or deception is related to the Antichrist.

In the twentieth century, more effort was put forth to bring peace on earth between men and nations than in all the preceding centuries of history. The League of Nations and peace conferences at Geneva, Paris, Camp David, etc., were held. The United Nations on Manhattan Island was to bring peace and understanding on earth, yet there is no peace. As in the days of Noah, violence is filling the world. The absence of peace now presents the probability of world destruction and human annihilation. Would the world accept a man, an international politician, who would promise peace in our time? Probably.

The rider on the white horse of Revelation 6 is given a crown and a bow. He appears at the very beginning of the Tribulation period, for he must make a covenant with Israel for seven full years (Dan. 9:27). The third stage in a world disarmament plan, set forth in U.S. Department of State Publication 7277, *Freedom from War,* is as follows:

> By the time Stage II has been completed, the confidence produced through a verified disarmament program, the acceptance of rules of peaceful international behavior, and the development of strengthened international peace keeping process within the framework of the U.N. should have reached a point where the states of the world can move forward to Stage III. In Stage III progressive controlled disarmament and continuously developing principles and procedures of international law would proceed to a point where no state would have the military power to challenge the progressively strengthened U.N. Peace Force and all international disputes would be settled according to the agreed principles of international conduct.
>
> The progressive steps to be taken during the final phase of the disarmament program would be directed toward the attainment of a world in which:
>
> (a) States would retain only those forces, non-nuclear armaments, and establishments required for the purpose of maintaining internal order; they would also support and provide agreed manpower for a U.N. Peace Force.

(b) The U.N. Peace Force, equipped with agreed types and quantities of armaments, would be fully functioning.

(c) The manufacture of armaments would be prohibited except for those of agreed types and quantities to be used by the U.N. Peace Force and those required to maintain internal order. All other armaments would be destroyed or converted to peaceful purposes.

(d) The peacekeeping capabilities of the United Nations would be sufficiently strong and the obligations of all states under such arrangements sufficiently far-reaching as to assure peace and the just settlement of differences in a disarmed world.

We are not proposing that the Antichrist will be a secretary–general of the United Nations. What we are saying is that economic, moral, political, and military realities in today's world make likely the appearance of the "man of sin" on the world stage in the near future.

Seal #2

Jesus said of the last days, " . . . ye shall hear of wars and rumors of wars: . . . nation shall rise against nation, and kingdom against kingdom . . ." (Matt. 24:6–7).

And when he had opened the second seal, I heard the second beast say, Come and see. And there went out another horse that was red: and power was given to him that sat thereon to take peace from the earth, and that they should kill one another: and there was given unto him a great sword.

—Revelation 6:3-4

Daniel prophesied regarding the Tribulation period, ". . . the end thereof shall be with a flood, and unto the end of the war desolations are determined" (Dan. 9:26).

Since Cain killed Abel, there has always been war, but Jesus, Daniel, and other prophets foretold a tremendous increase in the number and scope of wars in the last days. World War I and World War II of the twentieth century were international conflicts. Since 1774, the United States has been involved in 225 wars or military operations which required army involvement, but 124 of these military operations have occurred since 1990. According to statistics presented by LYCOS, there were nineteen major armed conflicts in the world as of February 24, 2003. In addition, there are twenty international terrorist organizations, most of them state sponsored. In the days of Noah before the flood, violence filled the earth; and Jesus said that as it was in Noah's day, so it would be when He returned.

In World War II, the Nazi regime of Germany killed 6 million Jews. One and a half million were children under twelve years of age. In addition to the millions of army personnel killed of the participating nations, 45 million civilians were killed in that war (*2003 World Almanac*, p. 481).

The Desert Storm war of 1990–91 is clearly prophesied in Isaiah 13 where an alliance of nations from the end of the earth come to destroy Iraq (Babylon). The warning is that when this happened "the Day of the Lord is near." When the Medes and Persians captured Babylon, no harm was done to the city, and these were two near neighbors. The Desert Storm war was the first time Isaiah's prophecy was fulfilled. But then at the end of the chapter where the prophet is in the Day of the Lord, Babylon will be destroyed like Sodom and Gomorrah. But this is just one of the wars that was to occur in the last days.

Today, United States troops are stationed around the world: 40,000 in South Korea; 80,000 in Germany; 10,000 in the Balkans; and some 300,000 at the present time in forty other nations. When Babylon fell, its armies were in other countries trying to keep the provinces under control; when Rome fell, its armies were spread from England to India, and one day Rome just wasn't there any more. The Soviet Union tried to hold a far-flung communist empire together, and it collapsed almost in one day. The United States is not learning from the lessons of history.

But as Jeremiah reported, the world cries peace, peace, but there is no peace. When the rider on the red horse of Revelation 6 appears upon the world scene, there will be wars in which two-thirds to three-fourths of the world's population will be killed. The rider of the red horse will indeed wield a "great sword." And, "... except those days should be shortened, there should no flesh be saved . . ." (Matt. 24:22).

Seal #3

And when he had opened the third seal, I heard the third beast say, Come and see. And I beheld, and lo a black horse; and he that sat on him had a pair of balances in his hand. And I heard a voice in the midst of the four beasts say, A measure of wheat for a penny, and three measures of barley for a penny; and see thou hurt not the oil and the wine.
—Revelation 6:5–6

The appearance of the rider of the black horse as the third seal is broken signifies two more agents of death that will visit humanity in the Tribulation period—famine and disease. Black is the color of famine, as those who die from hunger generally turn this color, or the absence of color. Oil and wine were the principal medicines in biblical times. The good Samaritan treated the wound of the injured man in Luke 10:33–34 with oil and wine. This would indicate that there will be a great need for medicines in the Tribulation period.

Jesus indicated that during the Tribulation there would be "famines, and pestilences" of pandemic proportions. There have been many famines and disease epidemics of the past, but these will pale in comparison to the ones that occur in the future.

One of the most severe famines of the last century was the one in the Ukraine that resulted from the forced communization of that country. Eleven million subsequently starved to death. Notes on famines taken from the Internet on February 25, 2003:

- Drought in Gujarat (India) worse in more than one hundred years . . . 50 million face famine.
- Drought in Pakistan worse than in one hundred years . . . 500 have died from disease caused by drought.

- Some 30 million Africans threatened with famine in the coming months.
- 830 million people worldwide go hungry as a result of natural disaster or extreme poverty, U.N. said.
- 100 million homeless children starving.
- 3.5 million North Koreans have starved to death since 1995.
- Shortage of water supplies threaten world peace.

When I was a boy on the farm, our family was self-sustaining in food supplies. We raised and stored potatoes, corn, peanuts, dried fruit, and my mother canned vegetables and beef. Pork was smoked and hams and bacon were kept in the smokehouse. Several kinds of beans were dried and kept for winter. Today, almost 100 percent of the population depends upon the local supermarket for every kind of food consumed, and most do not even know how to grow a hill of beans. If communications and transportation systems are severed in a world emergency, millions or billions will starve to death. Recently, the U.S. Homeland Security Department encouraged Americans to keep at least a two weeks' supply of food and water on hand in the event of natural disaster or a terrorist attack.

Quoting from the foreword in *The Coming Dark Age* by Roberto Vacca:

> Vacca shows how all the major systems on which we depend—transport, electrical, garbage removal, postal, telephone, and so on—are hopelessly overloaded, poorly planned, badly managed, and about to crack. The breakdown . . . will begin in the United States and Japan. A crisis in one system will aggravate the collapse of another, and then another—until the catastrophe becomes worldwide. Already, Vacca points out, we have seen the signs—massive power failures, fuel shortages, chronic traffic jams, deteriorating mail services.

Our nation has not recovered from the September 11, 2001, destruction of the Twin Trade Towers. What may we expect should another world war, even on a terrorist scale, occur?

But Jesus, as also indicated in chapter six, implied a severe shortage of food where a loaf of bread may cost an entire day's wages and medicines would be severely needed as pandemic epidemics rage.

A few decades ago, with the advances in medical sciences, it was predicted that mankind was overcoming disease. But with the change in diet and living circumstances, heart diseases, with the inclusion of an exponential rise in cancer, are killing more people today than the traditional diseases of the past. There has also been added an additional factor to world health—AIDS.

According to the Centers for Disease Control, as of January 2, 2001,

21.8 million had died of AIDS and another 36.1 million were infected. The AIDS-related death number does not include those who had AIDS, but due to their failing immune system, had died of tuberculosis, pneumonia, or some other disease. The Black Death that ravaged Europe in the Middle Ages claimed 25 million; therefore, AIDS is the most deadly epidemic to date to infect the human race.

According to page 9 of the *2003 World Almanac,* due to the threat of biological warfare, the entire civilized world is hostage. The anthrax scare after September 11, 2001, illustrates the terror that can be spread in all nations, because there are biological agents more deadly than anthrax.

Quoting from the cover of *The Coming Plague:*

> After four decades of assuming that the conquest of disease was "imminent" people on all continents now find themselves besieged by microbes. Tuberculosis, nearly eradicated from the industrial world by the 1970s, claims 3 million lives annually. Malaria, a disease the United States nearly vanquished by the early 1960s, leads to more than 105 million deaths a year. . . . The water we drink is improperly purified; the air we breathe potentially deadly; the food we eat possibly poisonous. How can this be? What went wrong?

God critically balanced man with the creation, but man has changed his food, his environment, the family structure, his moral conduct, his spiritual affiliations with each other and his Creator.

There are approximately one million forms of bacteria and over five thousand different types of virus entities. As declared in Romans 8, the whole creation, including the unseen microscopic world, groans and travails in pain, waiting to be delivered.

The scales in the hand of the rider of the black horse speaks of food rationing, possibly similar to that enforced in World War II. The penny in the Greek text is the Roman denarius, probably worth about twenty-five cents today. This amount was said to be a man's wages for one day, and a measure of wheat would be about what one person could eat at one meal. The same denarius would buy three measures of the cheaper grain, barley, enough for three meals. This again illustrates the coming scarcity of food and the great famine in the Tribulation period.

The scales could also indicate a different meaning: God's judgments ending man's day are about to begin, and the beginning of the Lord's Day is at hand.

". . . THOU ART WEIGHED IN THE BALANCES, AND ART FOUND WANTING" (Dan. 5:27).

Seal #4

As the fourth seal is broken, John sees a pale horse with a rider called Death. The word for pale in the Greek is *chloros,* interpreted "green" in other scriptures, or it could be interpreted "sallow," a word in Middle English used to describe the color of death.

Whether this rider brings judgments separate from the judgments that occur under the breaking of the first three seals, or new and separate judgments, is not clear. However, with additional judgments that are to come with the breaking of the seventh seal, I conclude that one-fourth of the earth's human population are killed by judgments unleashed by the first three seals.

In 1999 the earth's human population passed the 6 billion mark. This means that based on just the present population of the world, over 1.5 billion people will die with the breaking of the first four seals. We are not told if this number under the breaking of the first four seals will die in the first half or the second half of the Tribulation. Based on the overall context of the judgments unleashed by the breaking of all seven seals, I believe this is the number that will die in just the first half of the Tribulation. It appears to me that there will be wars increasing from the beginning to the end of the Tribulation. Those who believe the first half of the Tribulation will be a relatively peaceful time have difficulty in proving their case.

The only new judgment introduced with the breaking of the fourth seal is the beasts of the earth killing people. We again reference Romans 8, and other scriptures, which stress that the creation reacts against the sins of mankind. When the church is gone and only the unsaved are left, the spirit of iniquity will cover the nations, and even the animal world may rise up in rebellion. There are at present only certain countries where there are lions, tigers, and other wild, flesh-eating animals. However, almost every household today has a dog or other type of pet animal. If there is a great famine, even the dogs may band themselves into roving bands and attack people.

This may not be so far-fetched as it seems. There is historical precedent for domestic animals, such as dogs, becoming wild during times of famine and deprivation. In Grigori Medvedev's excellent book *The Truth About Chernobyl,* he relates the rescue and evacuation efforts launched by the Russian government during the aftermath of the nuclear disaster. During the evacuation of the area around Chernobyl, citizens were instructed to leave everything behind—including their pets. As a result, dogs and cats were left behind in the apartment complexes around the Chernobyl area. Since these animals were abandoned, they were left to their own devices with regards to obtaining food. Soon the previously domesticated dogs became "wild" and joined together in packs, first hunting down the cats, and then

And when he had opened the fourth seal, I heard the voice of the fourth beast say, Come and see. And I looked, and behold a pale horse: and his name that sat on him was Death, and Hell followed with him. And power was given unto them over the fourth part of the earth, to kill with sword, and with hunger, and with death, and with the beasts of the earth.

—Revelation 6:7-8

threatening the human rescue workers in the area. The Russian army was sent in to kill the packs of dogs that had become a threat to the rescue and construction workers who were attempting to seal off the damaged Chernobyl nuclear reactor.

In the event of a serious famine, people will be doing well to feed themselves, much less to feed their pets. As pets become increasingly neglected and abandoned, they will be left to their own devices for their survival, in much the same way as the pets of the Chernobyl disaster. It is reasonable to assume that the abandoned pet's behavior will change in a similar manner to those pets abandoned at Chernobyl.

Death, the rider of the pale horse, kills one-fourth of the world's population. We might say, Death kills more people than anything else we know about. But we notice that Hell also rides with Death. It appears to me that Isaiah 5:14–17 refers to this time, when afterward, war will be no more: "Therefore hell hath enlarged herself, and opened her mouth without measure: and their glory, and their multitude, and their pomp, and he that rejoiceth, shall descend into it. And the mean man shall be brought down, and the mighty man shall be humbled, and the eyes of the lofty shall be humbled: But the LORD of hosts shall be exalted in judgment, and God that is holy shall be sanctified in righteousness. Then shall the lambs feed after their manner, and the waste places of the fat ones shall strangers eat."

As we see the prophecies warning of the last days coming to pass before our eyes today, we should run, not walk, to tell the unsaved that Jesus Christ can save them, not only from the wrath of Satan in this world, but give them eternal life in Heaven where there is no sorrow, no war, no pain, only glory in serving our Lord forever.

The Fifth Seal

And when he had opened the fifth seal, I saw under the altar the souls of them that were slain for the word of God, and for the testimony which they held: And they cried with a loud voice, saying, How long, O Lord, holy and true, dost thou not judge and avenge our blood on them that dwell on the earth? And white robes were given unto every one of them; and it was said unto them, that they should rest yet for a little season, until their fellowservants also and their brethren, that should be killed as they were, should be fulfilled.

—Revelation 6:9–11

The rider of the first horse comes with a bow and a crown; the rider of the second horse comes with a great sword; the rider of the third horse comes with a pair of scales; the rider of the fourth horse comes with Death and Hell. But with the opening of the fifth seal, John is amazed to see a multitude of martyrs under the altar of Heaven crying out for vengeance.

The questions that immediately come to our mind are: who are these martyrs? when were they killed? how were they saved? As the results of the opening of the first four seals are appraised, it would seem that of the millions killed in the first half of the Tribulation, most of these souls died in their sins and go to hades to await the Great White Throne Judgment. However, the chronology in the opening of the fifth seal would also indicate that possibly millions of those who will die in the first half of the Tribulation will be saved to await their resurrection at the end of this seven-year period. In the Church age, as we have noted in our comments on chapters two and three, millions of Christians have died for believing the gospel and their testimony that Jesus Christ is both Savior and Lord. However, these would be in the resurrection and translation of the church before the Tribulation begins (1 Thess. 4:13–18). Dr. John Walvoord and Dr. Henry Morris both agree in their commentaries on Revelation that the fifth seal martyrs will have died in the first half of the Tribulation.

Even before the "mark of the beast" is enforced on penalty of death, millions will be killed for their faith in Jesus Christ. This fact seems to be indicated in the promise that they would be avenged when "their brethren, that should be killed as they were, should be fulfilled."

In the Old Testament, the blood of the innocent sacrificial animals was to be poured out in the bottom of the altar of burnt offering, which was a type of what is described here in Revelation 6 (Lev. 17:11). The souls of the martyrs are clothed with a temporary covering until the time of their resurrection given in Revelation 20:4.

It is difficult for us, even at this late hour, to fully understand what the world will be like when a world theocratic government with power over all nations is established by the Antichrist. Copies of my book on Petra are hidden in some of the caves in this city of refuge where a Jewish remnant will spend the last three and one-half years of the Tribulation. Then there are the thousands and millions of Bibles we have distributed in Russia, China, South America, Mongolia, and other nations. Then there are the Bibles that Christians will have left behind at the Rapture, and the *Left Behind* series by Dr. Tim LaHaye. In the first half of the Tribulation, it seems evident that millions will be saved and subsequently martyred for their faith, even though the church is gone.

We will discuss evangelism in the Tribulation in more detail in our comments on chapter seven.

The Sixth Seal

E. W. Bullinger wrote concerning the breaking of the first six seals: "... a summary of the judgments distributed over the whole book; a brief summary of what will occur in 'the day of the Lord,' up to the time of His actual Apocalypse, or unveiling in chapter six."

I agree, with the exception that subsequent judgments will kill more than just one-fourth of the world's population. Certainly, what John saw with the breaking of the sixth seal is a brief preview of what is yet to come concerning signs in the sun, moon, and earthquakes on earth.

Isaiah prophesied of the day of the Lord's vengeance:

> For the indignation of the LORD is upon all nations, and his fury upon all their armies . . . he hath delivered them to the slaughter. Their slain also

And I beheld when he had opened the sixth seal, and, lo, there was a great earthquake; and the sun became black as sackcloth of hair, and the moon became as blood; And the stars of heaven fell unto the earth, even as a fig tree casteth her untimely figs, when she is shaken of a mighty wind. And the heaven departed as a scroll when it is rolled together; and every mountain and island were moved out of their places.

—Revelation 6:12–14

And the kings of the earth, and the great men, and the rich men, and the chief captains, and the mighty men, and every bondman, and every free man, hid themselves in the dens and in the rocks of the mountains; And said to the mountains and rocks, Fall on us, and hide us from the face of him that sitteth on the throne, and from the wrath of the Lamb: For the great day of his wrath is come; and who shall be able to stand?

—Revelation 6:15–17

> shall be cast out, and their stink shall come up out of their carcases, and the mountains shall be melted with their blood. And all the host of heaven shall be dissolved, and the heavens shall be rolled together as a scroll: and all their host shall fall down, as the leaf falleth off from the vine, and as a falling fig from the fig tree.
>
> —Isaiah 34:2–4.

We read also in Isaiah 24:20–21: "The earth shall reel to and fro like a drunkard. . . . And it shall come to pass in that day, that the LORD shall punish the host of the high ones that are on high, and the kings of the earth upon the earth."

We read in Isaiah 13:10 that in the day of the Lord, the sun will become dark and the moon likewise, but in Isaiah 30:26 we read that the sun will become seven times hotter and the light from the moon as the light of the sun. The same solar and lunar phenomena in the Tribulation is declared in the second chapter of Joel. Jesus said that at the close of the Tribulation, the sun would become dark and the moon would not give light (Matt. 24:29). We read also under the trumpet and bowl judgments in Revelation that the sun will become hot, then dark, and the light from the moon will be as blood.

What does this mean? By checking an astronomy textbook, the reader will find that when a small or average-sized star novas, it becomes hot and bright for a period of seven to fourteen days. Our sun is an average-sized star. The atoms are then stripped of their shells and the entire mass collapses into a ball from thousands of miles in diameter to less than fifteen miles in diameter. The gravity becomes so intense that even light cannot escape. The moon reflects the light of the sun, and if the sun becomes seven times hotter, the light from the moon will become as the light of the sun. If the sun becomes dark, then of course the moon will become dark. There are more than thirty novas of stars in our Milky Way galaxy occurring annually. It is evident from the prophetic Word that in the Tribulation our sun will nova, else how could the prophets two or three thousand years ago describe this solar occurrence so accurately? What happens after that solar event is God's business, so let us let Him take care of it.

Angelic beings are often referred to as stars in the Bible, so when John saw the "stars of heaven" fall upon the earth (Rev. 6:13), this will be God's judgment against the fallen angelic host described in Isaiah 24:21 and Revelation 12:4.

Not only did Jesus say that in the Tribulation there will be ". . . signs in the sun, and in the moon, and in the stars . . ." (Luke 21:25), He said there would be ". . . fearful sights and great signs . . . from heaven . . ." (Luke 21:11). In the same verse He said, "And great earthquakes shall be in divers places. . . ." Two years ago I made a study of the increase in earthquakes, and it is submitted for the readers' consideration:

On the following page is a chart showing the number of earthquakes, worldwide, from 1987 through 1999 (total figures for 2000 not available). This chart is from the National Earthquake Information Center, U.S. Geological Survey. Preterists who try to deceptively manipulate statistics to support their false claims that all prophecy was fulfilled by A.D. 70 cannot deny these figures, which show that in the past thirteen years earthquakes have doubled. Partial statistics provided by the National Earthquake Information Center for the year 2000 shows there were nine super-quakes, two in the 8.0-plus Richter scale range.

In the seven years preceding 1993 there were two 8.0-plus quakes on the Richter scale. In the seven years after 1993, there were eleven earthquakes of 8.0-plus. These quakes originate usually from twenty miles to two hundred miles deep in the earth along earth-plate separation lines. If this indicates anything, it is that the earth-plates are shifting and becoming increasingly unsteady. Geological consensus is that the land mass of the earth was at one time on one plate, but something happened to break the land mass into separate plates and these plates drifted apart, creating continents and islands. The Bible indicates this happened at the flood, and the separation occurred over two hundred years in the days of Peleg.

Since the first three months of 2001, the rate of earthquake increases has not lessened. It is interesting that the Seattle earthquake of 7.1 on the Richter scale occurred, and shown on television, as Mr. Gates and the large staff of Microsoft were holding an important meeting in Seattle. Also, Boeing, the largest worldwide airplane corporation, is located in Seattle.

Another notable earthquake was the 7.9 earthquake on January 26, 2001, in India that reportedly killed tens of thousands, which occurred on Republic Day, not only an Indian holiday, but a day when millions of Hindu worshippers were trying to wash away their sins in the dirty water of the Ganges while praying to demonic Hindu gods and spirits.

Earthquakes are not only warnings, but judgments from God. As this generation proceeds ever nearer to the coming Tribulation, repudiation from God's creation upon a Christ-rejecting world will increase (Rom. 8:19–23).

Number of Earthquakes Worldwide 1990–2000, and Mortality Figures													
Magnitude	**1987**	**1988**	**1989**	**1990**	**1991**	**1992**	**1993**	**1994**	**1995**	**1996**	**1997**	**1998**	**1999**
8.9-9.9	0	0	1	0	0	0	1	2	3	1	0	2	0
7.0–7.9	11	8	6	12	11	23	15	13	22	21	20	14	23
6.0–6.9	112	93	79	115	105	104	141	161	185	160	125	113	123
5.0–5.9	1437	1485	1444	1635	1469	1541	1449	1542	1327	1223	1118	979	1106
4.0–4.9	4146	4018	4090	4493	4372	5196	5034	4544	8140	8794	7938	7303	7042
3.0–3.9	1806	1932	2452	2457	2952	4643	4263	5000	5002	4869	4467	5945	5521
2.0–2.9	1037	1479	1906	2364	2927	3068	5390	5369	3838	2388	2397	4091	4201
1.0–1.9	102	118	418	474	801	887	1177	779	645	295	388	805	715
0.1–0.9	0	3	0	0	1	2	9	17	19	1	4	10	5
no mag.	2639	3575	4189	5062	3878	4084	3997	1944	1826	2186	3415	2426	2096
Total	11290	12711	14585	16612	16516	19548	21476	19371	21007	19938	19872	21688	20832
Deaths	1080	26552	617	51916	2326	3814	10036	1038	7949	419	2907	8928	22711

Those who argue that earthquakes are not increasing should present their case to the National Earthquake Information Center rather than to me.

In viewing the judgments coming upon the world in the Tribulation, it is no wonder that John concludes chapter six with this warning: "For the great day of his wrath is come; and who shall be able to stand?"

Christians can take comfort from Paul's references to the judgments coming upon the unsaved in view of the Lord's return in 1 Thessalonians 5:9: "For God hath not appointed us to wrath, but to obtain salvation by our Lord Jesus Christ."

Chapter Seven

The Saved Out of Tribulation

If I were shown the judgments coming upon the earth with the opening of the first six seals, I would begin to wonder if anyone in the Tribulation period could be saved out of it. However, there appears to be a time-out after the opening of the sixth seal to show the apostle that many will indeed be saved, possibly millions or even hundreds of millions.

There are some ministers and pastors who believe that according to Paul's preachments in 2 Thessalonians 2:6–12, that no one who has heard the gospel, but misses the Rapture, can be saved in the Tribulation. However, Paul is referencing in this scripture the revealing of Antichrist to all the world after the beginning of the Tribulation. There is a question as to whether he is even referring to pre-Rapture or pre-Tribulation time. Nevertheless, I would never want anyone to delay being saved thinking they can be saved in the Tribulation even if they miss the Rapture. Also, I am convinced there will be millions in liberal churches who will indeed worship the Antichrist as their god and be forever lost in hell.

John is shown four angels standing on the earth's four corners holding back the north, south, east, and west winds, "after these things." Keep in mind that the chronology of this event is at the beginning of the Tribulation. Four is the number of the world, but how does a round earth have four corners? Dr. Henry Morris states on page 126 of his book, *The Revelation:*

> . . . accurate, modern geodetic measurements in recent years have proved that the earth actually does have four "corners." There are protuberances standing out from the basic "geode," that is, the basic spherical shape of the earth. The earth is not really a perfect sphere, but is slightly flattened

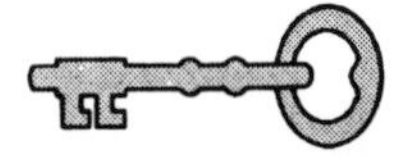

Key #17: The Wind

And after these things I saw four angels standing on the four corners of the earth, holding the four winds of the earth, that the wind should not blow on the earth, nor on the sea, nor on any tree. And I saw another angel ascending from the east, having the seal of the living God: and he cried with a loud voice to the four angels, to whom it was given to hurt the earth and the sea, Saying, Hurt not the earth, neither the sea, nor the trees, till we have sealed the servants of our God in their foreheads.

—Revelation 7:1–3

at the poles. Its equatorial bulge is presumably caused by the earth's axial rotation, and its four "corners" protrude from that. . . . The angles located in four different key positions on the earth, perhaps are able to control the great atmospheric circulation which governs the winds of the earth.

A NASA picture taken from outer space on a mission from earth to the moon does indeed show four corners on a round planet. But why would the angels want to hold back the winds? I live in Oklahoma City, the second windiest city in the nation according to the U.S. Weather Bureau (the windiest city being Lubbock, Texas). When I go to a part of the world where there is little or no wind, I hyperventilate, thinking that I have missed the Rapture and the world is coming to an end. It is difficult for me to imagine a world with no wind, no clouds moving, no tornadoes, no rain, etc.

Why? There are terrible and disastrous judgments in store for the nations of the world during the Tribulation, including deadly atomic explosions with equally deadly fallout spread by the winds. But nature is calmed and nothing moves until 144,000 of God's servants and witnesses for this hour are sealed in their foreheads. How long will the angels hold back the winds? We are not told, but probably not more than a few hours or days, because many things have to happen before the kingdoms of men become the Kingdom of our Lord Jesus Christ.

Key #18: The "Y" Chromosome

And I heard the number of them which were sealed: and there were sealed an hundred and forty and four thousand of all the tribes of the children of Israel. Of the tribe of Juda were sealed twelve thousand. Of the tribe of Reuben were sealed twelve thousand. Of the tribe of Gad were sealed twelve thousand. Of the tribe of Aser were sealed twelve thousand. Of the tribe of Nepthalim were sealed twelve thousand. Of the tribe of Manasses were sealed twelve thousand. Of the tribe of Simeon were sealed twelve thousand. Of the tribe of Levi were sealed twelve thousand. Of the tribe of Issachar were sealed twelve thousand.

—Revelation 7:4–7

144,000 Racially Pure Jews

John, in the continuing vision of things to come, sees an angel coming from the east to seal 144,000 servants of God in their foreheads. This sealing of these servants of God takes place at least three years before the Antichrist marks his servants on their foreheads or in their hands.

We are plainly told that all 144,000 are Israelites (Jews). Not an American, Englishman, Frenchman, Chinaman, or Ubangi among them. Paul informed us that in Christ there is neither Jew nor Greek, male nor female. So why in this assembly of God's servants depicted in Revelation 7, are there only Jews, and male Jews at that? Because the Tribulation period is not an extension of the Church age. The church is gone. The Tribulation period will once again be under the message of the Kingdom promise where the responsibility to bring the Gentiles into the Kingdom is that of Israel. If this were still the Church age, then these 144,000 Jews would be sealed with the Holy Spirit until the day of their redemption (Eph. 1:13; 4:30).

In Ezekiel 9 the prophet saw in a vision the sealing in the forehead of men in Jerusalem who abhorred the idolatry and sinfulness of the people. All who were not marked in the forehead were killed—men, women, and children. Ezekiel's vision seems to relate more to the Jerusalem of the Tribulation than to the Jerusalem of 586 B.C.

Of the tribe of Zabulon were sealed twelve thousand. Of the tribe of Joseph were sealed twelve thousand. Of the tribe of Benjamin were sealed twelve thousand.

—Revelation 7:8

But we are informed most definitely that there will be twelve thousand sealed from twelve tribes of Israel: 12 x 12 = 144,000. The tribal order in which each of the twelve divisions are sealed is as follows:

1. Judah	5. Nephtali	9. Issachar
2. Reuben	6. Manasseh	10. Zebulon
3. Gad	7. Simeon	11. Joseph
4. Asher	8. Levi	12. Benjamin

The sons of the Jewish father were to be assigned their birthright and blessing according to the order of their birth. Reuben was the first born of Jacob. Judah was the fourth son; yet, here we find Judah first and Reuben second. The reason is that Reuben failed to uphold his honored place, because he defiled his father's bed (1 Chron. 5:1–2). Judah prevailed as a leader, and from Judah was to come the "scepter" (Gen. 49:10). Gad, the seventh son, is elevated to third because the tribe of Gad was faithful to Moses and in obedience to the Lord more than others. Although the tribe of Gad suffered heavily, we read of their blessing in Genesis 49:19, "Gad, a troop shall overcome him: but he shall overcome at the last." Therefore, Gad is elevated to third. Benjamin, the youngest of Jacob's sons, is in the proper order, being sealed last. Others within the roster may be out of their birth order, but in searching the Scriptures we find their obedience, or disobedience, to the commandments of God according to Deuteronomy 28–30 determine their positions.

Now in the sealing listing we find Levi and Joseph. The tribe of Levi was not assigned a portion of land, because the Levites could choose where they lived from all the cities of Israel. This is why so many Levites lived in beautiful Jericho and the Judean Hills. The lot given to Joseph was divided between his two sons, Manasseh and Ephraim. In the listing, Manasseh maintains his place, but Ephraim is missing, as is Dan.

It is easy to understand why the tribe of Dan is absent from those Israelites called to serve God in the Tribulation. We read of Dan in Genesis 49:17, "Dan shall be a serpent by the way, an adder in the path, that biteth the horse heels, so that his rider shall fall backward."

Under Jeroboam, the golden calf was erected in both Dan and Bethel, in the tribe of Ephraim. Both apostatized and forsook the God of Israel. From Amos 5:18–19, some believe the Antichrist will come from the tribe of Dan. In any event, both the tribes of Dan and Ephraim suffered greatly in the Assyrian invasion and captivity period of 720 B.C. Foreigners were brought into their lands to intermarry with the Israelites left in the land. It was mainly from Ephraim that the Samaritans, half-Jew and half-Gentile, came. We read just from the book of Hosea:

5:9: "Ephraim shall be desolate in the day of rebuke. . . ."
6:10: "I have seen an horrible thing in the house of Israel: there is the whoredom of Ephraim, Israel is defiled."
7:8: "Ephraim, he hath mixed himself among the people; Ephraim is a cake not turned."
8:11: ". . . Ephraim hath made many altars to sin. . . ."

There are thirty-six condemnations of Ephraim in the book of Hosea alone, and at least fifty more in other books. Both Ephraim and Dan will occupy their tribal lands in the Millennium (Ezek. 48:1–6). Dan will also have a gate in the New Jerusalem, but Ephraim will not (Ezek. 48:30–35).

We are told much about the 144,000 sealed Jewish servants of God in the seventh chapter. However, we are given added information about them in chapter fourteen, where we learn the following things:

1. They have God the Father's Name written on their foreheads.
2. They were redeemed from the earth, and probably raptured or taken up into heaven at the middle of the Tribulation.
3. They sang a new song which only these Jewish redeemed can sing.
4. They are virgins, not being defiled by or with women.
5. They follow the Lamb, Jesus Christ, wherever He goes.
6. They are the firstfruits of the Tribulation and of Israel in resurrection.
7. They are blameless before the Throne of God; therefore, they must have placed their faith in Jesus Christ, the Lamb of God, who died for their sins.

Some who put the ministry of the two witnesses in the first half of the Tribulation believe that the 144,000 are converted to a belief in Jesus Christ as Messiah by the two witnesses. While this could be possible, we are not told this in any scripture. Others believe they are messianic Jews who did not make the Rapture, or relatives of messianic Jews. All we can safely conclude is that after the Rapture and the appearance of Antichrist, they come to saving faith in Jesus Christ as the true Messiah and their Savior.

Most who have written commentaries on the Revelation state without qualification that the 144,000 are Jewish men who have never been married, and who have never had a sexual relationship with a woman. I am of the opinion that the reference to their virginity has nothing at all to do with sex. No Israelite was ever commanded not to marry. In fact, members of the Sanhedrin had to be married. Aaron, the first high priest, had children and so did the judges and Levites.

To explain, let us first consider just the Aaronic priesthood. God covenanted with Aaron that his priesthood would be continued forever through his sons and their descendants, "And he shall have it, and his seed after him, even the covenant of an everlasting priesthood . . ." (Num. 25:13; also read Exod. 28:1; 29:9, etc.).

These promises were made to Aaron between 3,300 and 3,400 years ago. How can it possibly be known that the Cohens today are direct bloodline descendants of Aaron? If they are not, then there is no everlasting Aaronic priesthood to be continued in the Millennium.

It was discovered by biological science some 150 years ago that every cell in the body has a microscopic blueprint of that person. This blueprint is within forty-six chromosomes. Two of the forty-six chromosomes determine sex: female—XX chromosomes; male—XY chromosomes. Within each chromosome there are thousands of genes.

The psalmist was scientifically correct when he wrote that all his body parts were predetermined, even from the womb (Ps. 139:13–16). Jesus was also correct when He said that even the hairs on our head are numbered (Matt. 10:30).

When the male sperm unites with the female egg, twenty-three chromosomes from the woman and twenty-three chromosomes from the man unite to determine the characteristics, including sex, of the new life. This is the biological process by which the identity of Aaron has been passed down through his "Y" chromosome to his descendants today.

But the Jewish woman has had an important part in all this. A Cohen must not marry a Gentile, else his priestly line is cut off. Preferably, a Cohen is to marry a Jewish female also in the line of Aaron. We read in Luke 1:5–6 that Elizabeth, the wife of Zacharias, was of the daughters of Aaron, walking uprightly in all of God's commandments.

A Cohen cannot marry a divorcee, or a female, even from Aaron, who has had sex with another man previously.

There is a maze of additional restrictions too numerous to mention. Quoting from *THE TRIBE—The Cohen-Levi Family Heritage:* "A Cohen must be careful in selecting a proper mate, so as to pass his line and tradition to his children, and not to cause a break in the genealogical chain from Aaron."

We quote again from an article entitled, "The DNA Chain," from *THE TRIBE:*

> . . . The genetic information on a Y chromosome of a man living today is basically the same as that of his ancient male ancestors. . . . In the first study as reported in the prestigious British science journal, *Nature* (January 2, 1997), 188 Jewish males were asked to contribute some cheek cells from which their DNA was extracted. . . . Participants from Israel, England, and North America were asked to identify whether they were a Cohen, Levite, or Israelite, and to identify

> their family background. The result of the analysis of the Y chromosome markers of the Cohens and non-Cohens were indeed significant. A particular marker (YAP-) was detected in 98.5 percent of the Cohens.

The article continues to report there was also a second test in which 97 out of 106 Cohens tested had the Aaronic Y chromosome. It is indeed amazing that from the time Aaron and Moses led the children of Israel out of Egypt, over thirty-three hundred years ago, 95 to 99 percent of the Cohens can still be identified as descendants of Aaron and candidates for the priesthood when temple worship is restored. The percentage of Cohens who possessed the Y marker from Aaron from among the Sephardic and Ashkenazi Jews were the same. Additional tests proved that Ashkenazi Jews had no racial connection with the Khazars of southern Russia, something that I have consistently disputed on historical evidence.

In this same article we read that Jews with no ancestors from Aaron or Levi were tested, and we quote, "The finding was less than one-third." In other words, the Y identifications from the other tribal fathers like Judah or Gad showed up in only one-third of the male Jews. The Jewish father continues to pass the Y chromosomes on to his sons even though the mother may be a Gentile or part Jewish. But a Jewish mother who marries a Gentile cannot pass the Jewish Y chromosome on to her sons. The mother determines Jewish identity, but as we read from the article, "Tribe membership follows the father's line." The 144,000 are called in the Tribulation by tribal identification, but two-thirds of the Jews today can in no way know which tribe they belong to, even by DNA testing. The women of Israel over the past thirty-three hundred years have intermarried to the extent that tribal connections have been lost by 66.6 percent. The 144,000 will know their tribal identity, or at least God will know. The 144,000 will be virgins in the sense of their original tribal identifications; they will not have been defiled, or corrupted, by women. This does not mean the 144,000 Jewish males are virgins in the sense they are not married.

The word for virgin in Revelation 14 is *parthenos,* meaning to be separated as the church is to be a chaste virgin, separated from the world.

Considering that two-thirds of the Jews today have no tribal identification or association, Zechariah 13:8–9 is most interesting:

> And it shall come to pass, that in all the land, saith the LORD, two parts therein shall be cut off and die; but the third shall be left therein. And I will bring the third part through the fire, and will refine them as silver is refined, and will try them as gold is tried: they shall call on my name, and I will hear them: I will say, It is my people: and they shall say, The LORD is my God.

Tribulation Martyrs

The Apocalyptic scene in John's visions shifts suddenly from the 144,000 Israelites and their mission once more to the throne. Evidently gathered around and before the throne are millions clothed in white robes, indicating they are in Heaven in spiritual bodies before receiving their resurrected and glorified bodies. This fact alone should indicate they are not members of the church. We know they have been martyred for their faith in Jesus Christ, because we are so informed by the apostle John. Also, one of the elders asked who they are, and if they were members of the church, the elder would have known this.

The martyrs are evidently the completed number who will be killed by the Antichrist in the Tribulation, because we read of the martyrs of the first half of the Tribulation being told that ". . . they should rest yet for a little season, until their fellowservants also and their brethren, that should be killed as they were, should be fulfilled" (Rev. 6:1). Evidently, there will be many more killed by the Antichrist in the last half of the Tribulation, called the Great Tribulation, than in the first half. The martyrs of the first half of the Tribulation seem to be killed on a regional basis, but in the second half the martyrs come from every nation, language, and race. We are told in Revelation 13:7 that the Antichrist will have power over all nations, races, and tongues.

We believe these are the martyrs of the second half of the Tribulation, because we are told that they came out of Great Tribulation. Jesus said the days of the Great Tribulation, meaning the closing days of the Tribulation, must be shortened or no one could be saved (Matt. 24:21–22). Some of the martyrs also seem to have been burned by the sun, something that will occur only at the closing days of the Tribulation.

As the millions of martyred saints praise the Lord for their salvation, the entire angelic host fall down and worship God for these souls who are now in Heaven. There is joy in the presence of angels over one saved sinner (Luke 15:10), so John witnesses overflowing jubilation and joy from the angelic host in this scene.

Are the Tribulation martyrs of Revelation 7 the fruit of the mission of the 144,000 Jewish servants of God? We are not specifically told that they are, but the chronology seems to indicate that they will be. Else, why would God go to all the trouble to keep the 144,000 in the world during the reign of Antichrist?

A movie produced and released in 2003 titled *Gods and Generals* tells the story of the Civil War and the sufferings and tragedy that came out of this terrible conflict. Yet in spite of the horror and unspeakable misery, a revival swept both opposing armies and hundreds of thousands were saved. Out of ashes can come beauty (Isa. 61:3). Likewise, out of the greatest time of

After this I beheld, and, lo, a great multitude, which no man could number, of all nations, and kindreds, and people, and tongues, stood before the throne, and before the Lamb, clothed with white robes, and palms in their hands; And cried with a loud voice, saying, Salvation to our God which sitteth upon the throne, and unto the Lamb. And all the angels stood round about the throne, and about the elders and the four beasts, and fell before the throne on their faces, and worshipped God, Saying, Amen: Blessing, and glory, and wisdom, and thanksgiving, and honour, and power, and might, be unto our God for ever and ever. Amen. And one of the elders answered, saying unto me, What are these which are arrayed in white robes? and whence came they? And I said unto him, Sir, thou knowest. And he said to me, These are they which came out of great tribulation, and have washed their robes, and made them white in the blood of the Lamb. Therefore are they before the throne of God, and serve him day and night in his temple: and he that sitteth on the throne shall dwell among them. They shall hunger no more, neither thirst any more; neither shall the sun light on them, nor any heat. For the Lamb which is in the midst of the throne shall feed them, and shall lead them unto living fountains of waters: and God shall wipe away all tears from their eyes.

—Revelation 7:9-17

tribulation and human suffering the world will ever know, millions will be saved and glorify God with their lives forever. There will forever be a special relationship of love, mercy, comfort, peace, and joy between Jesus Christ and Christian martyrs. And as we behold our own circumstances and tribulations in consideration of the brevity of our sojourn on this planet, we can conclude as we look forward to Heaven: It's all over but the shouting!

Chapter Eight

The Seventh Seal

Returning to chapter five, we remember the seven-sealed book. Only Jesus Christ in Heaven or on earth will be able, and worthy, to open all seven seals. When all seven seals are opened, then the kingdoms of this world will become the Lord's Kingdom. We read again the catastrophic judgments that are determined with the opening of the sixth seal, "For the great day of his wrath is come; and who shall be able to stand?" (Rev. 6:17).

Therefore, with the opening of the seventh seal, the final judgments of the Great Tribulation—the time that never was or ever shall be—must begin. Whether the judgments of the seventh seal encompass the last forty-two months of the Tribulation, or just a part of the final forty-two months, is not certain. Some believe they will take place in one hour, but this cannot be proved either.

However, out of the seventh seal come seven angelic trumpeters, and from the sounding of the seventh trumpet come the seven vial judgments. Therefore, the seventh seal is the trumpet and vial judgments.

Most commentaries on Revelation reference extrabiblical books and come up with names for the seven angelic trumpeters. As far as I know, there are only two, and possibly three, angelic personalities identified by name in the Bible: Michael, Gabriel, and possibly Lucifer (who fell and became the enemy of God and man, Satan). All the millions of angels probably have names, but God evidently thought it not important that we know all their names before we get to Heaven. When we, the members of Christ's called-out assembly, are telling the angels to "pick it up here and put it there," then we can learn their names (1 Cor. 6:2–3).

While Michael and Gabriel may be two of the seven angels who can play the trumpet, we are not so informed. There is an old Southern gospel song with lyrics that go something like this:

> Gabriel don't you blow; Gabriel don't you blow;
> Gabriel don't you blow your horn, ho, ho.

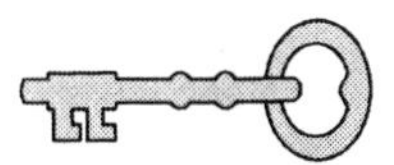

Key #19: Gabriel Don't Blow!

And when he had opened the seventh seal, there was silence in heaven about the space of half an hour. And I saw the seven angels which stood before God; and to them were given seven trumpets. And another angel came and stood at the altar, having a golden censer; and there was given unto him much incense, that he should offer it with the prayers of all saints upon the golden altar which was before the throne.

—Revelation 8:1–3

The lyrics to this gospel song were probably based on Revelation 8:1 where God demands total silence for one-half hour in Heaven before the first trumpeter can blow his trumpet.

In checking what Morris, Hindson, and Walvoord said about the half-hour silence in Heaven, I was surprised that neither took advantage of the tired pun that there will be no women in Heaven because women could not be silent for one-half hour. My observation would be that if the judgments to be unleashed will be so stunning as to keep the women in Heaven quiet for one-half hour, they must be real whizbangers.

How long is a half-hour in Heaven? Could it be based on the ratio that one day is with God as a thousand years? If so, then one day would be with God as 365,250 days; or thirty minutes would be something like 317 days, or about ten months . . . but we are not sure, so let's stick with just the approximate thirty minutes.

I have lived in Oklahoma all my life with the exception of three years in the Army in the South Pacific in World War II, and the times I have been out of the country on Bible tours and missions. Due to its geographic location, in the spring and summer months Oklahoma is known as Tornado Alley. About one-half hour before a tornado will strike a town or community, the wind stops completely and there is a strange and eerie silence. The silence is a warning that you are in the path of a dangerous tornado. This is the time to seek a storm shelter or move at right angles away from the storm. As the tornado approaches, a moving sound like a freight train gets louder and louder and then twisting winds between two hundred and three hundred miles an hour hit, blowing cars and leveling houses. The silence in Heaven preceding the blowing of the first trumpet is a warning of coming destruction upon the world.

Also, during this time of silence in Heaven, a very serious matter is to be addressed—the unanswered prayers of the saints. We read in Hebrews 8:5, and other scriptures, that the furniture and service in the temple were an example, or shadow, of the true temple in Heaven. A solemn service in the temple was the burning of frankincense on the altar of incense at the time of oblations and prayers. The smoke that arose from the incense represented the prayers that were ascending to the throne of God. The incense was so sacred that anyone using it for personal pleasure suffered the penalty of death (Exod. 30:34–38). Only Jesus at His birth was holy and worthy enough to receive a gift of frankincense.

We read in Luke 1:9–10 that the incense was burned with coals from the altar of sacrifice as prayers were being offered by the people outside the temple. When the people saw and smelled the smoke rising from the incense, they were assured that their prayers were ascending to the Lord. The Temple Institute is restoring the temple furniture for future worship when the temple is restored. The golden altar of incense is one of the items that is now ready.

Now . . . whose prayers and what kind of prayers are in the censer before the throne of God? We don't know . . . exactly. Some Revelation commentary authors believe they are the cries of the martyrs referenced in Revelation 6:10. However, these are cries for vengeance, and Jesus Himself instructed us to pray for our enemies' good, not evil. I am much more comfortable in presenting the probability that these are the prayers of all who have prayed as Jesus taught the disciples, "Thy kingdom come. Thy will be done, in earth, as it is in heaven." The Kingdom of Jesus Christ will not be established on this earth where His will shall be done in every nation until all the judgments under the seven seals are unleashed and finished on this planet. If the reader has prayed this prayer, then his or her prayer may be held in a heavenly deposit and be offered before the throne of God just before the first angelic trumpeter sounds his instrument.

In verse four we notice that the prayers of the saints are released and God evidently will take note of every petition. Certainly, every prayer offered in the Name of Jesus Christ is important. However these are all the prayers relating to one thing, and the one thing that can answer all these prayers is the breaking of Satan's hold on this present world. If the reader prayed for his or her sore toe to get well, or for a neighbor to quit parking their car in front of your house, God's will for these types of prayers has already been exercised.

And the smoke of the incense, which came with the prayers of the saints, ascended up before God out of the angel's hand. And the angel took the censer, and filled it with fire of the altar, and cast it into the earth: and there were voices, and thunderings, and lightnings, and an earthquake. And the seven angels which had the seven trumpets prepared themselves to sound.

—Revelation 8:4-6

We notice in verse five that the angel with the censer, after the prayers have been released, fills it with fire from the altar and then throws it upon the earth. What kind of fire is taken from the altar before the throne of God? I believe it is atomic fire.

In 1945 I was on Luzon, the northernmost of the Philippine islands. Although my unit was a sixteen-gun, 90-mm, antiaircraft battalion, we were assigned to the First Armored Calvary Division for artillery duty. As I was the only one in my unit who had training and experience in field artillery fire direction, I directed our guns in their firing missions. Once the island has been taken and secured, our unit pulled back into position at Clark Field. We were waiting, we thought, to get ready for the invasion of Japan. As July came and went, we began to worry as no preparation for the invasion was evident. We knew it would not be good to try to invade Japan in the winter months.

The splitting of the atom and the development of atomic bombs had been kept a secret. But on August 6, 1945, we learned why we were not getting ready to invade Japan. News came over the radio that the United States had dropped an atomic bomb on Hiroshima, a city of 350,000, destroying most of the city, and killing a large percentage of the population. Demands were made for Japan to surrender unconditionally. With the dropping of another atom bomb on Nagasaki, Japan gave up the fight. Here we had been fighting for three years, from New Caledonia, through New Guinea, and the Philippines, and now some egghead scientists had won the war in three days. How disgusting; how anticlimactic. But on August 6, 1945, the world changed. The human race has been on hold, waiting for man to use the fire from God's altar to destroy itself. Stars, including our sun, are atomic fusion instruments, and it is this power that the angel of Revelation 8:5 will cast upon the earth in the Tribulation. The apostle Paul prophesied of this time:

> Seeing it is a righteous thing with God to recompense tribulation to them that trouble you; And to you who are troubled rest with us, when the Lord Jesus shall be revealed from heaven with his mighty angels, In flaming fire taking vengeance on them that know not God, and that obey not the gospel of our Lord Jesus Christ.
>
> —2 Thessalonians 1:6–8

We notice also in verse five that as the result of the angel casting fire from the altar upon the earth, John heard voices. We are not told whether these are voices of those around the throne of God where there has been silence for one-half hour, or voices from earth in response to what is happening. We assume from the context these voices are concerns of the world masses, as Jesus warned, "hearts failing them for fear and for looking after those things which are coming on the earth . . ." (Luke 21:26). In the Revelation, John hears voices forty-six times. A psychiatrist may conclude that John had a mental problem and was hallucinating. However, every voice that John heard was associated with, or a fulfillment of, biblical prophecy in the preceding sixty-five books of the Bible. In studying the Revelation, as concluded by the early church fathers, the construction of the book itself proves that it was a revelation from God.

The First Trumpet

The first angel sounded, and there followed hail and fire mingled with blood, and they were cast upon the earth: and the third part of trees was burnt up, and all green grass was burnt up.

—Revelation 8:7

From where John stood in history in the year A.D. 96, the most dangerous weapons were the bow that would shoot an arrow about two hundred yards or a catapult that would cast a twenty-pound rock one hundred yards. Yet the apostle dared to prophesy that in the Tribulation, reaching 24,000 miles around the earth, one-third of the trees and all green grass would be burned up. True, this could be a catastrophic solar judgment, but considering the fact that Jesus is going to destroy those who intend to destroy the earth, we must at least consider nuclear warfare.

According to the *World Almanac* (2003, p. 7), the United States and

Russia have an estimated 10,000 nuclear bombs each. The Center for Defense estimates the United States has 35,000 nuclear weapons. The actual number may be somewhere in between. The A-bomb dropped on Hiroshima had the power of 20,000 tons of TNT. H-bombs in the arsenals of Russia and the United States have the power of 460 million tons of TNT, 35,000 times more powerful. Just one of these bombs creates an inferno that will burn trees, grass, automobiles, and buildings, within one hundred miles of detonation. Twenty-five bombs of this magnitude could practically destroy the United States within minutes, leaving few if any alive.

In 1987 in Goiania, Brazil, a city of one million, scrap hunters cut open an abandoned radiation therapy machine. The resulting cleanup operation filled 125,000 drums, 125,000 boxes, 85 houses were destroyed, 100,000 residents were decontaminated, and four died. Even those who might survive an initial nuclear explosion will face slow death and a miserable existence.

Is it conceivable that one-third of the trees and all the green grass on earth could be burned up in the next war? It is indeed possible. The Revelation is indeed not only a prophetic scenario of things to come, it is a believable one that has just been so in the last fifty years. Sir Winston Churchill observed, "War began to enter into its kingdom as the potential destroyer of the human race in the twentieth century."

The Second Trumpet

And the second angel sounded, and as it were a great mountain burning with fire was cast into the sea: and the third part of the sea became blood; And the third part of the creatures which were in the sea, and had life, died; and the third part of the ships were destroyed.

—Revelation 8:8–9

Dr. Henry Morris in his commentary on Revelation favors the opinion that the "great mountain burning" that plunges into the sea will be a giant meteorite, asteroid, or an orbiting satellite, possibly carrying hydrogen bombs. There has been much conjecture in recent years concerning an asteroid hitting the earth from outer space. Several have missed the earth in recent years by a few hundred thousand miles. Others have hit the earth in the past, leaving evidences like Crater Lake. Some even believe that the Gulf of Mexico was created by a giant asteroid.

It is interesting to note also that John does not name the sea, and he references sea in the singular noun. Could this be a particular body of water like the Mediterranean Sea or the Arabian Sea? Could these specific seas have one-third of all the ships?

We read of the coming battle of Armageddon in Zechariah 14:2, ". . . I will gather all nations against Jerusalem to battle. . . ." We also read in Revelation 16:14 that the armies of the kings of the earth will be gathered together for this great coming battle. According to a "Status of the U.S. Navy" report on the Internet dated March 10, 2003, of the eight aircraft carriers in service, five are either in the Arabian Gulf or the Mediterranean Sea. Of the thirty U.S. Amphibious Navy Task Groups, which includes destroyers and cruisers, twenty-one are in the Arabian Gulf, Gulf of Aden, Gulf of Oman, or the Mediterranean Sea.

Not only are the armies of the world to be gathered together in the Middle East, the navies of the world are already assembling in waters surrounding this area as a vanguard for gathering forces.

According to the U.S. Navy Status Report of March 10, 2003, there are forty-three submarines in service of three categories: guided missile submarines, attack submarines, and fleet ballistic missile submarines. All have nuclear weapons delivery systems, but the pride of the Navy is the eighteen submarines of the Trident class. Quoting from the Fact File of the United States Navy, March 10, 2003:

> Ohio-class/Trident ballistic missile submarines provide the sea-based "leg" of the triad of U.S. strategic deterrent forces. The 18 Trident SSBNs (each carrying 24 missiles), carry 50% of the total U.S. strategic warheads.

It has been calculated that one Trident submarine with twenty-four nuclear missiles has more destructive power than was unleashed in seven years of World War II. And if we consider the nuclear weapons the ships of other countries carry, the awesome destructive power becomes unimaginable. Russia has forty-seven submarines, and then there are England, China, Israel, and other nations with large numbers of both surface and submarine vessels carrying nuclear weapons.

While representatives of 191 nations meet at the United Nations to supposedly work for world peace, their military leaders at home meet to plan war. The following article is just an example of Jesus' warning that in the last days there would be wars and rumors of wars:

> **Russia Promises Weapons to China to Destroy U.S. Navy**
> NewsMax.com
> Thursday, Nov. 16, 2000
>
> In the event of hostilities between mainland China and Taiwan, top Russian military and political officials want China to have the potential of "guaranteed destruction of any U.S. navy aircraft carrier strike groupings" and have pledged to supply Beijing with the weapons it needs to accomplish this, Russia's *Nezavisimaya Gazeta* newspaper reports.
>
> According to the Hong Kong TaiYang Pao, Red China's military brass are developing a new five-year plan to enable the People's Liberation Armed Forces [PLA] to have "the strength to win a high-tech war against intervening foreign [U.S.] military forces while force is used against Taiwan," along with "the capability to counter-attack the hegemonist [U.S.] military forces, including the nuclear weapons capability."

It is reasonable to assume that in the event of another world conflict that one-third of sea life and one-third of the ships on the oceans could be destroyed in minutes.

The Third Trumpet

This judgment is as a great star burning like a lamp poisoning one-third of the earth's freshwater rivers and lakes. This could be the aftermath of an asteroid, or it could be the result of terrorist activities. The greater possibility is nuclear fallout from atomic warfare.

And the third angel sounded, and there fell a great star from heaven, burning as it were a lamp, and it fell upon the third part of the rivers, and upon the fountains of waters; And the name of the star is called Wormwood: and the third part of the waters became wormwood; and many men died of the waters, because they were made bitter.
—Revelation 8:10-11

It is interesting that the "great star" is named Wormwood. On April 26, 1986, the Chernobyl nuclear power plant in the Ukraine blew up. In spite of every effort to control the fallout, over 800,000 within a one hundred-mile area were killed or suffered nuclear poisoning. Even ten years later babies were being born without eyes, legs, or arms. On October 23, 1990, before the General Assembly of the United Nations, Mr. Kravchanka of Byelorussia made the following comment within a report on the nuclear tragedy:

> Then there was this new ordeal: Chernobyl, the Calvary of the twentieth century for the Byelorussian people. As I stand at this rostrum, in my mind I can hear the now stilled voices of my people cry out over and over again the same question: why? why? In Slavic languages, including the Ukrainian and Byelorussian languages, there is a word "chernobyl" which means wormwood, bitter grass. This has striking relevance to the Chernobyl tragedy. I am no fatalist. I do not believe in the blind inevitability of fate, but who can fail to be moved by these tragic and elegiac words from Revelation, which must leave their indelible imprint on the heart: ". . . and there fell a great star from heaven, burning as it were a lamp, and it fell upon the third part of the rivers, and upon the fountains of waters; And the name of the star is called Wormwood: and the third part of the waters became wormwood; and many men died of the waters, because they were made bitter" (The Holy Bible, Revelation 8:10–11).

Once again we see how the judgments coming upon the earth that John was shown can have a literal fulfillment in these last days. Should the fresh water supplies be contaminated with nuclear fallout, we cannot begin to consider the consequences.

The Fourth Trumpet

We have already commented on the mysterious solar and lunar activity with the opening of the sixth seal. Perhaps the sounding of the fourth trumpet is the actual result of what had been pre-written in the seven-sealed book. In any event, we summarize again what the Bible says about judgments from the sun and moon during the Tribulation:

And the fourth angel sounded, and the third part of the sun was smitten, and the third part of the moon, and the third part of the stars; so as the third part of them was darkened, and the day shone not for a third part of it, and the night likewise.

—Revelation 8:12

The Sun

The apostle John was shown an apocalyptic vision of the world during the last days of the Great Tribulation, and he wrote that because of the sun, ". . . men were scorched with great heat . . ." (Rev. 16:9).

The prophet Isaiah wrote of this time, ". . . the light of the sun shall be sevenfold, as the light of seven days . . ." (Isa. 30:26).

Jesus said: "Immediately after the tribulation of those days shall the sun be darkened . . ." (Matt. 24:29).

The prophet Joel predicted that when the great and terrible day of the Lord would come, "The sun shall be turned into darkness..." (Joel 2:31).

For many years astronomers concluded that our sun could maintain its present heat-energy output for at least five billion more years, because its hydrogen supply was only about half exhausted. However, more recently, astronomers have reappraised this theory, and now believe that once a star (our sun is a medium-sized star) has expended half its hydrogen, it is in danger of experiencing a nova. Larger stars supernova (blow up), and smaller stars, like our own sun, nova—get brighter and hotter for seven to fourteen days, and then become darker. There are about thirty novas a year in the observable universe. Some astronomers now believe that increased sunspot activity is a sign that our own sun may be about to nova. The nova of our sun would most assuredly: (1) cause the sun to become unusually bright (as Isaiah prophesied), (2) become seven times hotter (as John prophesied), (3) and then become dark (as Joel and Jesus prophesied).

The Moon

Isaiah prophesied, ". . . the light of the moon shall be as the light of the sun . . ." (Isa. 30:26).

Joel said of this time, "The sun shall be turned into darkness, and the moon into blood . . ." (Joel 2:31).

Jesus said, ". . . the sun shall be darkened, and the moon shall not give her light . . ." (Matt. 24:29).

Inasmuch as the moon has no light of its own, and reflects only that light which it receives from the sun, the prophetic Word is in perfect harmony with science. It naturally follows that when the sun becomes seven times brighter, as Isaiah prophesied, its reflected light upon the earth will make the night as hot and as bright as an average day. Then, when the sun becomes dark, as Jesus said it must, the moon will naturally give off no light. However, Joel indicates that at this time the moon will be turned into blood, or become red in appearance.

Another possible reason the third part of the stars, sun, and moon become darkened and the losing of one-third of the day could be the smoke from the obvious conflagrations taking place. We also remember what happened when Saddam Hussein of Iraq set the oil fields of Kuwait on fire in 1991. Thick smoke spread out and hid the earth from the sun for hundreds of miles. Isaiah indicated that this could happen in the Tribulation on a wider scope. Suppose all the oil fields of the Middle East caught on fire: "For it is the day of the LORD's vengeance, and the year of recompenses for the controversy of Zion. And the streams thereof shall be turned into pitch, and the dust thereof into brimstone, and the land thereof shall become burning pitch" (Isa. 34:8–9).

The loss of one-third of a day in the Tribulation could also possibly refer to the speeding up of the rotation of the earth, and there will be sixteen-hour instead of twenty-four–hour days. This could also be what Jesus meant when He said that, ". . . except those days should be shortened, there should no flesh be saved . . ." (Matt. 24:22).

Immanuel Velikovsky in *Worlds in Collision* and Donald Patton in *Catastrophism in the Old Testament* both suggest that in the past when Mars' orbit intersected Earth's orbit, there could have been a near collision and the orbits and rotation of both planets altered. Such an event may also explain why the ancients lived hundreds of years.

Woe! Woe! Woe! Have a Nice Day? Probably Not!

In the Old Testament "woe," Hebrew *oy*, means a pronouncement of judgment for bad or evil actions or deeds. We find this word used in twenty-two different scriptures. The Hebrew word *ho* is also interpreted "woe" in thirty-six Old Testament scriptures. But *ho* does not necessarily mean "woe." It could mean anything from "have a nice day" to "go jump in the lake."

And I beheld, and heard an angel flying through the midst of heaven, saying with a loud voice, Woe, woe, woe, to the inhabiters of the earth by reason of the other voices of the trumpet of the three angels, which are yet to sound!

—Revelation 8:13

Woe in Revelation 8:13 is the Greek word *ovai,* which means in the vernacular, "You dirty dog; you are really going to get it." In other words, the judgments of the last three trumpets will be far greater than the first three, if that is possible.

Chapter Nine

The First Woe

And the fifth angel sounded, and I saw a star fall from heaven unto the earth: and to him was given the key of the bottomless pit. And he opened the bottomless pit; and there arose a smoke out of the pit, as the smoke of a great furnace; and the sun and the air were darkened by reason of the smoke of the pit.
—Revelation 9:1-2

As noted previously, in the Old Testament under the Kingdom promise, angelic activity was common: Genesis 6; Sodom and Gomorrah; Israel's wilderness wanderings; etc. In the four gospels, both angelic and demonic activity were in evidence. Jesus offered the messianic Kingdom age, and even the demons wanted to know why He had come to judge them before their time. But there is no evidence of direct angelic activity after Acts 12:11 until the Tribulation. However, we are told that in the last days, not only would the direct intervention of God's angels increase, but also demonic activity would increase, because the devil would know his time was short.

As the fifth angel blows his horn, John sees a "star" fall from Heaven down to the earth. This is not a literal star, because this star is referenced in the same verse with a masculine pronoun "him." Spirit beings are often referred to as stars in the Bible. This may be the same event later described by John in Revelation 12:9 when Satan and his angels are cast down to the earth. Jesus also prophesied of this same future defeat of Satan in Luke 10:18, "And he said unto them, I beheld Satan as lightning fall from heaven."

We are not informed specifically that the "star" that falls from Heaven is Satan, but the evidence seems to indicate that it is. Also, we are not told just who gives this angel (who is probably Satan) the key to the bottomless pit. In the dissertation of Josephus on hades, it is explained that according to Jewish understanding, hades was divided into two compartments. Those who died in the messianic hope were in one compartment called "Abraham's bosom," or Paradise, awaiting their redemption. The other compartment was hell where the lost await final judgment. A wide gulf, or an abyss, was in between. This abyss could be the bottomless pit mentioned in Revelation 9:1. We know that the "rich man" looked over the gulf and saw Lazarus in Abraham's bosom.

In Luke 8:31 we read that the devils, or demons, begged Jesus not to send them "into the deep," which would seem to mean the bottomless pit.

We also read in Jude 6 that the angels which "kept not their first estate" are kept in chains of darkness until their future judgment.

In Luke 10 we read that Jesus sent seventy disciples out to preach the gospel of the Kingdom. While the number of the disciples was not 144,000, they did what the 144,000 will do in the Tribulation. Let us note the conversation that Jesus had with the seventy when they returned:

> And the seventy returned again with joy, saying, Lord, even the devils are subject unto us through thy name. And he said unto them, I beheld Satan as lightning fall from heaven. Behold, I give unto you power to tread on serpents and scorpions, and over all the power of the enemy: and nothing shall by any means hurt you.
>
> —Luke 10:17–19

Now here in the ninth chapter of Revelation Satan opens the bottomless pit and devils, or demons, come out the pit in the shape of scorpions and serpents, but they cannot hurt the 144,000 who have the seal of God in their foreheads. The Tribulation could have begun at Christ's crucifixion, but for the sake of the unsaved Gentile world, it has been postponed now for two thousand years.

At the sounding of the fifth trumpet, the bottomless pit is opened, and a plague of strange creatures John identifies as locusts with the stinging power of scorpions come out of the smoke. The eighth plague that Moses brought on Egypt was that of locusts. We read in Exodus 10:14–15:

> And the locusts went up over all the land of Egypt, and rested in all the coasts of Egypt: very grievous were they; before them there were no such locusts as they, neither after them shall be such. For they covered the face of the whole earth, so that the land was darkened; and they did eat every herb of the land, and all the fruit of the trees which the hail had left: and there remained not any green thing. . . .

The locust plague in the Tribulation is added evidence that Moses may be one of the two witnesses of Revelation 11. But these locusts described by John are not the grasshopper-type locusts that ate all of the green vegetation in Egypt, because we read there never would again be on earth this kind of locust. The Greek word for locust in Revelation 9:3,7 is *akris,* the same word used for locust in Matthew 3:4 and Mark 1:6, so the King James Version gives the correct meaning. Yet, they are indeed a strange type of insect, or monster, as John described them. But let us see what we can know about these creatures:

1. They come out of the bottomless pit.

And there came out of the smoke locusts upon the earth: and unto them was given power, as the scorpions of the earth have power. And it was commanded them that they should not hurt the grass of the earth, neither any green thing, neither any tree; but only those men which have not the seal of God in their foreheads. And to them it was given that they should not kill them, but that they should be tormented five months: and their torment was as the torment of a scorpion, when he striketh a man. And in those days shall men seek death, and shall not find it; and shall desire to die, and death shall flee from them. And the shapes of the locusts were like unto horses prepared unto battle; and on their heads were as it were crowns like gold, and their faces were as the faces of men. And they had hair as the hair of women, and their teeth were as the teeth of lions. And they had breastplates, as it were breastplates of iron; and the sound of their wings was as the sound of chariots of many horses running to battle.

—Revelation 9:3–9

And they had tails like unto scorpions, and there were stings in their tails: and their power was to hurt men five months. And they had a king over them, which is the angel of the bottomless pit, whose name in the Hebrew tongue is Abaddon, but in the Greek tongue hath his name Apollyon. One woe is past; and, behold, there come two woes more hereafter.

—Revelation 9:10-12

2. They do not eat grass or any green herbs or trees.
3. They have stingers much like scorpions.
4. While painful, their stings are not deadly.
5. They sting everyone except the 144,000 sealed Jews.
6. They live for five months.
7. Their shape is like a warhorse.
8. They have something like gold crowns on their heads.
9. They have faces like men.
10. They have hair like women.
11. They have breastplates (chest protectors) that look like iron.
12. They have wings.
13. When they fly, the sound is like stampeding horses.
14. They have teeth like lions.

Some types of insects appear every so many years. I remember when I lived on an acreage, that a long, six-inch, black and yellow larvae took over my cataba trees by the thousands. Within a few days the trees were stripped. I found out that one thing these huge worm-like things were good for was fish bait. I even gathered them by the gallons and froze them for future use. Since then, in the spring and summer, I look at every cataba tree I pass, hoping to find some more of these larvae for bait. This was in 1965, and I have not seen another one to this date.

But John does not give us even a hint as to just how big these creatures that come out of the bottomless pit will be. We are not sure if they are some kind of insect, or a type of human that looks like an insect. Soldiers wearing gas masks do have the appearance of a horse's head. Dressed in full battle gear with helmets, to John they may have appeared to be huge insects. That they have hair like women could mean that they are women. Women now serve in the armed services of most nations, especially Israel, the United States, and Russia.

Of course, another possibility is that the creatures that John saw are chimeras. It would be fairly easy for microbiologists to mix different life forms by recombinant DNA and come up with a life form such as John describes. As I document in my book *The New Creators,* scientists have been developing various life forms for the past fifty years. Scientists in China have no moral scruples against such Frankenstein procedures. If microbiologists can mix a firefly and a tobacco plant, which they have, and come up with a plant that glows in the dark, then they can do anything they imagine. According to a recent television program I watched about the future, designer human beings for space travel are being developed. More than twenty years ago scientists were working on these projects. In my book *The New Creators,* I included an article from the prestigious publication *Parent Magazine* of May 1981:

> Taking the concept of "gene therapy," as it is called, one step further has led others to think about creating new, improved beings by using other than human genes to give people traits they never had before. These hypothetical combinations of humans and other species referred to by scientists as *chimeras,* an ancient Greek name for a monster who was part lion, part goat, and part serpent. . . . The world is changing so rapidly that scientists are searching for ways to give us a helping hand. It is rumored that one American scientist is trying to develop humans with patches of chlorophyll so they can make food as plants do. And another researcher would like to create human beings who, like cows, can live on hay rather than the scarce food we now must eat. In a less complex experiment, in the late sixties, Chinese surgeon Dr. Ji Yongxiang successfully fertilized a chimp with human sperm to create a "near-human ape" to perform simple tasks. The pregnancy was terminated when rioters destroyed his lab, but Dr. Yongxiang, who believes that the world is ready for animal-human hybrids, advocates trying again.

Chimeras could be designed to live five months, or, if these creatures cannot eat as indicated, then they may not be able to live longer than five months. In this particular vision, John could have seen fleets of army helicopters bristling with guns and electronic gear. How could anyone in A.D. 96 describe helicopters except as monstrous flying locusts. However, without supporting evidence relating to what John actually saw, we must accept what the Scriptures report—demons out of the bottomless pit.

The fact that the torment during these five months will be so great that men will want to die, but cannot, seems rather strange. However, the Bible is replete with examples where individuals have been turned over to Satan for punishment, or even death (1 Cor. 5:5). As we read at the end of chapter nine, these are unregenerate sinners whom God allows to be punished so that they might repent. In this particular situation, Satan has been given the power of death (Heb. 2:14).

The Second Woe

We notice in Revelation 9:11 that the demons, and these doubtless include many of the angels who followed Satan and left their first estate, have a king over them. He is called Abaddon in Hebrew and Apollyon in Greek. It is apparent that before Satan fell from a superior status in God's Kingdom, possibly an archangel, he had his own angelic bureaucracy that followed him in his rebellion. Another of Satan's cohorts is Baalzebub, so spelled in the Old Testament and Beelzebub in the New Testament, called the prince of devils, and the lord of the flies. The name also has a relationship to dung in the Hebrew.

And the sixth angel sounded, and I heard a voice from the four horns of the golden altar which is before God, Saying to the sixth angel which had the trumpet, Loose the four angels which are bound in the great river Euphrates. And the four angels were loosed, which were prepared for an hour, and a day, and a month, and a year, for to slay the third part of men.

—Revelation 9:13–15

And the number of the army of the horsemen were two hundred thousand thousand: and I heard the number of them. And thus I saw the horses in the vision, and them that sat on them, having breastplates of fire, and of jacinth, and brimstone: and the heads of the horses were as the heads of lions; and out of their mouths issued fire and smoke and brimstone. By these three was the third part of men killed, by the fire, and by the smoke, and by the brimstone, which issued out of their mouths. For their power is in their mouth, and in their tails: for their tails were like unto serpents, and had heads, and with them they do hurt.

—Revelation 9:16–19

When the sixth angel sounds his trumpet, the second woe is announced. With the sounding of each succeeding trumpet the judgments become more severe. When the sixth trumpet sounds, the action that is to follow is announced by a voice that comes from the four horns of the golden altar. Horns signify kings, or absolute authority. Four is the number of the world. A perpetual fire was maintained in the altar. The fire signified God's eternal anger against sin, or His judgment for sin. Therefore, the priests were commanded to put some of the blood from the sacrifice on the four horns of the altar to signify that sin could only be covered, or forgiven, by the blood (Lev. 4:16–18). But the voice coming from the four horns of the altar is a warning to every sinner in the world that God will execute judgment against all whose sins are not covered by the blood of Jesus Christ.

As the sixth angel sounds his trumpet, four angels that have been bound in the Euphrates River are loosed. These must be angels of Satan, as only fallen angels are bound (Jude 6). If they had been under God's control, then they would not have needed to have been bound. But why would four angels of Satan be bound in the Euphrates River? We know that the city of Babylon was built upon the same foundation, or ground, upon which the Tower of Babel was erected. It was on this site that Nimrod defied God's will. It was here that God confounded man's language and scattered the human race by many races and languages throughout the world. Perhaps the four angels were Satan's angels who helped to build the tower that would reach into Heaven. But there must be some reason why on this spot the Tower of Babel and a counterfeit New Jerusalem, Babylon, was built; and why this area will one day be destroyed forever like Sodom and Gomorrah (Isaiah 13).

We know according to Revelation 16:12 that the Euphrates River must be dried up to make way for a huge army from the East to come to Armageddon. The specific number of this army is given as two hundred thousand thousand, or 200 million. Mao Tse-tung of China, when alive, was quoted as bragging he could raise an army of 200 million. Whether he actually made this statement or not, we do not know. However, it would be quite easy today for the nation of China alone to put this number in uniform, if not more. China in 2003 had a population of 1.3 billion; India's population has exceeded one billion; and there are at least another billion in the other oriental nations.

When I first went to China in 1978 it was the most backward nation in the world. The cities were hidden in smog; almost everyone rode bicycles; everyone wore drab Mao clothing; there were old black buildings; people earned commune labor wages—fifteen dollars a month. Today there are all-new airports; six- and eight-lane roads; traffic problems; all new airplanes; one hundred skyscrapers in Shanghai alone, and two hundred more going up. Service goods made in China now flood markets around the world. Yes, China could easily raise an army of 200 million.

We read that God has predetermined an exact year, month, day, and hour for these four angels to be unbound. We read in Galatians 4:4 that Jesus was born in the fullness of time, which was exactly four thousand years after Adam was created. Jesus said that neither Himself, nor any angel, nor any man, knew when He would come back to this earth. However, he said the Father knew. Therefore, there is an exact year, month, day, and hour for Jesus to return. While we cannot know this exact day, Jesus said we could know that it was near by the prophetic signs of the times. God knows the exact minute the Tribulation will begin and the exact minute it will end. From current signs in the Middle East, the time for the release of the four angels in the River Euphrates must be near.

John's description of this 200 million-man army:

1. They are horsemen—meaning men, not demons.
2. They evidently are mounted on horses (or vehicles).
3. They wear breastplates of fire, jacinth, and brimstone.
4. The heads of the horses appear as lions.
5. Fire, smoke, and brimstone come from the horses' mouths.
6. They have tails and heads like serpents.
7. This army kills one-third of the population left alive at the time.

It seems obvious that what John saw in the vision was a modern army with tanks, rifles, missiles, artillery, and an assortment of other contemporary weapons. Nine hundred years before the apostle John, the prophet Joel wrote about this same army in the Day of the Lord, the Tribulation. I suggest the reader read the book of Joel and see how it parallels the Revelation.

Why, when the earth's population will have been exterminated by at least 50 to 60 percent, will those left alive still not repent of their sins? The apostle Paul tells us why:

> And even as they did not like to retain God in their knowledge, God gave them over to a reprobate mind, to do those things which are not convenient; Being filled with all unrighteousness, fornication, wickedness, covetousness, maliciousness; full of envy, murder, debate, deceit, malignity; whisperers, Backbiters, haters of God, despiteful, proud, boasters, inventors of evil things, disobedient to parents, Without understanding, covenantbreakers, without natural affection, implacable, unmerciful: Who knowing the judgment of God, that they which commit such things are worthy of death, not only do the same, but have pleasure in them that do them.
>
> —Romans 1:28–32

And the rest of the men which were not killed by these plagues yet repented not of the works of their hands, that they should not worship devils, and idols of gold, and silver, and brass, and stone, and of wood: which neither can see, nor hear, nor walk: Neither repented they of their murders, nor of their sorceries, nor of their fornication, nor of their thefts.

—Revelation 9:20–21

We live in an age when knowledge has increased as Daniel prophesied. The sciences of mathematics, astronomy, chemistry, physics, and biology testify that this universe, this earth with all its millions of forms of life, with every entity of life from the elephant to the smallest virus having its own peculiar method of procreation, could not possibly have happened by evolutionary chance. Men will not acknowledge a Creator because they would then have a responsibility to this Creator. Today, man refuses to acknowledge that there is anything or anyone greater than himself—man himself is the product of his own godless, evolutionary process. This is why in the Tribulation, even in the face of disaster and extinction, men and women will find it impossible to bow their knee to Jesus Christ and confess Him as their Lord and Savior. Yet, throughout the book of Revelation we find that the judgments of God are righteous and merciful because,

> The Lord is not slack concerning his promise, as some men count slackness; but is longsuffering to us-ward, not willing that any should perish, but that all should come to repentance.
>
> —2 Peter 3:9

Chapter Ten

The Little Book

Chapter ten evidently continues the vision given to John in chapter nine about the demons loosed from the bottomless pit and the army of 200 million. After the judgment of the two woes, men and women left alive on earth do not repent, and John sees in the vision a "mighty angel" come down from Heaven. John describes the angel's appearance:

1. Clothed with a cloud;
2. A rainbow around His head;
3. His face as the sun;
4. His feet as pillars of fire.

Dr. John Walvoord and Dr. Ed Hindson both, in their commentaries on Revelation, say that the mighty angel is not Jesus Christ but could possibly be the angel Michael. Dr. John Morris in his book on Revelation expresses his belief that the mighty angel is Jesus Christ. On this particular scripture I agree with Dr. Morris.

No angel, including Michael and Gabriel, is so described elsewhere in the Bible. Daniel saw a preincarnate appearance of Jesus as described in the book of his prophecy, Daniel 10:5–6:

> Then I lifted up mine eyes, and looked, and behold a certain man clothed in linen, whose loins were girded with fine gold of Uphaz: His body also was like the beryl, and his face as the appearance of lightning, and his eyes as lamps of fire, and his arms and his feet like in colour to polished brass, and the voice of his words like the voice of a multitude.

If you were to ask an artist to draw this picture of the person that Daniel described, then the one that John described in Revelation 1:13–16, and the one that John saw in Revelation 10:1, and many other descriptions of the

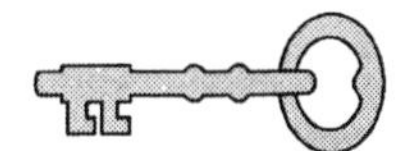

Key #20: The Sealed Little book

And I saw another mighty angel come down from heaven, clothed with a cloud: and a rainbow was upon his head, and his face was as it were the sun, and his feet as pillars of fire: And he had in his hand a little book open: and he set his right foot upon the sea, and his left foot on the earth, And cried with a loud voice, as when a lion roareth: and when he had cried, seven thunders uttered their voices.

—Revelation 10:1-3

glorified and risen Lord in other scriptures, all the pictures would appear much the same.

Dr. J. A. Seiss said of the mighty angel of Revelation 10:1:

> This person I take to be Lord Jesus himself. He is called an angel, but there is nothing in that to prove him a created being. Angel is a title of office, not of nature. In the Old Testament the Son of God is continually described as Jehovah-angel. . . . We do know that he appears in the Apocalypse as a Lamb, as a Lion, and as an armed Warrior, and there is nothing to hinder his appearance as an angel.

Dr. Seiss quotes the scholarship of his day (1860) to use the definite article "the" instead of the indefinite "a" in reference to the rainbow upon the head of the "mighty angel," pointing out this was not just any rainbow, but "the" rainbow. The first rainbow, as far as we know, appeared after the flood. In reading Genesis 9:9–17, not only was the rainbow the sign that God would never destroy the earth again by water, but also a sign of an everlasting covenant with mankind as long as "the bow shall be in the cloud." We note that the mighty angel was clothed with a cloud and the rainbow was in the cloud. The message again is, as we read in chapter nine, that Jesus is not coming back to destroy the earth, but to destroy those who would destroy the earth.

Peter saw Jesus as He will come a second time (2 Pet. 1:16–18), and His appearance is described thusly in Matthew 17:2: ". . . his face did shine as the sun, and his raiment was white as the light." So every description of Jesus Christ in His glory identifies with the mighty angel that John saw coming down to the earth.

John notes for us that the mighty angel has a little book in his hand. John also tells us that the book is open, indicating that it had been closed. The Greek for little here is *bibliaridion*, meaning a booklet. This "little book" could be the book of Daniel that was sealed to the time of the end, but now open (Dan. 12:9). It could be the seventh seal of the seven-sealed books. The "little book," whatever its contents or message, must have something to do with the title deed to the world. Adam and Eve relinquished dominion over the earth to Satan, subsequently referred to as the prince of this world. The fact that the mighty angel puts one foot in the sea and one foot on the earth signified taking possession of this entire planet.

Dr. Seiss comments:

> This was a distinct and deliberate act, and is full of significance. To set one's foot in a place, expresses a purpose to take possession of that place. Jehovah said to Israel, "Every place whereon the soles of your feet shall tread shall be yours."

Jesus Christ ascended back to Heaven from the Mount of Olives. When He returns He will come back to the same Mount of Olives. We read in Zechariah 14:4, "And his feet shall stand in that day upon the Mount of Olives. . . ."

During the closing days of Jesus' ministry on earth at His first coming, it came time for Him to tell the disciples that He must go away. He then revealed the signs of His return: "And as he SAT upon the mount of Olives, the disciples came unto him privately, saying, Tell us, when shall these things be? and what shall be the sign of thy coming, and of the end of the world?" (Matt. 24:3).

If Jesus were to be the received Messiah and bring in His Kingdom on earth, that was the time to do it. However, we note that He SAT down on the Mount of Olives as an indication that He knew it was not to be at His first coming.

In verse three of this chapter in Revelation we read that when the mighty angel stands on the earth and sea, he booms with a voice of seven thunders.

King David sang:

> The voice of the LORD . . . thundereth
> The voice of the LORD is powerful
> The voice of the LORD is full of majesty
> The voice of the LORD breaketh the cedars
> The voice of the LORD divideth the flames of fire
> The voice of the LORD shaketh the wilderness
> The voice of the LORD maketh the hinds to calve
>
> —Psalm 29

When the male lion moves to a new territory with his pride, he will roar several times to let the other male lions in the area know that this is now his territory. When Jesus returns, He will indeed come as the lion of the tribe of Judah. He will take charge. He will know what to do.

Walvoord, Seiss, Morris, and Hindson all seem to agree in that if John were told not to write the aftereffects of the seven thunders, then the readers should not be concerned. They seem to indicate that the seven thunders are a secret withheld by God, so let us not worry about them. Perhaps all four theologians are correct, but evidently John knew what they were, because he was ready to write about them just as he wrote about the four horsemen, the seven-sealed book, and the seven trumpets. I am somewhat jealous that John knew and I don't.

And when the seven thunders had uttered their voices, I was about to write: and I heard a voice from heaven saying unto me, Seal up those things which the seven thunders uttered, and write them not.

—Revelation 10:4

In the book of Revelation God shares with us terrible judgments that will shock the world in the Tribulation: earthquakes; millions lost at sea;

millions starving to death; millions killed in a nuclear war; millions beheaded for not taking the mark of the beast; millions dying of pandemic diseases. Yet, I think the judgments of the seven thunders will be even more terrible than any of these, and that is why John could not write them down. These judgments will be so horrible they are beyond mental comprehension.

Will the judgments of the seven thunders be more terrible than:

1. The crucifying of one thousand Jews every day before the walls of Jerusalem in the Roman siege (Josephus)?
2. Parents eating their children as well as animal dung during the same siege (Josephus)?
3. Nero covering Christians with tar and lighting the streets of Rome with their burning bodies?
4. Millions of Christians burned at the stake in the Dark Ages for defying the authority of the pope?
5. The Black Death killing 25 million in Europe in 1348–50?
6. The killing of at least 150 million in the wake of Communist revolutions in Russia and China in 1917–1975?
7. The murder of 100,000 residents of Nanking by the Japanese in 1935?
8. The sudden extermination of 80,000 in Hiroshima by a nuclear bomb in August of 1945?
9. The slow death of 36 million AIDS victims?
10. The sudden death of three thousand at the World Trade Towers on September 11, 2001, mostly by burning gasoline?

YES! YES! YES! The judgments of the seven thunders will be worse than any of the preceding human tragedies, or all of them combined, because both Daniel and Jesus Christ said of the Tribulation:

> . . . there shall be a time of trouble, such as never was since there was a nation even to that same time. . . .
>
> —Daniel 12:1

> For then shall be great tribulation, such as was not since the beginning of the world to this time, no, nor ever shall be.
>
> —Matthew 24:21

If the reader has not made a decision yet to put his or her faith in Jesus Christ as Lord and Savior, today is the day to be saved. Tomorrow may be too late.

> For God so loved the world, that he gave his only begotten Son, that whosoever believeth in him should not perish, but have everlasting life.
>
> —John 3:16

One objection raised by some to the mighty angel being Jesus Christ is that He swore by the Creator of Heaven and earth. Of course, we read in many scriptures that by and for Jesus Christ were all things created. Would Jesus swear an oath by Himself? This objection is answered in the following scriptures:

> The Lord GOD hath sworn by himself, saith the LORD the God of hosts, I abhor the excellency of Jacob. . . .
>
> —Amos 6:8

> For when God made promise to Abraham, because he could swear by no greater, he sware by himself, Saying, Surely blessing I will bless thee, and multiplying I will multiply thee. . . . Wherein God, willing more abundantly to shew unto the heirs of promise the immutability of his counsel, confirmed it by an oath."
>
> —Hebrews 6:13–14,17

And the angel which I saw stand upon the sea and upon the earth lifted up his hand to heaven, And sware by him that liveth for ever and ever, who created heaven, and the things that therein are, and the earth, and the things that therein are, and the sea, and the things which are therein, that there should be time no longer.

—Revelation 10:5-6

Jesus Christ has sworn an oath by Himself that He is coming back to take charge of this earth, which makes it an immutable promise, a promise that cannot be changed or broken. This fact in itself proves that the mighty angel is Jesus Christ. An angel could not make this promise.

We note in verse six the mighty angel ends his oath with the statement, "there should be time no longer." We know that the Tribulation period must be seven years, and the Millennium be one thousand years. So the time and dating process must continue. The word in Greek for "time" in this verse is *chronos,* which means delay. At Nineveh God changed His mind when Nineveh repented. However, we read in the last two verses of chapter nine that men on earth were determined not to repent. Therefore, God is justified in completing the judgments for the last half of the Tribulation. There would be no further delay in ending man's inhumanity to man and lifting nature from the curse of sin.

When the seventh angel sounds his trumpet, the seven bowls of God's wrath will be emptied upon the earth. The Lord Jesus Christ will return, and the mystery of God will be made known. I am sure the readers of this book have many questions about the mystery of God:

But in the days of the voice of the seventh angel, when he shall begin to sound, the mystery of God should be finished, as he hath declared to his servants the prophets.

—Revelation 10:7

> Why did God create this earth?
> Why did God create the devil?

And the voice which I heard from heaven spake unto me again, and said, Go and take the little book which is open in the hand of the angel which standeth upon the sea and upon the earth. And I went unto the angel, and said unto him, Give me the little book. And he said unto me, Take it, and eat it up; and it shall make thy belly bitter, but it shall be in thy mouth sweet as honey. And I took the little book out of the angel's hand, and ate it up; and it was in my mouth sweet as honey: and as soon as I had eaten it, my belly was bitter.

—Revelation 10:8–10

Why did God make a man who could sin?
Why would God send anyone to hell?
Why does God allow little children to suffer?
How can God raise us from the dead?
Why won't God give me a new car?
Why did God allow my husband to die?
Why did God allow Hitler to kill 6 million Jews?

There are many mysteries about God that I would like to know myself. But be assured in verse seven that God has revealed a plan to the prophets. These prophets revealed God's plan and purpose for this earth and the human race in the prophetic books of the Bible. This plan and purpose will be fulfilled, and when this is done, all these incidental questions about God will be answered. I am just as impatient as the reader, but we will just have to wait. According to Peter, we can take assurance from the fulfillment of prophecy that everything else will be taken care of, because God knows how to do it (2 Pet. 1:19–21; 2:9).

In this vision in chapter ten of Revelation, John is told by a voice from Heaven to go and take the little book that is in the hand of the mighty angel. As John takes the little book, he is told to eat it and that it would be sweet to his taste but bitter in his stomach.

I remember during the Great Depression days when practically everything we ate was raised on the farm. The first vegetable in the garden to mature was snow peas. We would be so hungry for green vegetables, and we would eat snow peas for a week. Then early Irish potatoes would mature, and we would eat potatoes for a week, then the early corn, etc. The first fruit to become edible was early apples. Us kids would be hungry for fruit, and so we would get a salt shaker and knives and go to the apple trees before they were ripe. The green and sour apples were delicious, but they would give us a severe stomachache.

Of course, we know that John did not literally eat the book. King David said the Word of God was sweeter than honey (Ps. 19:10). Ezekiel found the book he was given to eat to be bitter with mourning and woe, because it was about the sufferings that would come upon Israel. Eating a book symbolically simply means to mentally digest it. That God has a plan and purpose to make this world a more beautiful, safer, and kinder place for man to live is certainly sweet, but there will be untold suffering and death before this happens.

And he said unto me, Thou must prophesy again before many peoples, and nations, and tongues, and kings.

—Revelation 10:11

Based on the statement in Revelation 10:11 that John must prophesy again before many people, nations, languages, and kings, Tertullian in A.D. 210 and Origin in A.D. 228, both believed that John would be one of the two witnesses, and Elijah would be the other. Seiss does not even comment on this verse. Hindson quotes Mounce as believing that this means that John was to complete the prophecy of Revelation; Morris agrees, stating that up to this point, John's writing of the Revelation is only half completed. Walvoord quotes an ambiguous reference by Swete stating that the second half of the Revelation involves many nations and races. To this consensus I will simply add that John did go back to Ephesus and completed the mission given to him by the Lord. Victorinus (A.D. 280) wrote:

> For when Valentinus, Cerinthus, Ebion, and others of the school of Satan were scattered abroad throughout the world, all of the bishops assembled together to John from the neighboring provinces and compelled him to draw up his testimony.

Iranaeus (A.D. 180) wrote of John:

> There are also those who heard from [Polycarp] that John, the disciple of the Lord, went to bathe at Ephesus. But realizing that Cerinthus was within, John rushed out of the bath house without bathing. Instead, he exclaimed, "Let us fly, lest even the bath house fall down, because Cerinthus, the enemy of the truth is within."

John did indeed finish the Revelation, and he also went back to Asia and bore witness of Jesus Christ to bishops, pastors, ministers, and rulers. He was called home to be with the Lord in about A.D. 100, and a tomb where his body was buried is located in the foundation of the Church of St. John at Ephesus, or so the sign reads.

As to John being one of the two witnesses of Revelation 11, I doubt it. But, I have been wrong before.

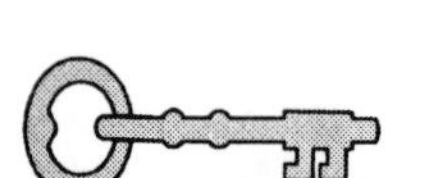

Key #21: Who? How? Why?

And there was given me a reed like unto a rod: and the angel stood, saying, Rise, and measure the temple of God, and the altar, and them that worship therein. But the court which is without the temple leave out, and measure it not; for it is given unto the Gentiles: and the holy city shall they tread under foot forty and two months.

—Revelation 11:1-2

Chapter Eleven

The Two Witnesses

In chapter eleven we are first confronted with a temple in Jerusalem. This presents an immediate problem, because there has been no Jewish temple in Jerusalem for almost two thousand years. Next, we are presented with two mysterious witnesses with unusual powers, and we wonder just who they are; how do they do what they do; and why do they do it?

Jesus said of the temple in Jerusalem in the Olivet Discourse that it would be destroyed and not even one stone would be left on another. This occurred in A.D. 70. But here in chapter eleven of the Revelation John sees another temple standing in Jerusalem.

Solomon's Temple. The first temple was built during the administration of King Solomon, but most of the money and materials had already been set aside by King David, Solomon's father. The cost was 108 talents of gold, 10,000 darics of gold, and 1,017,000 talents of silver. The size was approximately 100 feet long, 30 feet wide, and 45 feet high. The work was done with 150,000 Canaanites and 30,000 Israelites. According to Ussher, it was completed and the ark of the covenant placed in the Holy of Holies in the year 1004 B.C., exactly one thousand years before Jesus Christ was born of the Virgin Mary. The fourth millennium began with the completion of the first temple. Solomon's Temple was robbed and burned by the Babylonians on the ninth of Av, 586 B.C. The temple was completely overlaid with gold on the inside. This gold ended up in Babylon on the image of Nebuchadnezzar (Dan. 3).

Zerubbabel's Temple. After the fall of Babylon to the Medo-Persian Empire, Cyrus of Persia permitted the Jews in captivity who wished to return and rebuild their temple to do so under the leadership of Zerubbabel. Although there are no specific dimensions of Zerubbabel's Temple available, the new temple seemed to follow the outline of the former temple. The precious metals were provided by a freewill offering from the Jews. The new temple was completed in 515 B.C., but it was not nearly as beautiful as Solomon's Temple. The workmen and costly materials that went into building the first temple were simply not available. Cyrus allowed the Jews to take back the furnishings and vessels of Solomon's Temple that had been in storage in Babylon. However there was no ark in the second temple. No mention in Scripture is made of the ark after the visit of the Queen of Sheba to Solomon. There is some indication that either the queen or her son by Solomon took the ark to Ethiopia. Other unverified accounts place the ark in a cave on the west side of Mount Nebo or underneath the Temple Mount.

Herod's Temple. There is a difference of opinion as to whether Herod's Temple was an enlargement of Zerubbabel's Temple or an entirely new temple. There are some indications that Herod, being a mighty builder and a supreme egotist, would have torn the old temple down and erected one that was completely his. In any event, Herod's Temple was almost twice as big as either of the former temples. It was also more beautiful and ornate, as the disciples pointed out to Jesus. Herod began the rebuilding of the temple in Jerusalem in 20 B.C., and according to Josephus, it was not completed until A.D. 45, long after King Herod had died. We read in John 2:19–20, "Jesus answered and said unto them, Destroy this temple, and in three days I will raise it up. Then said the Jews, Forty and six years was this temple in building, and wilt thou rear it up in three days?"

This occurred within a year after Jesus began His ministry at thirty years of age. Counting the four-year error in the calendar, the year would have been A.D. 26, and adding twenty years to the time of John 2:19, the temple would have indeed been under construction for forty-six years.

In any event, Herod's Temple was completely destroyed by the Romans, as Jesus prophesied in A.D. 70, forty years after He foretold the event. Forty is the number of testing or judgment. Josephus, an eyewitness to the destruction of the temple, recorded in *Wars of the Jews,* book six, chapter five:

> So Titus retired into the tower of Antonia, and resolved to storm the temple the next day, early in the morning, with his whole army, and to encamp round about the holy house; but, as for that house, God had for certain long ago doomed it to the fire; and now that fatal day was come, according to the revolution of ages: it was the tenth day of the month Lous [Ab], upon which it was formerly burnt by the king of Babylon; although these flames took their rise from the Jews themselves, and were occasioned by them; for upon Titus's retiring, the seditious lay still for a little while, and then attacked the Romans again, when those that guarded the holy house fought with those that quenched the fire that was burning in the inner [court of the] temple; but these Romans put the Jews to flight, and proceeded as far as the holy house itself. At which time one of the soldiers, without staying for any orders, and without any concern or dread upon him

> at so great an undertaking, and being hurried on by a certain divine fury, snatched somewhat out of the materials that were on fire, and being lifted up by another soldier, he set fire to a golden window, through which there was a passage to the rooms that were round about the holy house, on the north side of it. As the flames went upward the Jews made a great clamor, such as so mighty an affliction required, and ran together to prevent it; and now they spared not their lives any longer, nor suffered anything to restrain their force, since that holy house was perishing, for whose sake it was that they kept such a guard about it.

Josephus continued to report that Titus rushed to save the temple and put out the fire, but the noise and confusion was so great that the soldiers either did not hear him, or ignored his orders. Josephus also notes that God had already ordained that the temple be destroyed, and what happened was the fulfillment of this prophecy. But the only prophet who prophesied the destruction of that temple was Jesus Himself (Matt. 23:38; 24:2). This statement lends proof that Josephus did indeed acknowledge Jesus Christ as Messiah:

> Now, there was about this time, Jesus, a wise man, if it be lawful to call him a man, for he was a doer of wonderful works,—a teacher of such men as receive the truth with pleasure. He drew over to him both many of the Jews, and many of the Gentiles. He was [the] Christ; and when Pilate, at the suggestion of the principal men amongst us, had condemned him to the cross, those that loved him at the first did not forsake him, for he appeared to them alive again the third day, as the divine prophets had foretold these and ten thousand other wonderful things concerning him; and the tribe of Christians, so named from him, are not extinct at this day.
>
> —*Antiquities of the Jews,* book 18, chapter 3

The common calendar of Josephus' day gave the date for the destruction of both temples as the tenth of Lous, or Ab. The Jewish calendar today notes for the ninth of Ab, "Feast of the 9th of Ab—Day of mourning—both the first and second temples were destroyed on this day." The ninth of Ab in 2003 fell on August 7.

After A.D. 70, there were attempts to rebuild the temple but none succeeded, and the temple site became a garbage dump after A.D. 200. The Moslems under Omar conquered Jerusalem around A.D. 700, cleaned the temple site, and the Dome of the Rock was erected by Omar the Second. In 1967 the Israeli army took possession of the Temple Mount, but because the leadership of Israel at the time was primarily agnostic and atheistic, there was no interest in rebuilding the temple. The Temple Mount was left under the control of Jordanian and Muslim authority.

Some religious Jews continue to engage in efforts to rebuild the temple and others believe they should wait until the Messiah comes and let Him build the temple. The Temple Mount Faithful organization has attempted to get Jews interested in taking possession of the Temple Mount and then rebuild the temple. The Temple Institute has made all of the temple furnishings and vessels with the exception of the ark of the covenant; this organization is also training Levites and Cohens in the conducting of Jewish sacrificial temple worship services. "For the children of Israel shall abide many days without a king, and without a prince, and without a sacrifice. . . . Afterward shall the children of Israel return, and seek the LORD their God, and David their king; and shall fear the LORD and his goodness in the latter days" (Hos. 3:4–5).

The prophet provides us an indication of just how many days Israel would be without a temple in Hosea 6:1–2: "Come, and let us return unto the LORD; for he hath torn, and he will heal us; he hath smitten, and he will bind us up. After two days will he revive us: and in the third day he will raise us up, and we shall live in his sight."

Israel has been torn, smitten, and without a temple for two thousand years. If we consider one day as a thousand years with God (Ps. 90:4; 2 Pet. 3:8), then it must be time for another temple.

Chronology Check

Before we proceed in chapter eleven, let us see at what point we are in the Tribulation in our study. We have assumed, and I think correctly so, that the ministry of the 144,000 is in the first half of the Tribulation. In Revelation 9:4 we find the 144,000 are still in the world. In Revelation 14:1–4, the 144,000 have been translated from earth to Heaven. In Revelation 11:3 John sees the ministry of the two witnesses for three and one-half years about to begin. In Revelation 11:1–2 John sees a Jewish temple on Mount Moriah with services evidently in progress. Inasmuch as the Antichrist will stop Jewish service in the temple at the middle of the Tribulation (Dan. 9:27), then verses two and three of chapter eleven must be either the beginning of the Tribulation, or the very end of the first half of the Tribulation. Larkin and Walvoord put the ministry of the two witnesses in the second half; most others who have written commentaries on Revelation put them in the first half. I will explain in more detail as to why I favor putting the two witnesses in the first half of the Tribulation in the consideration of verses thirteen and fourteen of chapter eleven.

In Revelation 11:1 John is instructed by the mighty angel to take a reed and measure the temple, the altar, and the people who worship at the temple. It is evident that there is more involved than linear or vertical measurements. The reed is like a rod, a standard measuring stick of 15.05 feet, or about ten cubits. God evidently takes stock of the people who worship, why they are worshipping, what god are they worshipping and why. For the first time in Jewish history, King Herod allowed Gentiles to worship, or at least visit, in an outer court of the temple on Mount Moriah. The same will evidently be true in at least the first half of the Tribulation. Jerusalem was trodden down by the Gentiles for almost two thousand years. In 1967 Israel regained control of the Old City of Jerusalem, but there have been many proposals before the United Nations to make it an international city. This may become a reality when the Antichrist makes the seven-year agreement with Israel (Dan. 9:27).

And I will give power unto my two witnesses, and they shall prophesy a thousand two hundred and threescore days, clothed in sackcloth. These are the two olive trees, and the two candlesticks standing before the God of the earth. And if any man will hurt them, fire proceedeth out of their mouth, and devoureth their enemies: and if any man will hurt them, he must in this manner be killed. These have power to shut heaven, that it rain not in the days of their prophecy: and have power over waters to turn them to blood, and to smite the earth with all plagues, as often as they will.

—Revelation 11:3-6

The Return of Elijah

The mighty angel, whom we have already understood to be Jesus Christ, tells John about the coming Tribulation temple (or tabernacle as indicated in Amos 9, or Holy Place, as indicated in 2 Thessalonians 2). But then the mighty angel immediately goes from the temple into the matter of two witnesses. These are just not any two witnesses, but MY two witnesses. The two witnesses that testified of Christ's first coming were ". . . the prophets and the law . . ." (Matt. 11:13). Inasmuch as the two witnesses of Revelation 11 are to be flesh and blood, we would assume that one would be a foremost Old Testament prophet and one would be the foremost representative of the law. And, inasmuch as Jesus immediately turned from the temple to the two witnesses, we would also assume that they would have a connection with the temple. The time period of their ministry is to be forty-two months of thirty days each, or three and one-half years. Their attire of sackcloth indicates bad news for sinners and enemies of God.

The two witnesses are not named. Although unlikely, they could be two people of contemporary identity, but more likely, two Old Testament personalities. Jesus provides a clue to their identity in verse four: two candlesticks and two olive trees ". . . standing before the God of the earth."

In Zechariah 4 the prophet saw one candlestick and two olive trees "... that stand by the Lord of the whole earth" (vs. 14). Zechariah was told that the candlestick stood for Zerubbabel, the builder of the second temple. The two olive trees stood for the "two anointed ones" who would perform their ministry ". . . Not by might, nor by power, but by my spirit, saith the LORD of hosts" (vs. 6).

Again, the representative symbolism that associates Zechariah 4 and Revelation 11 is that the two witnesses will have something to do with the rebuilding of the Tribulation temple and be anointed with the Holy Spirit, which is above all power on earth.

What the two witnesses will do for three and one-half years:

- Fire out of their mouths will destroy their enemies
- Whoever tries to kill them will themselves be killed
- They will stop the rain on earth for three and one-half years
- They will turn water into blood
- They will bring many judgments as required

God speaks of a special "messenger" to Israel in Malachi 3:1–2:

> Behold, I will send my messenger, and he shall prepare the way before me: and the Lord, whom ye seek, shall suddenly come to his temple, even the messenger of the covenant, whom ye delight in: behold, he shall come, saith the LORD of hosts. But who may abide the day of his coming? and who shall stand when he appeareth? for he is like a refiner's fire, and like fullers' soap.

This is not just any messenger; it is "my messenger." Verse one refers to Christ's first coming; verse two refers to His Second Coming. But will He also come to the Tribulation temple at His Second Coming? Possibly, but it will be only to destroy it, because then He will build His own temple (Zech. 6:12).

The last three verses of Malachi, the last message from God to Israel for four hundred years, identifies the messenger who is to come before the Lord as Elijah:

> Remember ye the law of Moses my servant, which I commanded unto him in Horeb for all Israel, with the statutes and judgments. Behold, I will send you Elijah the prophet before the coming of the great and dreadful day of the LORD: And he shall turn the heart of the fathers to the children, and the heart of the children to their fathers, lest I come and smite the earth with a curse.

Here we read that Moses, the lawgiver, and Elijah, the prophet, are connected with the second coming of Jesus Christ. The apostles wanted proof, not only that Jesus was the Messiah, but that He would come again. Jesus took them upon a high mountain and was transfigured into the appearance He would be when He did return. We read in Matthew 17:3 that both Moses and Elijah not only appeared with Jesus, but that they were talking with Him. Now we are told what Jesus, Moses, and Elijah were discussing, but notice what loud-mouth and impetuous Peter said when he interrupted them: "Then answered Peter, and said unto Jesus, Lord, it is good for us to be here: if thou wilt, let us make here three tabernacles; one for thee, and one for Moses, and one for Elias" (Matt. 17:4).

It is obvious that Jesus, Moses, and Elijah, in their conversation, brought up the subject of the tabernacle or temple. The Greek word used for tabernacle is *skene,* which means dwelling place. In reference to the Lord's dwelling place, it could be interpreted the Lord's House, or temple. But Peter impetuously broke in: "Lord, if you want a temple, then it is a good thing that we came up here with you. We will not only build you a temple, we will also build one for Moses and Elijah!"

Some object to Moses being one of the two witnesses, because it is recorded in Deuteronomy 34:5 that Moses died and was buried in the land of Moab. However, it is also noted that no man knows where he was buried. We also read in Jude 9 that Michael and the devil evidently had an argument about who was to get the body of Moses.

As to Elijah being one of the two witnesses, we are not informed specifically that he will be one of them. However, evidence indicates that he will be.

1. Elijah withheld rain for three years in Israel.
2. Elijah brought fire down from Heaven on Mount Carmel.
3. Elijah confronted wicked King Ahab with his sins.
4. Elijah stood against the evil works of Jezebel, the queen.
5. Elijah challenged the prophets of Baal.
6. Elijah's ministry led seven thousand to reject Jezebel's false god.
7. Elijah was caught up to Heaven in a fiery chariot.

Likewise, in the Tribulation Elijah will turn, we believe, 144,000 in Israel to the true God. He will with fire destroy his enemies. It will not rain for three and one-half years during his ministry. As he stood against Ahab and Jezebel, he will also stand against the Antichrist and the Great Whore, the false church. He will be killed, but resurrected and taken up to Heaven. As prophesied, he will come before the last half of the Tribulation, noted as the Great Tribulation, the time of Jacob's trouble.

Some so-called scholars contend that Elijah will not come back because John the Baptist fulfilled the prophecy of Elijah's coming to prepare the way for the Messiah. Jesus said of John the Baptist: ". . . This is he, of whom it is written, Behold, I send my messenger before thy face, which shall prepare the way before thee" (Matt. 11:10). "For all the prophets and the law prophesied until John. And if ye will receive it, this is Elias, which was for to come" (Matt. 11:13–14).

The key phrase in this scripture is "if ye will receive it," meaning Jesus as the Messiah who would bring in the Kingdom. On another occasion Jesus was asked if He were the Messiah, where was Elijah who was to come first, "And his disciples asked him, saying, Why then say the scribes that Elias must first come? And Jesus answered and said unto them, Elias truly shall first come, and restore all things. But I say unto you, That Elias is come already, and they knew him not, but have done unto him whatsoever they listed . . ." (Matt. 17:10–12).

John the Baptist did fulfill in type the mission of Elijah at Jesus' first coming. John announced Jesus as the Christ: ". . . Behold the Lamb of God, which taketh away the sin of the world" (John 1:29). Just as Elijah stood up and challenged Ahab and Jezebel, so did John the Baptist condemn Herod for living with his brother Philip's wife, Herodias, in an adulterous relationship. John was beheaded by Herod just as Elijah will be beheaded by the Antichrist. As Jesus said, if Israel had accepted Him as the Messiah, then John the Baptist would have fulfilled the mission of Elijah. But because Israel did not, "then Elijah must truly come first." There is an interesting account of John the Baptist's execution in *Antiquities of the Jews* by Josephus, book eighteen, chapter five.

It is obvious that Moses, the lawgiver, could also be one of the two witnesses of Revelation 11. He turned water into blood in Egypt and brought all kinds of plagues on Pharaoh. There is also no other explanation as to why Michael and Satan argued over the body of Moses. The objection that many who have written commentaries on Revelation have to Moses being one of the two witnesses is that he died. Therefore, they think Enoch will be one because " . . . it is appointed unto men once to die . . ." (Heb. 9:27), and Enoch never died. Yet these same authors have no trouble at all accepting the bringing back to life of Lazarus even after his body was decaying, or the widow's son, or others. It is apparent that they later died and are awaiting the resurrection. On the other hand, those Christians alive when the Rapture comes will never die. Did God bring Moses back to life and Michael took him to Heaven to await with Elijah their mission in the Tribulation? This is one of those mysteries of God that will be cleared up when we all get to Heaven.

At the conclusion of their ministry, God withdraws His protection from the two witnesses and the "beast" of Revelation 13 kills them. The "beast" has not been mentioned by John in any previous chapter, and this again illustrates that the visions that the apostle were shown overlap. However, John would have known about the "beast" from Daniel 7:7–8. The death of the two witnesses will remove the last obstacle for the Antichrist to have complete control over the nations of the world.

Inasmuch as we read in Revelation 20:4 that the method of execution used against all who oppose the Antichrist will be beheading, we assume this is the method by which the two witnesses will die. It will be at the midway point of the Tribulation that the Antichrist will stop the Jewish worship in the temple, and it will probably be at this time that the two

And when they shall have finished their testimony, the beast that ascendeth out of the bottomless pit shall make war against them, and shall overcome them, and kill them. And their dead bodies shall lie in the street of the great city, which spiritually is called Sodom and Egypt, where also our Lord was crucified. And they of the people and kindreds and tongues and nations shall see their dead bodies three days and an half, and shall not suffer their dead bodies to be put in graves.

—Revelation 11:7-9

And they that dwell upon the earth shall rejoice over them, and make merry, and shall send gifts one to another; because these two prophets tormented them that dwelt on the earth. And after three days and an half the Spirit of life from God entered into them, and they stood upon their feet; and great fear fell upon them which saw them. And they heard a great voice from heaven saying unto them, Come up hither. And they ascended up to heaven in a cloud; and their enemies beheld them. And the same hour was there a great earthquake, and the tenth part of the city fell, and in the earthquake were slain of men seven thousand: and the remnant were affrighted, and gave glory to the God of heaven. The second woe is past; and, behold, the third woe cometh quickly.

—Revelation 11:10–14

witnesses will be killed in Jerusalem. When Jesus knew that His time for crucifixion was at hand, He said, ". . . I must walk to day, and to morrow, and the day following: for it cannot be that a prophet perish out of Jerusalem" (Luke 13:33).

The dead bodies of the two witnesses will be allowed to lie in the streets of Jerusalem for three and one-half days. But why will God allow their bodies to stay in the streets this long before He raises them up? Today, when someone stops breathing and is apparently dead, a physician or coroner comes and officially pronounces them dead and signs a death certificate for legal and insurance reasons. In Bible times this was not possible, so relatives or civic authorities would allow three days to pass before the deceased was declared officially dead. In Israel this three-day waiting period was strictly observed. This is why Jesus waited until the fourth day to raise Lazarus from the tomb (John 11:17). This is also why Jesus Christ lay in the tomb a full seventy-two hours and was raised at the beginning of the fourth day. He was crucified on Wednesday before the High Sabbath, which was the first day of Passover on Thursday. He could not have been crucified on Friday as is commonly believed. Likewise, the two witnesses cannot be raised from the dead until the fourth day.

However, for three and one-half days, or eighty-four hours, the major TV services, possibly including CNN, will show their dead bodies to world audiences. As indicated by John, there will be great rejoicing, beer parties, and dancing in the streets. We remember witnessing the dancing in the streets in some Islamic nations when the Twin World Trade Towers in New York City were destroyed and three thousand innocent victims died. Those left alive on earth will be so happy they will send each other presents—now their own messiah, the Antichrist, can bring in his own government and all restraints against sin and lust will be gone. But all at once, as the eyes of the world are upon them, the two witnesses suddenly stand on their feet, and before anyone can turn the volume down on their TV sets, this great booming voice shouts, "Come up to Heaven!" A cloud catches them up and they go out of sight. The word used for cloud in this scripture is *nephele,* meaning a small, bright, moving cloud. This is the same type of cloud that Moses and Elijah came down on the Mount of Transfiguration to talk with Jesus (Matt. 17:5).

Possibly with TV cameras still beaming pictures to all the world, an earthquake will occur in Jerusalem in which seven thousand men will die, which means there will probably be twenty-one thousand men, women, and children die. The merrymaking all over the world will suddenly turn to shock, awe, and fear. This will conclude the judgments of the sixth trumpet, or the second woe.

As we briefly consider another chronology check, John has witnessed the opening of the seven-sealed book in Heaven by Jesus Christ. Out of the opening of the first four seals came four horsemen bringing war, famine, disease, and natural disasters that will be the judgments of God in the first half of the Tribulation. At the opening of the fifth seal, millions will be martyred for their faith in Jesus Christ; at the opening of the sixth seal, the terrible judgments coming upon the nations and their governments are revealed; and out of the opening of the seventh seal, the judgments of the first six trumpets will appear. With the sounding of the seventh trumpet the following events will occur in the last half of the Tribulation:

1. The kingdoms of men will be taken into the Kingdom of Jesus Christ as foretold in Daniel 2.
2. Jesus Christ will reign forever over all kingdoms in Heaven and on earth.
3. The host of Heaven worship and praise God for using His mighty power to put all nations, kingdoms, and men and angels under His authority.
4. The nations will rebel at the battle of Armageddon to defy God's will and purpose.
5. Jesus Christ will return with the armies of Heaven to destroy the rulers of nations under Antichrist and their armies.
6. The temple of God will be opened in Heaven and out of the ark will come lightnings, thunderings, and earthquakes—a revelation of the wrath of God that will be unleashed upon a Christ-rejecting world.

The tabernacle with all its contents, including the ark of the covenant, were examples of the true in Heaven. Whether the ark of the covenant that was in the tabernacle, and later in Solomon's Temple, is the one that is in the Temple of Heaven, is a matter of opinion. Dr. Henry Morris believes that the ark that was in the tabernacle is now in Heaven.

Perhaps no better concluding commentary to chapter eleven can be composed or referenced than the Second Psalm:

The Holy Spirit Speaks

Why do the heathen rage, and the people imagine a vain thing? The kings of the earth set themselves, and the rulers take counsel together, against the LORD, and against his anointed, saying, Let us break their bands asunder, and cast away their cords from us. He that sitteth in the heavens shall laugh: the Lord shall have them in derision. Then shall he speak unto them in his wrath, and vex them in his sore displeasure.

Jehovah speaks

Yet have I set my king upon my holy hill of Zion.

And the seventh angel sounded; and there were great voices in heaven, saying, The kingdoms of this world are become the kingdoms of our Lord, and of his Christ; and he shall reign for ever and ever. And the four and twenty elders, which sat before God on their seats, fell upon their faces, and worshipped God, Saying, We give thee thanks, O Lord God Almighty, which art, and wast, and art to come; because thou hast taken to thee thy great power, and hast reigned. And the nations were angry, and thy wrath is come, and the time of the dead, that they should be judged, and that thou shouldest give reward unto thy servants the prophets, and to the saints, and them that fear thy name, small and great; and shouldest destroy them which destroy the earth. And the temple of God was opened in heaven, and there was seen in his temple the ark of his testament: and there were lightnings, and voices, and thunderings, and an earthquake, and great hail.

—Revelation 11:15-19

Christ speaks

I will declare the decree: the LORD hath said unto me, Thou art my Son; this day have I begotten thee. Ask of me, and I shall give thee the heathen for thine inheritance, and the uttermost parts of the earth for thy possession. Thou shalt break them with a rod of iron; thou shalt dash them in pieces like a potter's vessel.

The Holy Spirit speaks

Be wise now therefore, O ye kings: be instructed, ye judges of the earth. Serve the LORD with fear, and rejoice with trembling. Kiss the Son, lest he be angry, and ye perish from the way, when his wrath is kindled but a little. Blessed are all they that put their trust in him.

Chapter Twelve

Satan's Fight with Israel

Chapter eleven is primarily related to the Jewish temple and the two witnesses, the foremost representatives of Israel from the law and the prophets. In the continuing prophetic visions that John is shown, in the particular sequence revealed in chapter twelve he sees the comprehensive historic and prophetic efforts of Satan to prevent the birth and crowning of the Messiah as King of Kings and Lord of Lords.

While we can know that the woman of the first two verses is Israel, subsequent verses leave no doubt that she is representing Israel. The preterists and reformed covenant churchmen will try to make the woman the church. British-Israel people, the Mormons, Jehovah's Witnesses, and other cultic groups also have their own interpretations, but the woman can be no other than Israel.

We read of one of the dreams of Joseph in Genesis 37:9: "And he dreamed yet another dream, and told it his brethren, and said, Behold, I have dreamed a dream more; and, behold, the sun and the moon and the eleven stars made obeisance to me." We note that Joseph said that eleven stars honored him, so the stars represented all the twelve sons of Jacob. If the stars represent the twelve brothers, then the sun and moon must represent national Israel.

The woman clothed with the sun projects God's will that Israel put on His righteousness. The moon under the woman's feet represents God's will that Israel reflect His glory as the moon has no light of its own but reflects the light of the sun. To this date Israel has not yet fulfilled God's plan and purpose for the nation, but in the future Millennium it will.

In verse two John notices that the woman is pregnant and is experiencing labor pains. We will learn in the upcoming verses that this child that is

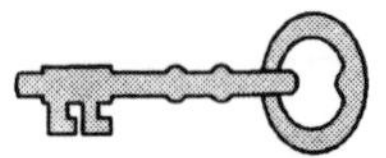

Key #22: Birth Pains

And there appeared a great wonder in heaven; a woman clothed with the sun, and the moon under her feet, and upon her head a crown of twelve stars: And she being with child cried, travailing in birth, and pained to be delivered.

—Revelation 12:1-2

And there appeared another wonder in heaven; and behold a great red dragon, having seven heads and ten horns, and seven crowns upon his heads. And his tail drew the third part of the stars of heaven, and did cast them to the earth: and the dragon stood before the woman which was ready to be delivered, for to devour her child as soon as it was born. And she brought forth a man child, who was to rule all nations with a rod of iron: and her child was caught up unto God, and to his throne.

—Revelation 12:3-5

to be born is not just any child. It is to be a special male baby whose birth was prophesied four thousand years earlier.

The first wonder was a star-crowned woman in Heaven. The second wonder is a red dragon in Heaven. The word "wonder" is more often used in conjunction with other words with similar meaning like "signs and wonders" or "miracles and wonders." The word *semeion* by itself more correctly could mean "a sign." The woman may be represented by the sign of "Virgo" (virgin) and the red dragon by the sign of "Draco" (Dragon) in the constellations (see *The Witness of the Stars* by E. W. Bullinger).

Another prophecy that is related to the woman as a sign of Israel is Isaiah 66:7, "Before she travailed, she brought forth; before her pain came, she was delivered of a man child."

Israel gave birth to the Messiah without knowing it. The birth of Christ was prophesied in Genesis 3:15. In the Old Testament it was prophesied that the Messiah would be born of a virgin; what town He would be born in; what tribe He would come from; how He would grow from a child to manhood; that He would make the blind to see, the dumb to speak, the deaf to hear, and the lame to walk; how and why He would die; and that He would be raised from the grave. Yet, Israel never knew or recognized Him as the Christ. As Jeremiah prophesied, Israel did not know the time of their visitation, and in the time of their visitation, they were cast down. So concerning the Messiah, there were no birth pains. But in these last days, Israel is looking for their Messiah, and the birth pains are just now beginning. The travailing birth pains come in the Tribulation. As the prophecy declares, Israel's birth pains came after the Messiah was born.

Also as declared in verse three, Satan had a great empire within God's universal Kingdom. He was then known as Lucifer, the bright and shining one (Isa. 14:12). Verse four, and other related scriptures, indicated that Satan, who possibly ruled over one-third of God's Kingdom, determined not to bow his knees to the one that God preordained to be Lord of Lords and King of Kings. Satan then drew (enticed, not forced) one-third of the angelic host to follow him in his rebellion (Jude 6). Satan in his sublime pride is determined that Jesus Christ bow down to him and not he bow and worship Jesus. On the Mount of Temptation Satan offered Jesus all the kingdoms of this world if He would bow down and worship him.

As indicated in verses four and five, Satan planned ahead to destroy the Messiah as soon as He was born. It was doubtless Satan who motivated Herod to kill all the children around Bethlehem. Demonic activity was intense during the ministry of Jesus Christ to Israel, and the Jews cried out to the Roman authority, "Crucify Him." But God raised Jesus Christ from the grave, and as verse five declares, He ascended back to the Father. Yet, He is destined to rule all nations with a "rod of iron." We read of the second coming in Revelation 19:15, "And out of his mouth goeth a sharp sword, that with it he should smite the nations: and he shall rule them with a rod of iron...."

Jesus says: "I will go and return to my place, till they acknowledge their offence, and seek my face: in their affliction [tribulation] they will seek me early" (Hos. 5:15).

Israel says: "Come, and let us return unto the LORD: for he hath torn, and he will heal us; he hath smitten, and he will bind us up. After two days [two thousand years] will he revive us: in the third day [third millennium] he will raise us up, and we shall live in his sight" (Hos. 6:1–2).

We should notice that Israel is simply called the "woman." This "woman" has twelve sons, and the face of God has shined upon her. Nowhere in chapter twelve is this woman referred to as the "bride." Israel's past, present, and future is earthly. The church's past is anchored in the cross. The present is to be heavenly minded, and the future is to be at home with the Lord forever in heavenly places (Eph. 2:4–7). When Jesus Christ claims His bride (Rev. 19:7–10), the Old Testament saints have not been resurrected and living Israel is still on earth. Therefore, it is difficult to see how Israel could be the bride of Christ as some claim.

And the woman fled into the wilderness, where she hath a place prepared of God, that they should feed her there a thousand two hundred and threescore days.

—Revelation 12:6

It is interesting that in Revelation 12 the apostle John follows the example of the Old Testament prophets. He goes directly from the cutting off of Messiah, and the Jewish nation, into the Tribulation period, just as if there was no Church age. In Revelation 12 John goes from the ascension of Jesus after His resurrection to the flight of Israel to a hiding place for forty-two months. Jesus clearly prophesied that this would occur when the Antichrist stopped the Jewish worship in the temple and broke his covenant with Israel:

> When ye therefore shall see the abomination of desolation, spoken of by Daniel the prophet, stand in the holy place, (whoso readeth, let him understand:) Then let them which be in Judea flee into the mountains: Let him which is on the housetop not come down to take any thing out of his house: Neither let him which is in the field return back to take his clothes. And woe unto them that are with child, and to them that give suck in those days! But pray ye that your flight be not in the winter, neither on the sabbath day: For then shall be great tribulation, such as was not since the beginning of the world to this time, no, nor ever shall be.
>
> —Matthew 24:15–21

In Revelation 12 as in Matthew 24, a difference is made between the Jews in the land and the Jews in other nations. The national regathering will not take place until Jesus Christ returns and sets up His Kingdom on earth. According to Zechariah 13:8–9, only one-third in "all the land" (meaning the nation of Israel) will be saved. Two-thirds of the Jews in the land will be killed in the last half of the Tribulation. Combining the accounts of the flight of the Jews in Revelation 12 and Matthew 24, it can be determined that the one-third who escape into the mountains will be protected by God for three and one-half years until Jesus comes back with the angels of Heaven and destroys the Antichrist and the armies gathered at Armageddon.

Most authors of commentaries on Revelation conveniently ignore the question of where some million or more Jews are going to hide from the Antichrist for three and one-half years. While some may conclude that it is impossible to know, I believe the Bible sheds considerable light on where it will be. I believe it will be Petra, also called Mount Seir in the Bible.

After Jacob traded Esau out of his birthright, Esau took his lesser inheritance and went down to Mount Seir in Edom, chased the Horites out from Mount Hor, and took over this mountainous and rugged area of cave dwellings that covers thirty or more square miles. *Hor* in Hebrew means caves (Deut. 2:10–12). The enmity that was created over Esau losing his birthright would be an everlasting hatred between the descendants of Esau and the descendants of Jacob. When Moses led the children of Israel out of Egypt the first problem he had was with Amalek, a descendant of Esau (Exod. 17). Then another problem arose when Moses attempted to go through Edom to the Promised Land. The king of Edom, a descendant of Esau, not only refused passage, but fought against Israel with his army.

Throughout the history of Edom and Israel, there was war between them. However, when the Babylonian Empire was spreading westward, Edom and Israel made a mutual assistance treaty. But Edom not only refused to help Israel, but joined the Babylonians in destroying Jerusalem and the temple (Ps. 137). And, as was the frequent custom of that time with the conquering dictator, the Edomites were moved out of Petra to replace the Jews that had been killed or taken into captivity. Then the Nabateans, descendants of Ishmael through Nebajoth (Gen. 25:13), came up from Arabia and settled at Mount Seir (called Petra by the Greeks). Josephus records the many problems the Jews had with the Edomites in the land after returning from Babylon. They were called "I(E)dumeans" by the Romans. Josephus reported that in just one incident the Edomites killed seventy-five hundred in Jerusalem. The Romans could not trust the Jews to follow Caesar's orders, so the Edomites were put in charge. The Herods were Edomites. After A.D. 70 when the Jews were either killed, sold into slavery, or escaped to other nations, the Edomites were left in the land. The so-called Palestinian

Arabs today are really the descendants of Esau, or Edomites. We read this prophecy in Ezekiel 36:5:

> Therefore thus saith the Lord GOD; Surely in the fire of my jealousy have I spoken against the residue of the heathen, and against all Idumea, which have appointed my land into their possession with the joy of all their heart, with despiteful minds, to cast it out for a prey.

We also read in Ezekiel 35:1–7 that God's judgment will be on the Edomite race forever, because they have a "perpetual hatred" for Israel. Continuing on into the next chapter, God says that the Edomites will say the land of Israel belongs to them, but He will declare to the world that it belongs to His chosen people.

During the time of the Roman Empire, Petra was an important commercial metropolis for Rome. When the Roman legions left the Middle East in about A.D. 500, the city declined and the Nabateans either died out or faded back into Arabia. As the Jews began to go back to Israel after 1860, Petra was rediscovered and tourists from all over the world began visiting this lost city of Esau. The local residents became wandering Bedouin tribes who were neither Edomite nor Nabatean. When I first visited Petra in 1978 there was one hotel. Each time I have gone to Petra since, there are more hotels, paved roads, and utilities. At last count, there were sixty-seven hotels in Petra.

In Bible times Petra was designated as one of the cities of refuge where those who were unjustly persecuted could go and find food and shelter. David went to Petra on one occasion to find safety from the attempts of King Saul to kill him. It is also obvious that Paul went to Petra, which was at that time in North Arabia, for three years to escape the Jews who wanted to kill him (Gal. 1:17). Petra is in the highest mountain range that is close to, and accessible from, Jerusalem. There is plenty of water and large animal herds in the area. If God could feed and take care of over a million Jews in the wilderness desert for forty years, He is certainly able to care for a million or so Jews in a protected city for three and one-half years.

The plain message of Scripture is that Petra will be Israel's hiding place for the last half of the Tribulation. Psalm 60:1,9–12 states plainly that after God has regathered Israel, they will have a time of great trouble, but the Lord will preserve them in the strong city of Edom, which can be no place but Petra:

> O God, thou hast cast us off, thou hast scattered us, thou hast been displeased; O turn thyself to us again. . . . Who will bring me into the strong city? who will lead me into Edom? Wilt not thou, O God, which hadst cast

> us off? and thou, O God, which didst not go out with our armies? Give us help from trouble: for vain is the help of man. Through God we shall do valiantly: for he it is that shall tread down our enemies.

God even gave a heathen prophet, Balaam, a prophecy concerning the possession of Petra by Israel when the Lord God reigns on David's throne:

> He hath said, which heard the words of God, and knew the knowledge of the most High, which saw the vision of the Almighty, falling into a trance, but having his eyes open: I shall see him, but not now: I shall behold him, but not nigh: there shall come a Star out of Jacob, and a Sceptre shall rise out of Israel, and shall smite the corners of Moab, and destroy all the children of Sheth. And Edom shall be a possession, Seir also shall be a possession for his enemies; and Israel shall do valiantly. Out of Jacob shall come he that shall have dominion, and shall destroy him that remaineth of the city.
>
> —Numbers 24:16–19

And there was war in heaven: Michael and his angels fought against the dragon; and the dragon fought and his angels, And prevailed not; neither was their place found any more in heaven. And the great dragon was cast out, that old serpent, called the Devil, and Satan, which deceiveth the whole world: he was cast out into the earth, and his angels were cast out with him. And I heard a loud voice saying in heaven, Now is come salvation, and strength, and the kingdom of our God, and the power of his Christ: for the accuser of our brethren is cast down, which accused them before our God day and night. And they overcame him by the blood of the Lamb, and by the word of their testimony; and they loved not their lives unto the death. Therefore rejoice, ye heavens, and ye that dwell in them. Woe to the inhabiters of the earth and of the sea! for the devil is come down unto you, having great wrath, because he knoweth that he hath but a short time.

—Revelation 12:7-12

The sixty-third chapter of Isaiah also prophetically explains that Jesus Christ will come to Bozrah in Jordan to lead the remnant back to Jerusalem. Bozrah is the gateway on the King's Highway that leads to Petra, only a few miles to the north of the city. We were in Bozrah recently making a video. Both my book *Petra in History and Prophecy* and the video have been hidden in caves in Petra.

John was shown in this particular vision that there would be war in Heaven. There has doubtless been war in Heaven since Satan rebelled and one-third of the angels of Heaven followed him in an attempt to dethrone God. As I have noted before, there is reason to believe that the members of the glorified and resurrected church of Jesus Christ will take over the planets and solar systems now ruled by Satan and his angels. We read in Job 15:15, ". . . the heavens are not clean in his sight." The stars that are going into a supernova stage, or the ones that nova and implode, may be signs of the continuing war in the solar systems. It is interesting to think about how this final war between the angels will take place. Angels are spirit beings instead of physical beings. We wonder how General Michael will lead the angels of God against the forces of Satan. But the angelic army of God wins, and Satan and his angels are cast down to the earth. This is when Satan perhaps takes possession of the Antichrist who then becomes the devil incarnate.

Ezekiel 28:14–19 appears to reference the casting out of Satan from the heavens:

> Thou art the anointed cherub that covereth; and I have set thee so: thou wast upon the holy mountain of God; thou hast walked up and down in

> the midst of the stones of fire. Thou wast perfect in thy ways from the day that thou wast created, till iniquity was found in thee. By the multitude of thy merchandise they have filled the midst of thee with violence, and thou hast sinned: therefore I will cast thee as profane out of the mountain of God: and I will destroy thee, O covering cherub, from the midst of the stones of fire. Thine heart was lifted up because of thy beauty, thou hast corrupted thy wisdom by reason of thy brightness: I will cast thee to the ground, I will lay thee before kings, that they may behold thee. Thou hast defiled thy sanctuaries by the multitude of thine iniquities, by the iniquity of thy traffick; therefore will I bring forth a fire from the midst of thee, it shall devour thee, and I will bring thee to ashes upon the earth in the sight of all them that behold thee. All they that know thee among the people shall be astonished at thee: thou shalt be a terror, and never shalt thou be any more.

As we read in Revelation 12:10, the devil still has the freedom to accuse the saints before the throne of God. Job, who was an upright, moral, and godly man, was accused by Satan of serving the Lord for selfish reasons. And not only does Satan accuse the saints before God, he uses gossipers in the church to accuse us down here on earth. Even the best Christians will be accused of being too snooty, or too self-righteous. But when the devil is cast out of the heavens he will no longer be able to accuse us before the throne of God. And as we read in the next verse, there is no sin that Satan accuses us of that cannot be covered by the blood of Jesus Christ.

When Satan is cast down to this earth in the middle of the Tribulation, John tells us that he will become exceedingly vengeful. He will become subject to time and know that he has but three and one-half years before his judgment comes. This is why the last half of the Tribulation will be the most terrible time the world will see.

And when the dragon saw that he was cast unto the earth, he persecuted the woman which brought forth the man child. And to the woman were given two wings of a great eagle, that she might fly into the wilderness, into her place, where she is nourished for a time, and times, and half a time, from the face of the serpent. And the serpent cast out of his mouth water as a flood after the woman, that he might cause her to be carried away of the flood. And the earth helped the woman, and the earth opened her mouth, and swallowed up the flood which the dragon cast out of his mouth. And the dragon was wroth with the woman, and went to make war with the remnant of her seed, which keep the commandments of God, and have the testimony of Jesus Christ.

—Revelation 12:13–17

There will be rejoicing in the heavens, but terror here on earth as the seven bowls of the wrath of God are poured out and the Antichrist beheads all who will not take his mark and worship him as their god.

We understand that those who rejoice in the heavens are the angelic host and possibly the raptured church. If there are any other classes of beings in the heavens, they are not specifically revealed.

Verses thirteen and fourteen revert back to the middle of the Tribulation which show that the casting out of Satan and his angels from the heavens will come three and one-half years before the end of this horrible time. This is the time when Satan will attempt to kill all the Jews and one-third escape to Petra. In the fourteenth verse the period of Israel's hiding is measured in time, times, and one-half time. A time in Israel was from one Passover until the next, so this indicates that this final attempt to wipe out Israel will be on a national holiday, the Passover. This is not unusual as the attempt by Syria, Jordan, and Egypt to destroy Israel in 1973 began on Yom Kipper when even the army was off duty.

We notice in verse fifteen that as one-third of the Jews escape, Satan will attempt to drown them. The Ciq at Petra is notorious for trapping hundreds of drowning victims. The Ciq is a narrow gorge, about fifty feet wide with cliffs rising six hundred feet. The geology of the region funnels all the rain that falls in a ten square mile area into this narrow Ciq. There are times in this high mountainous region when there are virtual cloudbursts. The Ciq is six thousand feet long (over a mile), and anyone caught in this gorge at such a time will certainly be drowned. There have been reported incidents where entire caravans or groups of visitors have been drowned. One tourist, Harriet Martineau, described being caught in the Ciq at such a time:

> Within three minutes, before I had put off my wet clothes, I heard a shout: the torrent had come down. Down it came, almost breast high, rushing and swirling among the thickets and great stones in the water-course, giving us a river in a moment, where we had never dreamed of hoping to see one.

The government of Jordan has now built a dam to divert the water away from the Ciq. It is still possible in the event of a super rain for the Ciq to be flooded, but now it is more difficult.

After one-third of the Jews in the land escape to Petra, Satan motivates the Antichrist to kill those who remain in the land. Then he turns to kill the Jews in other nations who confess Jesus Christ as the Messiah—Lord and Savior.

Chapter twelve is a remarkable account of how God's plan and purpose for the nation of Israel will be realized in spite of Satan and every enemy that Israel has today. God is indeed the Almighty—He knows how to do it, and He has the power to do it. Trust Him!

Chapter Thirteen

The Antichrist and the False Prophet

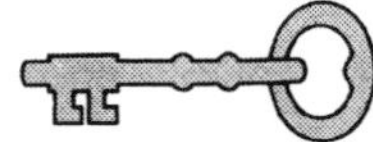

Key #23: No. 666

And I stood upon the sand of the sea, and saw a beast rise up out of the sea, having seven heads and ten horns, and upon his horns ten crowns, and upon his heads the name of blasphemy. And the beast which I saw was like unto a leopard, and his feet were as the feet of a bear, and his mouth as the mouth of a lion: and the dragon gave him his power, and his seat, and great authority.

—Revelation 13:1–2

Chapter thirteen is about two characters who will most certainly wear the blackest hats in the Tribulation—the Antichrist and the False Prophet. Not only could entire books be written about these two baddies, entire books have been written about them. To attempt to present an adequate summary of their rise, roles, and fall, in the most tempestuous time in the history of the world, in a few hastily written pages would be impossible. Therefore, we will ramble around a bit in the Bible and secular history and see what we can find out about this "beast" of Revelation who was, is, or will appear. Serious theologians down through the Church age without exception agree that there was, is, or will be, an Antichrist.

The definitive word "Antichrist" is found only four times in the Bible—three times in the first epistle of John and once in his second epistle. However, this person mentioned in Revelation is found by other names in both the Old Testament and the New Testament: son of perdition; man of sin; false christ; the prince that shall come; little horn; etc.

Justin Martyr said of the Antichrist: "He speaks strange things against the Most High . . . [and] do unlawful things against Christians" (A.D. 160).

Iranaeus (A.D. 180): "By means of the events that will occur in the time of the Antichrist, it is shown that he, being an apostate and robber, is anxious to be worshipped as God. . . . Daniel foresaw those [kings] upon whom the son of perdition will come."

Hippolytus (A.D. 205): "The Antichrist will be shameless, a war-monger, and a despot. . . . He will build the city of Jerusalem and restore the sanctuary."

Several of the early Christian theologians believed the Antichrist would come from the tribe of Dan; others believed he would be Nero whom the devil would bring back (see *Dictionary of Early Christian Beliefs* by Bercot). It seems rather odd that I could not find an early Christian authority who nominated Judas for the role of Antichrist. However, I did in fact throw Judas' hat into the ring in a book I wrote in 1976 entitled *Countdown for Antichrist.* The reader may be asking him or herself, "Surely, you can't be serious?" Okay, smarty pants, consider the following:

1. Jesus said in John 6:70, ". . . Have not I chosen you twelve, and one of you is a devil?" *Fausset's Bible Encyclopedia and Dictionary* says of this scripture in referring to Judas that "devil" here "does not merely mean demon, the Greek word always used for the evil spirit possessing a body, but 'devil' used only of Satan himself." The word for devil in the Greek used here is *diabolos,* rendered "devil," and not *daimonion* interpreted "demon".
2. In Acts 1:25 we read, ". . . of this ministry and apostleship, from which Judas by transgression fell, that he might GO TO HIS OWN PLACE." Where is Judas' own place? A reference made to no other person in the Bible.
3. John 17:12: "While I was with them in the world, I kept them in thy name: those that thou gavest me I have kept, and none of them is lost, but THE SON OF PERDITION. . . ." Not "a" son of perdition, but "THE" son of perdition, a title given but two people in the Bible, Judas and Antichrist: "Let no man deceive you by any means: for that day shall not come, except there come a falling away first, and that man of sin be revealed, THE SON OF PERDITION . . . so that he as God sitteth in the temple of God, shewing himself that he is God" (2 Thess. 2:3–4).
4. Ezekiel 21:25–27 and Psalm 55;109 prophetically foretell that the betrayer of the coming Christ would be Satan.
5. Dr. Arthur W. Pink, noted Bible expositor, said of the references to Judas in the gospels and psalms: "These verses describe not only the base treachery of Judas toward Christ, but they also announce how he shall yet, when reincarnated in the Antichrist, betray and desert Israel. . . ."

However, we do not definitely conclude that Judas will be the Antichrist. He is only worthy of consideration as a candidate. Martin Luther said that Pope Leo was the Antichrist. In 1933–34 some thought that President Franklin Roosevelt was the Antichrist. He had a great plan to feed the world and his NRA sign had to be on the door of every business. Even Congress became disturbed, and the sign was removed. My own civics teacher in Hugo High School, Mr. Os Doenges, had me convinced that FDR was the most evil man in the world. Being a freshman in high school, and rather overt, I took a black crayon and drew a beard, glasses, and horns on a monstrous picture of the president. The problem was that the huge picture was on the front porch of my uncle Henry, who lived on Cloudy Mountain, a food distributor to the needy for the Roosevelt administration. Consequently, I barely missed a load of birdshot from a twelve-gauge shotgun in the seat of my pants.

Some during World War II thought that perhaps Hitler or Mussolini was the Antichrist, and they had good reason to think so. Hitler and Mussolini were co-conspirators in the greatest war in history, which could have been Armageddon. Mussolini was with the pope in Rome, and Hitler made a contract with the pope whereby he could kill all the Jews in the world. He did end up killing 6.5 million Jews. Hitler's armies were marching down through the Balkans and into North Africa in a pincer movement to conquer Israel. The Nazi twisted cross was a good "mark of the beast" emblem, and WW II lasted seven years.

Satan has a definite plan whereby he can stand in the temple of God and exalt himself above God to all the world. Every serious type of Antichrist attempts to follow this plan. Hitler almost made it, and a few think he will try again. The reason that many look for a dead, evil ruler of the past to be the Antichrist is that we read the "beast" will receive a deadly wound and that he will ascend out of the bottomless pit. But though Mussolini, Hitler, and Franklin Roosevelt never made it to the high office of Antichrist, they did succeed in fulfilling an interesting last-days prophecy. In Zechariah 12 the prophet foretold the end of the age when Jerusalem would be a burdensome stone to all nations. In the preceding eleventh chapter is another end-time prophecy about the "day of slaughter" for the Jews, which is probably a reference to Hitler's killing of 6.5 million. In verse eight of this chapter there is a prophecy about three shepherds, which probably refers to three world leaders, who will die after the great slaughter of the Jews, in one month. The only time we can determine this ever happening was in April 1945, when Hitler, Mussolini, and Franklin Roosevelt, all died in that month.

Some believe the Antichrist will be a Jew; some believe he will be a Gentile; some believe he will be the president of the European Union, the Revived Roman Empire; some believe he will be a Syrian; some believe he will come from Spain; and some did even believe he is Henry Kissinger. Daniel indicated that he would make a covenant with Israel, so he must not be a Jew. And, we cannot identify him by his signing a treaty with Israel, because the U.N. has made more than fifty resolutions with Israel since 1948. The only sure way the Antichrist can be identified is by his breaking a treaty with Israel, then stopping the resumed Jewish worship service on the temple, and then demanding every person in the world take his mark and number or be beheaded . . . but Christians are not going to be around by then, so there is absolutely no way we can know that the Antichrist is in the world today, or who he might be. Nevertheless, it is most interesting to speculate. So, let us see what we can learn about the Antichrist, and his partner, the False Prophet, in Revelation 13.

The vision of Revelation 13 begins in verse one with John standing upon the sand of the sea. Daniel 7, which corresponds with Revelation 13, begins with the prophet seeing four beasts come up out of the "great sea." The "great sea" is usually the Mediterranean Sea in the Bible. As noted, predatory empires are given the names of wild beasts.

The beasts in successive appearance in Daniel 7 were a lion with eagle wings which were plucked off. Then, the lion is no longer a beast. The next beast was a bear, and the third a leopard with four wings of a fowl. The fourth beast was more terrible than any of the former three beasts, and its chief characteristic was iron teeth. The traditional interpretation is that the lion represents Babylon; the bear is Medo-Persia; the leopard is Greece; and the fourth beast is Rome. There could also be a second contemporary explanation in that the lion represents England, and England did control the Middle East and had possession of Israel until 1948. The wings could represent the United States, as the lion is the symbol of Great Britain and the emblem of the United States is an eagle with outstretched wings. The wings were plucked off, and the United States did replace England as the major power in the Middle East. The bear is the symbol of Russia, and Russia did exercise considerable influence in the Middle East in the three decades from 1960 to 1980. The leopard could represent Islam and the Arab alliance. The fourth and terrible beast is yet to appear, but without doubt it will be the kingdom of Antichrist.

Daniel mentions the beasts in order as the lion, the bear, and the leopard. John mentions the characteristics of the fourth beast in reverse order: leopard, bear, and lion. Daniel was looking forward in history; John was looking backward in history. Daniel was primarily interested in the fourth beast because this would be the empire in control of the world during the Tribulation when Israel would be brought into the messianic Kingdom. Because John is given a vision of this world empire that will produce the Antichrist for the Tribulation, he sees only the fourth beast of Daniel 7.

Daniel's fourth beast was adorned with ten horns, and we are informed in Daniel 7:24 that the ten horns represent ten kings. This is a nice arrangement; so far, so good. But then Daniel throws us a curve—a little horn comes up from among the ten horns and throws down three horns along with three kings. Okay, with a slight adjustment, now we have the Antichrist kingdom, with the little horn (the Antichrist himself) in charge, composed of seven kings plus an empire dictator. John throws us another curve by noting that the original ten kings sit on seven mountains. John clears up this mystery somewhat in the seventeenth chapter where he explains that the seven heads are seven mountains on which the Great Whore (false religious system) sits. The city of Rome was built on seven hills, so perhaps this means that the Roman Catholic church will bring forth the Antichrist and the pope will be the false prophet. But mountains in Scripture are also symbolic of governments, and John confuses us again by indicating in Revelation 17:10 that the seven mountains are seven kings; five of the kings had fallen, one is, and one is yet to come. Those who accept the historic interpretation give the seven mountains as Sumeria (Babel), Egypt, Assyria, Babylon, Medo-Persia, Greece, and Rome. If the historic interpretation is correct, then we would say that the seven mountains are: Egypt, Assyria, Babylon, Medo-Persia, Greece, Rome, and Revived Rome (Antichrist kingdom). But if we consider the seven mountains from a future date in the middle of the Tribulation rather than A.D. 96, then the identity of the seven kingdoms, or seven nations, would be open to speculation. In any event, if three of the ten kings are removed then we again have one king for one nation. If we have confused the reader in the identity of the seven mountains, then we apologize. We are simply attempting to cover all the bases and allow the reader to consider the options and arrive at his or her own conclusion. As the apostle Paul reminds us, on some difficult Bible questions, ". . . Now we see through a glass, darkly . . ." (1 Cor. 13.12). Therefore, let us major on what we can be sure: the ten kings, their kingdoms, and the three that will be pulled up. These are the identities in the Tribulation that are of primary importance.

In Revelation 13:3, John reports seeing one of the "heads" on the beast receiving a wound, "as it were," unto death. We notice first that it is a head, not a horn, that is wounded. Secondly, we notice the wound does not really kill the head, but only seems to kill it. Almost as many opinions as to who is wounded, and why, are found as there are commentaries and books on Revelation. Many believe that assassination attempts will be made to kill the Antichrist, and while the wound would be sufficient to kill an ordinary human being, he lives. Such a thing is not uncommon. We remember in recent history that President Ronald Reagan and Pope John Paul II both received deadly wounds and lived. Others believe that verse three references Nero, Judas, Hitler, Stalin, or some other Antichrist candidate of the past. If the wounded head is a nation or empire, then we have only two primary possibilities—Rome and Babylon. The two empires that destroyed the temple in Jerusalem were Rome and Babylon.

And I saw one of his heads as it were wounded to death; and his deadly wound was healed: and all the world wondered after the beast. And they worshipped the dragon which gave power unto the beast: and they worshipped the beast, saying, Who is like unto the beast? who is able to make war with him?

—Revelation 13:3-4

Rome seemingly died, yet it continued to live through the European colonial system. Even in its broken state, it continued to tread down the whole world. Rome is revived today through the European Union. During the Church age the city of Babylon was covered over with sand. The city has been restored by Saddam Hussein as a tourist attraction. As we write our commentary on this chapter, the armies of England and the United States are invading Iraq (Babylon) to destroy its head (government) and its king (Saddam Hussein) who is labeled as a beast. Saddam Hussein claims to be a reincarnation of Nebuchadnezzar. Present Iraq as "Babylon lives again" could fulfill the prophecy of Revelation 11:3 and Mystery Babylon of Revelation 18.

I was interested in the opinion of Dr. Joseph Seiss as to whether the "beast" of Revelation is a person, a government, or a system. Dr. Seiss had remarkable insight for someone who lived 150 years ago. He recognized the government, but without the Antichrist, he said the "beast" would not be a beast. Dr. Seiss pointed out that as we progress into the study of Revelation 13 the "beast" takes on the personality of a man: he blasphemes, he speaks, he reigns supreme on earth for forty-two months, he is worshipped as a god, and he is referenced by John with personal pronouns. Dr. Seiss concludes, ". . . this beast is an individual administration embodied in one particular man. Though upheld by ten kings or governments they unite in making the Beast the one sole Arch Regent of their time."

As Hitler was inseparably identified with Nazi Germany, so the Antichrist will inseparably be identified with the beast system in the last half of the Tribulation. Hitler after his many almost miraculous victories thought himself infallible and invincible. So will the unsaved world think of the Antichrist and worship him as a god, and likewise worship the entire beast system, including Satan who gives him evil powers. If man does not worship God as Creator then he will worship himself or the devil.

And there was given unto him a mouth speaking great things and blasphemies; and power was given unto him to continue forty and two months. And he opened his mouth in blasphemy against God, to blaspheme his name, and his tabernacle, and them that dwell in heaven.
—Revelation 13:5–6

Because of his successes in the first half of the Tribulation, the Antichrist will be given the power, or authority, to continue as world dictator for another forty-two months. We might say that he would be an American except in the United States we elect our president every forty-eight months. So who will give the Antichrist the right to another three and one-half–year term? The answer is the world beast system, which could be an outgrowth of the United Nations.

John sees this inhuman beast speaking great things and blasphemies. We read of the Antichrist (little horn) in Daniel 7:

1. A mouth speaking great things (vs. 8).
2. A mouth that spake very great things (vs. 20).
3. He shall speak great words against the most High (vs. 25).
4. Shall speak marvellous things against the God of gods (Dan. 11:36).

There will indeed be given to the Antichrist a great mouth. We imagine that the Antichrist will take over every radio and television station in the world. For twenty-four hours a day only recorded blasphemies and speeches by the Antichrist will be played on every station. For twenty-four hours a day only the videotaped programs by the Antichrist will be aired. No sports, no Oprah, no CNN, CBS, ABC, or NBC—only the Antichrist. And what will the radio and TV programs contain? Speeches condemning the two witnesses; speeches condemning the 144,000; speeches urging his followers to kill anyone who does not take his mark and number; speeches denying the Bible and the God of the Bible; and yes, speeches against those dirty, traitorous Christians who ran out on him before his reign began. We read of the Antichrist in Daniel 7:25, "And he shall speak great words against the most High, and shall wear out the saints of the most High. . . ."

And it was given unto him to make war with the saints, and to overcome them: and power was given him over all kindreds, and tongues, and nations. And all that dwell upon the earth shall worship him, whose names are not written in the book of life of the Lamb slain from the foundation of the world. If any man have an ear, let him hear.

—Revelation 13:7–9

During the first half of the Tribulation, millions will come to the awareness that this is what their friends, neighbors, or relatives who were Christians told them would happen. There is also the witness of the 144,000 who will go through the world with the gospel of the Kingdom, just as Jesus sent the seventy disciples to Israel with this message to repent and believe on Jesus Christ as the Messiah and Savior. The Antichrist cannot tolerate this if he is to promote his plan for the kingdom of darkness. He kills the two witnesses and then furiously plans to kill the 144,000 and anyone else who will not take his mark and number. However, before anyone takes his mark and number they must confess him as God. Often we are asked if the credit card numbers and the bar codes are not the mark and number of the beast. They are indeed precursors of the mark of the beast, but until someone threatens to kill those who refuses to take the mark, then credit or debit cards are not the mark of Antichrist.

Everyone whose names are not in the Book of Life will worship the Antichrist as their god, take his mark, and be eternally damned to punishment in hell. The apostle Paul was executed thirty years before John received the Revelation, and here is what he had to say about the Antichrist and those who would worship him as their god:

> And then shall that Wicked be revealed, whom the Lord shall consume with the spirit of his mouth, and shall destroy with the brightness of his coming: Even him, whose coming is after the working of Satan with all power and signs and lying wonders, And with all deceivableness of unrighteousness in them that perish; because they received not the love of the truth, that they might be saved. And for this cause God shall send them strong delusion, that they should believe a lie: That they all might be damned who believed not the truth, but had pleasure in unrighteousness.
>
> —2 Thessalonians 2:8–12

Asaph, who was in charge of the music services before the ark, had an atti-

He that leadeth into captivity shall go into captivity: he that killeth with the sword must be killed with the sword. Here is the patience and the faith of the saints.

—Revelation 13:10

tude problem. He served God faithfully, but seemingly he was not rewarded accordingly; yet, as he considered the ungodly, they were having all kinds of fun and pleasures even though they were serving the devil. But as Asaph testifies in Psalm 73:16–19,27–28, he found out that the wicked were not so fortunate and he was the one who was blessed:

> When I thought to know this, it was too painful for me; Until I went into the sanctuary of God; then understood I their end. Surely thou didst set them in slippery places: thou castedst them down into destruction. How are they brought into desolation, as in a moment! they are utterly consumed with terrors. . . . For, lo, they that are far from thee shall perish: thou hast destroyed all them that go a whoring from thee. But it is good for me to draw near to God: I have put my trust in the Lord GOD, that I may declare all thy works.

In the middle of Revelation 13 when it seems that the Antichrist and his worshippers will have everything their way, and those who are placing their faith in Jesus Christ are being killed and persecuted, God assures us in verse ten that He is still in control; the wicked will be eternally punished and the righteous will receive their eternal blessings and rewards.

And I beheld another beast coming up out of the earth; and he had two horns like a lamb, and he spake as a dragon. And he exerciseth all the power of the first beast before him, and causeth the earth and them which dwell therein to worship the first beast, whose deadly wound was healed. And he doeth great wonders, so that he maketh fire come down from heaven on the earth in the sight of men, And deceiveth them that dwell on the earth by the means of those miracles which he had power to do in the sight of the beast; saying to them that dwell on the earth, that they should make an image to the beast, which had the wound by a sword, and did live.

—Revelation 13:11-14

John the Baptist came to present Jesus Christ as the Lamb who would take away the sins of the world. The Antichrist will have the False Prophet to present him as the one whom everyone should accept as the true christ. Many (including the early church theologians) who voiced opinions about the False Prophet, think that he is the government of Antichrist or Satan. However, we read in Revelation 19:20 that "both" Antichrist and the False Prophet are cast alive into the lake of fire. If the Antichrist is a real person then the False Prophet will be a real person.

The Antichrist is from the sea; the False Prophet is introduced as Mr. Beast from the earth. In fact, John wants to make sure that we know that this is a beast from the earth:

Verse 11 "beast coming up out of the earth"
Verse 12 "and causeth the earth and them which dwell therein to worship the first beast"
Verse 13 "he maketh fire come down from heaven on the earth"
Verse 14 "he deceiveth them that dwell on the earth"

Although the "beast out of the earth" is not identified as the "false prophet" in Revelation 13, he is so called in Revelation 16:13; 19:20; 20:10. In all three references he is identified with the Antichrist.

John described the False Prophet as appearing on the world scene looking like a lamb, but then he says in effect, "My, what big teeth you have Rev. False Prophet!" This dude is a wolf in lamb's clothing. When he speaks, he does not sound like a sheep; he roars like a mean, flesh-eating Komodo dragon. He has the same amount of power from Satan as the Antichrist has, except the False Prophet uses his power to deceive the unsaved world to worship the Antichrist as a god.

The same Greek word (*therion*) is used for both the Antichrist and False Prophet. The word means "a dangerous animal." The power, calling, and mission of both are from Satan. As Dr. John Walvoord states in his commentary on Revelation, the Antichrist will probably be a Gentile as he comes from the sea, in this case, representing general humanity. And while the Israeli people are God's earthly people, the word for earth in Revelation 13:11 in the Greek text is *ge,* meaning land generally, or the whole earth. Therefore, we cannot say that the False Prophet will be a Jew. As noted in our study of Revelation 12, at the middle of the Tribulation the two witnesses will be killed, the 144,000 raptured, one-third in the land will escape to Petra, and two-thirds in the land will be killed. If the False Prophet is a Jew, he would have to be an apostate Jew from a country other than Israel. In the second place, inasmuch as the Antichrist tries to kill all the Jews in Israel, why would he want to work with a Jew as his right-hand religious guru?

Antichrist means "against Christ." The Antichrist and the False Prophet will not be atheists. They believe in God and they believe in Jesus Christ as Creator, else they would not bother to blaspheme their Names. They both simply deceive the world to believe that they are greater than God and that men do not have to believe in Jesus Christ to be saved. John made it very clear who and what an antichrist is in his first epistle:

> Who is a liar but he that denieth that Jesus is the Christ? He is antichrist, that denieth the Father and the Son.
>
> —1 John 2:22

> And every spirit that confesseth not that Jesus Christ is come in the flesh is not of God: and this is that spirit of antichrist, whereof ye have heard that it should come; and even now already is it in the world.
>
> —1 John 4:3

The March 1999 edition of *Current Thoughts & Trends* reported the results of an Easter poll in which 7,441 Protestant and non-Catholic ministers were asked if they believed the biblical account of the literal resurrection of Jesus Christ: 33 percent of American Baptist ministers said they did not; 30 percent of Presbyterian ministers said they did not; 35 percent of Episcopalians said they did not; 51 percent of Methodists said they did not. The percentage of ministers who do not believe that Jesus Christ was conceived by the Holy Spirit of a virgin approximates the preceding percentages.

According to the *Encyclopaedia Britannica,* earth's population passed 6 billion in the year 2000. In mid-2001, the religious population was as follows:

Buddhists of all national variations		750 million
Christians:		
Catholics	1.07 billion	
Non-Catholics	1.1 billion	2.17 billion
Hindus		820 million
Muslims		1.21 billion
New Age		103 million
Atheists and non-religious		921 million
Other minor religions		100 million

I was somewhat amazed recently to hear Bill O'Riley of Fox TV News arguing with Dr. Jerry Falwell of Liberty University that he believed, and his church also believed (Roman Catholic), that anyone could believe anything they wanted to and still go to Heaven. In other words, faith in Jesus Christ as the only begotten Son of God is superfluous; Mohammed, Buddha, or the Hindu gods can get a person to Heaven also. I researched item five of the Second Vatican Ecumenical:

> The non-Christian may not be blamed for his ignorance of Christ and his Church; salvation is open to him also, if he seeks God sincerely and if he follows the commands of his conscience, for through this means the Holy Ghost acts upon all men: this divine action is not confined within the limited boundaries of the visible Church.

In other words, 5 billion of the 6 billion on planet earth are going to Heaven, and only one billion are going to hell. But Jesus said only a few are going to Heaven and most are going to hell. Why? Because there is no other Name given among men whereby they must be saved, and there is no other Name but Jesus Christ whereby they must be saved.

The reason the Roman Catholic Church has changed its doctrinal position on salvation is that the Vatican plans to bring the vast majority of mankind under the authority of the pope. All who bow to the pope will be determined to be saved; all who do not will be determined to be lost. Also, the United Nations outline for world government cannot allow for Christians to be saved while Buddhists, Hindus, and Muslims are lost. The new one-world ecumenism preaches now that we are all going to the same place regardless of our religious beliefs. And, if there is to be a one-world government and a one-world religion under Antichrist, this is the message that the False Prophet must preach. According to the Bible, the Antichrist will be exalted above every god. Just as the Caesar of Rome was the chief god of the pantheon in Rome, the Antichrist will be declared by the False Prophet to be the god of the Revived Roman Empire.

Jesus said of the end time, and especially in reference to the Tribulation, the time of great trouble, "For there shall arise false Christs, and false prophets, and shall shew great signs and wonders; insomuch that, if it were possible, they shall deceive the very elect" (Matt. 24:24). Every prophecy relating to the administration of the Antichrist and False Prophet presents the same format. As we write this chapter, there are twenty-four–hour TV presentations showing cruise missiles and guided bombs raining down on Baghdad. Perhaps this is something similar to what John saw in his visions, or perhaps the False Prophet will be able to bring fire down from the sky by the power of Satan. Evidently the False Prophet will be able to stage his own "shock and awe" show for all the world to see. From the position of present-day military, scientific, and technological capabilities, it will have to be something ultra-spectacular to impress the world population of the last generation of this age.

We are informed in verse fourteen that those that dwell on the earth will make an image to the "beast" (Antichrist), and this image will speak. Those who do not fall down and worship the image as their god will be executed. When I first went to China, it seemed that on every street corner there was a huge picture of Mao Tse-tung glaring down on me. When I went to Iraq, huge pictures of Saddam Hussein lined the avenues, and there was even one on the Ishtar Gate at restored Babylon. When I went to Russia, not only were there huge pictures of Stalin everywhere, there were also statues of both Stalin and Lenin in front of public buildings. On Red Square in Moscow, the pickled body of Lenin is on display; on Tianeman Square in Beijing is the pickled body of Mao with a continuing line of thousands to view and worship it. Atheistic or anti-Christ nations must have their own gods to worship. Dictators like Hitler, Saddam Hussein, Stalin, or Mao also project the fear-factor through their statues or pictures: "I will kill you and your family if you do not obey me!" The words, image, images, imagery, appear one hundred times in the Old Testament and New Testament, in the King James Version. Different Hebrew and Greek words in the Textus Receptus and Masoretic Text were translated into image by the KJV translators. Some of these Greek and Hebrew words mean image, idol, picture, or reflection. The Greek word for image in Revelation 13:14,15 is *eikon,* meaning a likeness or reflection, as in Colossians 1:15, "[Jesus Christ] Who is the image of the invisible God. . . ."

And he had power to give life unto the image of the beast, that the image of the beast should both speak, and cause that as many as would not worship the image of the beast should be killed.

—Revelation 13:15

We certainly would not interpret image here to be a statue or an idol. In A.D. 96 there were statues of Caesar everywhere, but none of these idols could speak. I believe the "image" of Antichrist will simply be personal appearances daily on world television. Some believe that the "image of Antichrist" will be a computerized idol. Several years ago an exaggerated tale was widely spread that there was a giant computer called "the Beast" in a six-story building in Brussels that was controlling world commerce. It is possible that the "image of the beast" will be a giant computer, but I favor the television world telecast, which would be more effective for the Antichrist than all the pictures and statues that could be produced.

And he causeth all, both small and great, rich and poor, free and bond, to receive a mark in their right hand, or in their foreheads: And that no man might buy or sell, save he that had the mark, or the name of the beast, or the number of his name. Here is wisdom. Let him that hath understanding count the number of the beast: for it is the number of a man; and his number is Six hundred threescore and six.

—Revelation 13:16–18

Everyone today who works, buys, or sells in the United States must have a Social Security number. I was told in 1935 when I received my Social Security number that it would never be used on any federal or state record except to identify my Social Security pension account. Today, try to get a loan, a credit card, a driver's license, etc., without a Social Security number. Impossible!

With international security becoming intensely necessary, an international ID number is now extremely desirable. If there was a public announcement that a bar code or a computer number would help protect individuals from international terrorism, 99 percent of every church membership in America would be waiting in line on Monday morning for their mark and number. Computerization and security, nationally and personally, demands that every person on planet earth have instant identification.

Recently I began to notice that when I checked in for security clearance at the airlines, I was given a card with orange lettering (security danger) and told to wait in a certain line. While there would be dozens of international questionable types in one line, I, an eighty-year-old, meek-looking fellow, would be waiting by myself in the double security line to have every item in my bag checked, inspected, and minutely scrutinized, as well as everything on my person from my cap to the bottom of my shoes. When I mildly complained and asked why was I being selected every time I got on an airplane for a complete security check, the security person replied: "You are in the computer." When I asked who put me in the computer, the reply came: "We don't know who put you in the computer. We just do what the computer says." When I responded, "What if the computer tells you to shoot me; would you shoot me?" There was a shrug of the shoulders but no oral reply.

Today, we rely on computers for everything. The most terrible message today that we hear is: "The computers are down!" Computers are amoral. Who is to be blamed if the computer says, "This person does not have a bar code or computer number, cut his head off!" At the airport security check, the security person does not know who I am or what I have done to demand a security check, regardless how many times I have been checked. He or she is not to blame—they just do what the computer says. Maybe I am checked because I am a world traveler; maybe I have written something that irritated a bureaucrat in Washington D.C.; maybe it is because I am a fundamental, conservative Christian. I should be identified as the last person in the world who would blow up an airplane, but I am suspected as the one most likely to blow up an airplane—by the computer. This is where the world is headed—right into the Tribulation and the mark of the beast.

In 1986, our book *Computers and the Beast of Revelation* was published by Huntington House. In this book we traced the birth of the computer age.

> The magazine *Senior Scholastics*, September 20, 1973, startled students of prophecy when an article titled "Public Needs and Private Right—Who is Watching You?" stated in part:
>
> "All buying and selling in the program will be done by computer. No currency, no change, no checks. In the program, people would receive a number that had been assigned them tattooed in their wrist or forehead. The number is put on by a laser beam and cannot be felt. The number in the body is not seen with the naked eye and is as permanent as your fingerprints. All items of consumer goods will be marked with a computer mark. The computer outlet in the store which picks up the number on the items at the check stand will also pick up the number on the person's body and automatically total the price and deduct the amount from the person's 'Special Drawing Rights' account. . . ."
>
> In a long list of the evolving uses of computers given in the July 19, 1976, edition of *U.S. News & World Report* one is of particular note:
>
> "'Helping doctors to determine which terminally ill patient should die and which should live.' According to this article, computers are helping to determine which terminally ill patients in hospitals should be treated and which should be allowed to die. This is just one small step from the world of the Tribulation period when the image of the beast will determine who should live and who should die in all nations.
>
> "According to the revelation of the last days given to the apostle John, everyone will be required to have a mark, or a code mark, on their forehead, and/or a number in their hand. The code mark on the forehead could be the same as the number in their hand, because code marks are readily changed by a computer scanner to numbers that identify products, animals, or even people."

Even when secular sources were comparing the technology, economics, and prophetic significance of the arriving computer age, the vast majority of ministers and pastors were ignoring it. But even their silence and mockery was a fulfillment of Bible prophecy:

> KNOWING THIS FIRST, that there shall come in the last days scoffers, walking after their own lust, And saying, Where is the promise of his coming? for since the fathers fell asleep, all things continue as they were from the beginning of the creation.
>
> —2 Peter 3:3–4

John reported to us that the Antichrist can be known by the number 666, because it is the number of a man.

Six is the number of man:
Man was created on the sixth day.
Man's time is measured by:
Sixty seconds in a minute (10 x 6).
Sixty minutes in an hour (10 x 6).
Twenty-four hours in a day (4 x 6).
Twelve months in a year (2 x 6).
Man has:
Six major members and parts.
Six quarts of blood.
Six senses.
Six hundred body muscles.
Normal height is six feet.
Average birth weight is six pounds.
When he dies he is buried six feet under.

The number 666 indicates a claim to human perfection, but it also indicates a trinity of evil: False Prophet, Antichrist, and Satan.

Jesus told John that the number of the Antichrist's name would tell us who he is. Many Bible scholars believe that the Antichrist will appear out of the Revived Roman Empire. The Roman alphabetical numbering system was:

I	1
V	5
X	10
L	50
C	100
D	500
	666

By ignoring all other letters in names, many have identified certain popes as having a name adding up to 666. Martin Luther said that a pope would be the Antichrist. Others have come up with 666 in the names of politicians and world personalities.

There are also numerical values to certain letters in the Hebrew and Greek alphabets. It is uncertain if we are to calculate the number of Antichrist in Hebrew, Greek, or Latin, which makes it much more difficult to locate Mr. Antichrist.

By adding values to letters in the English alphabet, the sum total of Henry Kissinger's name can be made to total 666. As Dr. John Morris notes in his book on Revelation, by using the Greek numbering system, Lyndon Johnson's name totals 666. In fact, one in every ten thousand personal names (given and family) will total 666. This would mean that in the United States alone, there are thirty thousand potential antichrists. Is the Antichrist in the world today? If you try to identify him by number, be sure and stock up on plenty of pens and paper. Or, you might want to use your computer.

But one day, the Antichrist will appear. How do we know? Because Jesus Christ told the apostle John that the "beast out of the bottomless pit" would come. All those who refuse to take his mark and number will have their heads severed. I trust the reader has been born again by faith in Jesus Christ and will miss this most terrible event in human history.

Chapter Fourteen

The Lamb Victorious

And I looked, and, lo, a Lamb stood on the mount Sion, and with him an hundred forty and four thousand, having his Father's name written in their foreheads. And I heard a voice from heaven, as the voice of many waters, and as the voice of a great thunder: and I heard the voice of harpers harping with their harps: And they sung as it were a new song before the throne, and before the four beasts, and the elders: and no man could learn that song but the hundred and forty and four thousand, which were redeemed from the earth. These are they which were not defiled with women; for they are virgins. These are they which follow the Lamb whithersoever he goeth. These were redeemed from among men, being the firstfruits unto God and to the Lamb. And in their mouth was found no guile: for they are without fault before the throne of God.
—Revelation 14:1–5

In chapter seven John was shown a vision of 144,000 Israelites who were sealed in their foreheads with the seal of God. As we have previously noted, it is assumed that they are converts of the two witnesses, and consequently millions are saved by their ministry as they go throughout the world preaching the gospel of the Kingdom. The seal of God protects them from the judgments of war, famine, and disease that come upon the world. The last we read about the 144,000 is in Revelation 9:4 where those who have the seal of God in their foreheads will be protected from the sting of the demons that come out of the bottomless pit. Again, we assume these are the same 144,000, because they are the only ones mentioned in the Revelation who are sealed with the seal of God in their foreheads.

Here in chapter fourteen John is shown a vision of the 144,000 rejoicing with the Lamb on Mount Sion (Gr. *Sion*; He. *Zion*). Sion, or Zion, means fortress or refuge. The questions that need to be considered are:

1. Are the 144,000 of chapter fourteen the same 144,000 of chapter seven?
2. Is the Mount Sion in Revelation 14 the earthly Jerusalem, the millennial Jerusalem, or the heavenly Jerusalem?
3. Will the 144,000 be killed by the Antichrist? will they live through the entire Tribulation? or will they be translated to Heaven at the middle of the Tribulation?

The answer to question number one should be that the 144,000 of Revelation 14 are the same 144,000 of Revelation 7. While a few who have written commentaries of Revelation think they may be a different group of Israelis, most believe they are the same bunch. I see no reason to believe they could possibly be different.

The answer to the second question is somewhat more difficult. Perhaps

I should take the fifth, because I disagree with Dr. Walvoord, Dr. Morris, Dr. Hindson, and Dr. Seiss. All four believe that John is shown a vision of the 144,000 with Jesus Christ in Jerusalem after He returns. In other words, the 144,000 will be waiting for Jesus as His feet stand upon the Mount of Olives. There are a few who have written commentaries on Revelation who interpret the Mount Zion of Revelation 14 to be the heavenly Jerusalem. Zion was the hill in Jerusalem where the city of David was located and where David kept the ark until a temple could be built. Zion is the hill where Jesus observed the last supper with His disciples and where the disciples met in the upper room to await the coming of the Holy Spirit. Zion at times means all of Jerusalem, or the Jewish messianic hope. One commentary suggests when Zion is referenced alone it means Jerusalem, and when it is referenced as Mount Zion it means the heavenly Jerusalem. The *New Westminster Dictionary of the Bible* interprets the Mount Zion of Revelation 14 to be the New Jerusalem. One reason that I believe it is the heavenly Jerusalem also is that the 144,000 are rejoicing with the Lamb. When Jesus returns, He comes not as the Lamb, but as the Lion of Judah, King of Kings and Lord of Lords. The earthly Jerusalem was to be a type of the heavenly Jerusalem. We read in Hebrews 12:22: "But ye are come unto mount Sion, and unto the city of the living God, the heavenly Jerusalem, and to an innumerable company of angels."

My answer to the third question may not agree with the majority opinion, but to me it makes sense. According to Revelation 12:17, after the Antichrist commits the Abomination of Desolation, he kills the two witnesses, the remnant of Israel escapes to Petra, then he goes to wage war against the Jews ". . . which keep the commandments of God, and have the testimony of Jesus Christ." It seems to me the 144,000 are taken out of the world at this time before God pours out his bowls of wrath upon the earth. If there is such a thing as a "pre-wrath" Rapture theory, it involves the 144,000, not the church which is taken out of the world before the Tribulation begins.

I do not think the 144,000 will be on earth for the full seven-year Tribulation. When they are caught up to the throne of God, we read that they sing a new song that no other man can sing or understand. The reason is that their mission will be unique, their sealing in the forehead will be unique, and their translation will be unique.

In verse four John repeats the special characteristics of the 144,000, mentioning again that they are virgins and undefiled by women. This subject has been discussed in our comments in chapter seven. This is not to be understood within a sexual context; the subject is spiritual and racial purity. I agree with Dr. Seiss who commented:

> We are not to suppose with some that these 144,000 are all males who

> have never been married; for there is no more impurity in marriage than in abstinence from marriage. Celibacy is not the subject or virtue in their description, but purity, freedom from contamination by the corruption which prevail in their time.

We read also in verse four that the 144,000 are firstfruits unto God and the Lamb. In Israel the firstfruits were to be given to the Lord, but there were many different varieties of the firstfruits' harvest. There were firstfruits of the wheat, barley, grapes, oil, wine, etc. Paul referred to the first who were saved in a certain town as the firstfruits to the Lord in that particular place (Rom. 16:5). We read in 1 Corinthians 15:23 that Jesus Christ is the firstfruit of the first resurrection, then those who are His at His coming. We read in Romans 11:26, "And so all Israel shall be saved: as it is written, There shall come out of Sion the Deliverer, and shall turn away ungodliness from Jacob." All Israel who are alive at the end of the Tribulation will see Jesus Christ, and even the nail prints in His hands, when He returns. They will accept Jesus Christ, not only as their Messiah, but their Savior who shed His blood for them. They will be saved by faith in that He died for their sins. But the 144,000 will be the firstfruits of redeemed Israel to be presented to God.

And I saw another angel fly in the midst of heaven, having the everlasting gospel to preach unto them that dwell on the earth, and to every nation, and kindred, and tongue, and people, Saying with a loud voice, Fear God, and give glory to him; for the hour of his judgment is come: and worship him that made heaven, and earth, and the sea, and the fountains of waters.

—Revelation 14:6-7

With the two witnesses and the 144,000 gone, the world is left without an effective witness except the gospel revealed in creation as referenced by Paul in Romans 1:17–20. But God has never left unsaved mankind without a message and a messenger for very long. Therefore, we read that in the last half of the Tribulation God will send an angel, flying in the air around the world, reaching every nation with the everlasting gospel. The Greek word for angel is as elsewhere in the Bible: messenger. Could this "messenger" be a satellite broadcasting the gospel message of salvation? Possibly! Our daily ministry is not only heard over shortwave and a network of radio stations, it is also broadcast over Sky Angel from Jerusalem to all the world (channel 9773 at 3:00 p.m. and 3:00 a.m. EST). There is the gospel of the Kingdom which entails Jesus Christ ruling all nations with a rod of iron from Jerusalem, and there is the gospel of grace, God's offer of salvation by faith in His Son who died for sin to everyone regardless of race or language. Then there is the everlasting gospel presenting Jesus Christ who created all things and in whom there is no other Name whereby sinners must be saved. The animals which provided the skins for Adam and Eve, and the blood sacrifices in the Old Testament, looked forward to the cross. It is the Lamb of God, slain from the foundation of the world, who saves. This is the everlasting gospel (Rev. 13:8). The theory of evolution refutes the Son of God who died for our sins, because it denies Him as Creator. If Jesus was not Creator of all things, then He could not die for our sins. The greatest need in the world today is to present Jesus Christ once more to our children as the One in whom we breathe and have our being. In the Tribulation the remaining population on planet earth will be given one more opportunity to worship the Lord as Creator.

The fourteenth chapter of Revelation presents a preview of the main events that are to occur in the last half of the Tribulation. The translation of the 144,000 is the first event. The second event is to give the unsaved world another opportunity to be saved. The third announcement is the fall of Babylon. In the Revelation we have two Babylons in view during the Tribulation: the Babylon on the Euphrates and Mystery Babylon. According to Isaiah 13 and many other prophecies relating to Babylon, the Babylon on the Euphrates is to be destroyed as Sodom and Gomorrah were destroyed. According to Revelation 18, Mystery Babylon is to be destroyed in one hour and made desolate. During the Church age, the Babylon on the Euphrates became deserted, the bricks were partially taken for other building purposes, and the city was covered under the shifting sands. I was in Babylon in 1978 and saw the restoration of the city in progress, and in 1987 Iraq announced to the world that Babylon lived again. Whether Mystery Babylon is the revived old Babylon, or a world religious system, or perhaps the United States, will be discussed in more detail in our studies of chapters seventeen and eighteen. Nevertheless, the chronology of coming events in chapter fourteen indicates the destruction of Babylon is not the same as the battle of Armageddon, and probably precedes Armageddon by at least a year.

And there followed another angel, saying, Babylon is fallen, is fallen, that great city, because she made all nations drink of the wine of the wrath of her fornication.

—Revelation 14:8

A third messenger follows the second with a final warning to everyone on earth, in a **loud** voice, not to worship the Antichrist and then take his mark and number. The order of events here again indicates that to get a mark or number to make working, buying, or selling in the last half of the Tribulation possible, a man or woman must worship the Antichrist as their god.

And the third angel followed them, saying with a loud voice, If any man worship the beast and his image, and receive his mark in his forehead, or in his hand, The same shall drink of the wine of the wrath of God, which is poured out without mixture into the cup of his indignation; and he shall be tormented with fire and brimstone in the presence of the holy angels, and in the presence of the Lamb: And the smoke of their torment ascendeth up for ever and ever: and they have no rest day nor night, who worship the beast and his image, and whosoever receiveth the mark of his name. Here is the patience of the saints: here are they that keep the commandments of God, and the faith of Jesus.

—Revelation 14:9-12

In the book of Jude we read of certain religionists who know the truth, yet they consciously made a definitive decision not to accept and worship the Lord Jesus Christ, and not only so, but influence others to do likewise. For these apostates, Jude 13 says, " . . . is reserved the blackness of darkness for ever." The recipient of the "mark of the beast" must make a conscious decision to reject Jesus Christ and accept the Antichrist as their god; then they can qualify for a mark or number to work and get food. However, in doing so, they condemn themselves to an eternal hell forever. Yet, some well-meaning preachers and seminary professors today preach and teach that God would never send a person to an eternal place of punishment.

In Paul's first epistle to the church at Thessalonica, he concluded his letter with an account of the Rapture at the end of the dispensation of grace. Then in the next final chapter, he warns of the wrath of God that is to follow. But the Christians at Thessalonica did not quite understand the chronology. They were heavily persecuted, so they thought perhaps they had missed the Rapture and were in the Tribulation. They were troubled. So Paul writes to them in verses seven through nine of the first chapter of his second epistle:

> And to you who are troubled rest with us, when the Lord Jesus shall be revealed from heaven with his mighty angels, In flaming fire taking vengeance on them that know not God, and that obey not the gospel of our Lord Jesus Christ: Who shall be punished with everlasting destruction from the presence of the Lord, and from the glory of his power.
>
> —2 Thessalonians 1:7–9

In these verses Paul briefly explains what will happen to the unsaved when the Lord comes, including an everlasting separation from God and a consignment to everlasting punishment. But Paul said, "You Christians have nothing to be troubled about. This does not apply to you." If Paul had thought Christians would be in the Tribulation, he would have said, "now you Christians had better be diligent and not worship the Antichrist, and above all, don't take the mark of the beast." There is no place in any of the epistles to the churches, nor even in the letters to the seven churches in Revelation 2–3, where any Christian is warned not to take the mark of the beast. Why? Because no Christian will be in the Tribulation. Those saved in the Tribulation are warned not to take the mark of the beast, but not those saved before that time.

The apostle Paul continued in his second letter to the church at Thessalonica in chapter two to explain, "if you church members at Thessalonica were in the Tribulation as some of you fear, then you would see the Antichrist in the temple proclaiming himself to be god." Then Paul continues to explain further that the Antichrist will show up one day, as he told them when he was with them. In 2 Thessalonians 2:8–12, we read:

> And then shall that Wicked be revealed, whom the Lord shall consume with the spirit of his mouth, and shall destroy with the brightness of his coming: Even him, whose coming is after the working of Satan with all power and signs and lying wonders, And with all deceivableness of unrighteousness in them that perish; because they received not the love of the truth, that they might be saved. And for this cause God shall send them strong delusion, that they should believe a lie: That they all might be damned who believed not the truth, but had pleasure in unrighteousness.

Now some argue that verses twelve and thirteen prove that anyone who ever heard the gospel, and does not accept Jesus Christ by faith, and then is unsaved when the Tribulation comes, cannot be saved in the Tribulation. But Paul here is referencing the Tribulation when the Antichrist will be in the world. He says, "and then shall that Wicked be revealed"—future tense. In verse eleven Paul says, "for this cause God shall send them strong delusion"—future tense. Let's leave these verses in the Tribulation where they belong and not bring them back into the Church age. Millions will be given the opportunity in the Tribulation to be saved, but because most will not believe the truth, most will take the mark of the beast and be damned. Some will be saved.

In every letter to the seven churches of Revelation we read, "He that hath an ear, let him hear what the Spirit **saith unto the churches."** But nowhere in chapters four through nineteen do we read the admonition to "hear what the Spirit says to the churches." We only read, "He that hath an ear, let him hear." The reason is, of course, the church will not be in the Tribulation. Again, if the reader is a Christian and wants to go through the Tribulation, then be my guest.

John comforts those who refuse the mark of the beast but are killed for their faith. While those who worship the Antichrist will suffer eternally in hell, those who obey God and place their trust in Jesus Christ will live in glory forever. This should also be the comfort of every Christian today.

Dr. Walvoord writes of this and the preceding verse:

> The saints are described in verse 12 as those who "keep the commandments of God, and the faith of Jesus." Here is the proper link between works and faith, so necessary in all ages but especially in the great tribulation. . . . It is far better to be dead at the hand of the beast than to have favor as his worshipper.

And I heard a voice from heaven saying unto me, Write, Blessed are the dead which die in the Lord from henceforth: Yea, saith the Spirit, that they may rest from their labours; and their works do follow them.

—Revelation 14:13

Although verse thirteen applies specifically to those who die for their faith in the Tribulation, there is a general reference to everyone who are or will be saved from Abel to the end of the Millennium. It is true that Christians will be rewarded for good works done for the right reasons. Paul set the record straight in Ephesians 2:8–10:

> For by grace are ye saved through faith; and that not of yourselves: it is the gift of God: Not of works, lest any man should boast. For we are his workmanship, created in Christ Jesus unto good works, which God hath before ordained that we should walk in them.

What Paul has said in these three verses is that it is far better to do good works because you are saved, rather than to do good works to try to keep your salvation.

Verse thirteen is often used to encourage Christians to leave at least part of their earthly possessions to their church, missions, or a Christian organization in their wills. While I certainly would leave such matters to the concerns of the individual, I also think this is a worthy consideration for every Christian.

And I looked, and behold a white cloud, and upon the cloud one sat like unto the Son of man, having on his head a golden crown, and in his hand a sharp sickle. And another angel came out of the temple, crying with a loud voice to him that sat on the cloud, Thrust in thy sickle, and reap: for the time is come for thee to reap; for the harvest of the earth is ripe. And he that sat on the cloud thrust in his sickle on the earth; and the earth was reaped. And another angel came out of the temple which is in heaven, he also having a sharp sickle. And another angel came out from the altar, which had power over fire; and cried with a loud cry to him that had the sharp sickle, saying, Thrust in thy sharp sickle, and gather the clusters of the vine of the earth; for her grapes are fully ripe. And the angel thrust in his sickle into the earth, and gathered the vine of the earth, and cast it into the great winepress of the wrath of God. And the winepress was trodden without the city, and blood came out of the winepress, even unto the horse bridles, by the space of a thousand and six hundred furlongs.

—Revelation 14:14-20

As already noted, in this chapter John is given a visionary preview of the most important events that will occur in the last half of the Tribulation. In these verses John describes for us a heavenly view of the mother of all battles, the battle of Armageddon. We will try not to get too involved and carried away in our commentary, as we will want to discuss specifics of the earthly view of Armageddon when we get to the nineteenth chapter.

The best commentary on this section of chapter fourteen that I have read by others is from *The Revelation Record* by Dr. Henry Morris. It reads like my commentary from *Petra in History and Prophecy,* although I am sure Dr. Morris would not have plagiarized my work without giving me credit. I am sure this is just another case of good minds coming to the same conclusions.

In Israel there were three main harvests:

1. Harvest of firstfruits: This was when the first grain ripened fifty days after Passover. The first that matured was the best, and was to be given to the Lord.
2. Harvest of grain: This was the general harvest of the grain crops.
3. Harvest of grapes: The third harvest that occurred was the harvest of grapes, which could also include other types of fruits and melons.

In chapter fourteen we find three symbolic harvests. We read clearly in verse four that the 144,000 are considered to be the harvest of firstfruits.

We read about the second harvest of grain in Matthew 13:30, "... Gather ye together first the tares, and bind them in bundles to burn them: but gather the wheat into my barn." We read that there are three angels that John saw associated with these three harvests, and one of the angels had power over fire. The second harvest involves the separation of the saved and the lost at the end of the Tribulation.

The third harvest symbolized in this chapter is the destruction of the Antichrist and the armies that have gathered at the battle of Armageddon. This is the harvest of grapes. This is why there are three harvests in chapter fourteen.

Jesus Christ is described as the Son of man sitting on a cloud. The Greek word for cloud here is *nephele,* meaning a small thin cloud. Jesus must come back as the "Son of man" to reclaim what man gave to Satan. We read in

Matthew 24:30, "And then shall appear the sign of the Son of man in heaven: and then shall all the tribes of the earth mourn, and they shall see the Son of man coming in the clouds of heaven with power and great glory." The reader should now understand how every piece of the prophetic puzzle depicting the return of Jesus Christ fits so very perfectly.

Now why would an angel have to tell Jesus Christ that it is time to begin the final harvest of the earth? Because, Jesus Himself said that only the Father knows the hour He would return. Thus, an angel comes from the throne of God to give the Word to Jesus Christ to return, although this may be only a legal formality to fulfill what has already been said.

Babylon is destroyed first as recorded in Revelation 18; Jesus Christ returns to destroy the armies at Armageddon in Revelation 19. I have stood on top of the Mount of Megiddo many times. On a clear day I could see all the way from one end of the valley of Jezreel to the other—from Mount Carmel to the southern end of the Sea of Galilee. Napoleon, who had visions of conquering all the world, paraded his army below as he stood on Mount Megiddo and remarked that all the armies of the world could marshal on the Jezreel plain. Napoleon had won a tremendous victory previously in Egypt, and from Megiddo he attacked the fort at Acre that had been constructed by the Crusaders. Napoleon filled the first moat with the bodies of his soldiers, but he did not have enough men to fill the second moat. He returned to France in humiliation and defeat.

It is stated in many books that have been written about the coming battle of Armageddon that more men have been killed at the Mount of Megiddo than any other place on the earth. Megiddo guards the route from the north and west to Jerusalem and Egypt. The battles here in history are documented, yet the greatest battle is yet to come:

> I will also gather all nations, and will bring them down into the valley of Jehoshaphat. . . . Multitudes, multitudes in the valley of decision: for the day of the LORD is near in the valley of decision.
>
> —Joel 3:2,14

The Kidron Valley between Jerusalem and the Mount of Olives is the Valley of Jehoshaphat.

> For I will gather all nations against Jerusalem to battle. . . .
>
> —Zechariah 14:2

> And he gathered them together into a place called in the Hebrew tongue Armageddon.
>
> —Revelation 16:16

In the last verse of chapter fourteen the battle is described as raging for sixteen hundred furlongs. A furlong is approximately one-eighth of a mile. According to Revelation 9:16, there will be 200 million men at the battle of Armageddon just from the East and probably at least this many from the other nations. The battle will rage for a distance of 180 miles to 200 miles. Every soldier at the battle of Armageddon will be killed (Rev. 19:21). This means that approximately 500 million gallons of blood will be spilled. The symbolism of workers mashing grapes in a winepress is used by John. The battle will probably be fought from Mount Carmel at the western end of the Jezreel Valley to Petra where the remnant of Israel is hiding. Bozrah in Jordan is eighteen miles north of Petra on the King's Highway. The prophecy of Israel's Messiah coming to Bozrah to bring the redeemed of Israel back to Jerusalem is presented in Isaiah 63:1–4:

> Who is this that cometh from Edom, with dyed garments from Bozrah? this that is glorious in his apparel, travelling in the greatness of his strength? I that speak in righteousness, mighty to save. Wherefore art thou red in thine apparel, and thy garments like him that treadeth in the winefat? I have trodden the winepress alone; and of the people there was none with me: for I will tread them in mine anger, and trample them in my fury; and their blood shall be sprinkled upon my garments, and I will stain all my raiment. For the day of vengeance is in mine heart, and the year of my redeemed is come.

That Bozrah will be the southern anchor point at the battle of Armageddon is also foretold in Isaiah 34:5–6,8:

> For my sword shall be bathed in heaven: behold, it shall come down upon Idumea, and upon the people of my curse, to judgment. The sword of the LORD is filled with blood, it is made fat with fatness, and with the blood of lambs and goats . . . for the LORD hath a sacrifice in Bozrah, and a great slaughter in the land of Idumea. . . . For it is the day of the LORD's vengeance, and the year of recompences for the controversy of Zion.

God's covenant with Abraham, that He would bless them that blessed him and his seed and curse them that cursed him and his seed, is still in effect. At the battle of Armageddon God will finally settle the controversy He has with the nations over Israel, that little country not much bigger than the state of Vermont.

Chapter Fifteen

The Wrath of God

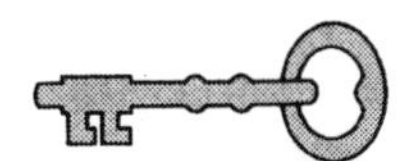

Key #24: Full Means Full

And I saw another sign in heaven, great and marvellous, seven angels having the seven last plagues; for in them is filled up the wrath of God.

—Revelation 15:1

Chapter fifteen is the smallest of all the twenty-two chapters in the Revelation. In the movie previews of shows to come, snacks and drinks that are available in the lobby are pitched, then there is a break of a few minutes where (management hopes) many will rush out and buy popcorn and Cokes at five times the regular prices. Chapter fourteen is the preview of things to come during the last half of the Tribulation, and chapter fifteen introduces the divine wrath administrators. If people left alive on earth are going to pop any popcorn, they had better do it between chapters fifteen and sixteen because God's patience is at an end.

Out of the seventh seal come seven angels with six trumpet judgments, and out of the seventh trumpet come seven vial judgments. In this first verse of chapter fifteen the angels who are to pour out the vials of God's wrath are introduced. The Greek word for vial (*phiale*) could be interpreted to be a vial, a bowl, a basin, or even a cup. John does not explain the size of the vessel, the shape of the vessel, or the volume of the vessel.

The containers of God's wrath are not identified until verse five, yet it is inferred in the first verse of chapter fifteen that vials, bowls, basins, or cups are involved. And, we notice that whatever the containers are, they are "filled up" with the wrath of God. We read in Galatians 4:4 that ". . . when the fulness of the time was come, God sent forth his Son. . . ." There was an exact day, hour, and minute for Jesus to be born. The fullness of the Gentiles will be when the last determined Gentile to be saved is saved. When God says a cup is full, that means that not even one more drop can be added to the cup without it overflowing. A full and complete measure of God's anger will be directed against the earth in the last seven judgments.

As the seven angels appear with vessels filled with the wrath of God, John sees, as it were, a sea of glass mingled with fire. This means, of course, that it was really not a sea and it was really not fire, but it appeared to look

And I saw as it were a sea of glass mingled with fire: and them that had gotten the victory over the beast, and over his image, and over his mark, and over the number of his name, stand on the sea of glass, having the harps of God. And they sing the song of Moses the servant of God, and the song of the Lamb, saying, Great and marvellous are thy works, Lord God Almighty; just and true are thy ways, thou King of saints. Who shall not fear thee, O Lord, and glorify thy name? for thou only art holy: for all nations shall come and worship before thee; for thy judgments are made manifest.

—Revelation 15:2–4

like a sea with fire in it. This scene doubtless represents a sea of people who came out of fiery judgments but are now at peace, because they have gained the victory over the Antichrist. We read again of those in the Tribulation who will gain the victory over the Antichrist in Revelation 12:11, "And they overcame him by the blood of the Lamb, and by the word of their testimony; and they loved not their lives unto the death." Those in the Tribulation who try to cling to their lives by taking the mark of the beast will go to an everlasting hell. Those who refuse to take the mark of the beast because they have been saved by faith in the blood of Jesus Christ will live forever.

There are some things to live for and some things to die for. As the song goes, we need to know when to hold 'em and when to fold 'em. It is extreme foolishness to give one's life for false promises. We think of the poor, deceived people who willingly died for Jim Jones in South America, or those in California who foolishly died in the Applewhite group, thinking they were going to latch on to a passing comet. Or the young Muslims who rush to blow themselves up for a promise of a harem of young virgins in paradise.

A pungent joke that comes out of Israel is about a young Muslim who kills himself in order to kill Israelis. As this young Palestinian male wakes up in the hereafter, he rushes up to Mohammed with great excitement and says, "Holy prophet, I just blew myself up on an Israeli bus and killed thirty Jews. Where is my harem of seventy-two beautiful virgins?" Mohammed responded, "Son, there has been a slight misunderstanding. It's not seventy-two virgins, but one seventy-two–year–old virgin."

The promises of God to all who put their faith in His only begotten Son extend even to those who will be killed in the Tribulation for refusing to take the mark of the beast. God confirms His promises with the fulfilling of Bible prophecy (2 Pet. 1:19), something that no man-made or false religion in the world can do.

The particular group of the redeemed from the earth that John describes as a sea of glass may be the saved of Israel, including the 144,000, because they sing a song of Moses. We assume the lyrics are taken from Exodus 15:1–7:

> Then sang Moses and the children of Israel this song unto the LORD, and spake, saying, I will sing unto the LORD, for he hath triumphed gloriously: the horse and his rider hath he thrown into the sea. The LORD is my strength and song, and he is become my salvation: he is my God, and I will prepare him an habitation; my father's God, and I will exalt him. The LORD is a man of war: the LORD is his name. Pharaoh's chariots and his host hath he cast into the sea: his chosen captains also are drowned in the Red sea. The depths have covered them: they sank into the bottom as a stone. Thy

> right hand, O LORD, is become glorious in power: thy right hand, O LORD, hath dashed in pieces the enemy. And in the greatness of thine excellency thou hast overthrown them that rose up against thee: thou sentest forth thy wrath, which consumed them as stubble.

We notice in verse seven of Exodus 15 that God in His wrath destroyed Pharaoh and his armies, and when all seven vials of the wrath of God are poured out, the Antichrist and his armies will likewise be destroyed.

And after that I looked, and, behold, the temple of the tabernacle of the testimony in heaven was opened: And the seven angels came out of the temple, having the seven plagues, clothed in pure and white linen, and having their breasts girded with golden girdles. And one of the four beasts gave unto the seven angels seven golden vials full of the wrath of God, who liveth for ever and ever. And the temple was filled with smoke from the glory of God, and from his power; and no man was able to enter into the temple, till the seven plagues of the seven angels were fulfilled.

—Revelation 15:5–8

In Revelation 11:19 we read that the temple of God in Heaven was opened just enough for John to see the "ark of his testament." Here in Revelation 15:5–6 the temple is opened wider for John to see the seven angels who are to be given the seven vials of God's wrath. In the Old Testament, the tabernacle was called "the tabernacle of the testimony" (Num. 10:11). The most important item in the ark of the covenant was the tablets of the law. Some commentaries on Revelation place the lost ark in the temple of God in Heaven, but that is looking for the lost ark in another realm, and I would not go that far. In any event, the tabernacle or temple and the tablets of the law were emblems of the true in Heaven. The law on tablets of stone set forth God's wrath against sin in definitive terms. We read in Romans 7:13, ". . . sin, that it might appear sin, working death in me by that which is good; that sin by the commandment might become exceeding sinful."

The law was to reveal sin, not to take away sin. The reader may go to the family doctor with a pain in the stomach. The doctor puts the patient before an x-ray machine. A malignant tumor shows on the x-ray negative. The x-ray machine does not take the tumor away; it only reveals the need to take it away. The patient has to go to a surgeon for the removal of the tumor. Only Jesus Christ can take away our sin.

God's law treasured in the temple of Heaven, as set forth by Moses on the tablets, states explicitly under the penalty of eternal death to have no gods before the true God; don't worship idols; don't commit murder; don't lie or steal, etc. Yet, in the Tribulation, the Antichrist and his world will hold the law of God in utter contempt and deny the Lord Jesus Christ who is able to save the uttermost all who come to Him by faith (Rev. 9:20–21; Heb. 7:25). The seven vials of wrath given to the seven angels are judgments determined for the world under the leadership of Antichrist that stands in complete rebellion against its Creator. The anger, or wrath of God, fills the temple in Heaven.

It does not take a husband long to find out that the kitchen is the wife's temple in the house. When the wife is angry, the kitchen is no place for the husband or the children to be. Likewise, no one is allowed in the temple in Heaven until God's righteous wrath is poured out by the seven angels of judgment.

It was said of Dr. Jonathan Edwards, president of Yale University, that when he preached his sermon "Sinners in the Hands of an Angry God," that grown men would cry out for mercy and women would faint. If the reader will look up the word "anger" in the concordance, this word is used approximately three hundred times in the Bible, and at least two out of three times it refers to the "anger" of God. We read in Isaiah 66:15–16,

> For, behold, the LORD will come with fire, and with his chariots like a whirlwind, to render his anger with fury, and his rebuke with flames of fire. For by fire and by his sword will the LORD plead with all flesh: and the slain of the LORD shall be many.

In the Bible, the reader will find the word "wrath" some two hundred times, and half of these words apply to the "wrath" of God. We read in Revelation 19:15 that when Jesus Christ returns He will tread ". . . the winepress of the fierceness and wrath of Almighty God."

The softhearted but soft-headed preachers today complain that we should not talk about hell, nor the anger and wrath of God. They say we are scaring little children into becoming Christians. But we read that all scripture is profitable for reproof, instruction, doctrine, and correction in righteousness (2 Tim. 3:16). We do indeed have a God of love, who loved us so much that He sent His only begotten Son to die in our place. But we also have a God of anger and wrath against those who blaspheme His name and murder and kill and rob and plunder and destroy the world.

Paul wrote to the Christians at Thessalonica:

> For yourselves know perfectly that the day of the Lord so cometh as a thief in the night. . . . But let us, who are of the day, be sober, putting on the breastplate of faith and love; and for an helmet, the hope of salvation. For God hath not appointed us to wrath, but to obtain salvation by our Lord Jesus Christ, Who died for us, that, whether we wake or sleep, we should live together with him.
>
> —1 Thessalonians 5:2,8–10

God has not appointed Christians to live through that time when His anger and wrath comes to the full and seven angels come out of the temple in Heaven to destroy them who would destroy the world. Has the reader made the decision to trust Jesus Christ as the One who died for him? If not, then pray this prayer:

> Dear God, I know that I am a sinner deserving of your wrath and anger. I understand that if I died I would go to hell. Will you forgive me of my sins as I place my faith in Jesus Christ who died for my sins on the cross, and in His name I pray.

Chapter Sixteen

The Grapes of God's Wrath

And I heard a great voice out of the temple saying to the seven angels, Go your ways, and pour out the vials of the wrath of God upon the earth.
—Revelation 16:1

There was a book written in the 1930s, and a movie by the same name, titled *The Grapes of Wrath*. The book and the movie were about the refugees from an environmental disaster, the Oklahoma Dust Bowl. When the seven vials of God's wrath are poured out upon the earth, the remaining population will be harvested in God's winepress as we learned from our study of chapter fourteen.

Many of the early church theologians did not believe that God could be angry or manifest wrath. They reasoned that anger was an emotion resulting from a person's will or property being challenged or threatened. Wrath, according to the dictionary's definition, is action resulting from anger, or divine retribution. However, the early Christian writers reasoned that since God was omnipotent, He could not be challenged or contested; therefore, He could not be angry.

In the Old Testament, the Hebrew word *aph,* meaning anger, is used repeatedly in God's attitude regarding the wicked, sinners, and Israel. In the New Testament, the Greek word *orge,* meaning anger or wrath, is used only once in reference to either Jesus or God, and that is in Mark 3:5. In this dispensation, God is dealing with mankind in mercy and grace. In the many places in the New Testament where God in His wrath is referenced, it nearly always looks forward to God's judgments during the Tribulation period. The Greek words for wrath, *thumos* and *orge,* meaning the action and result of wrath, are both used in Revelation 16. The example of the father spanking his son and saying, "This is going to hurt me more than it hurts you" probably does not apply in God pouring out His wrath during the last half of the Tribulation. These judgments are righteous, predetermined

And the first went, and poured out his vial upon the earth; and there fell a noisome and grievous sore upon the men which had the mark of the beast, and upon them which worshipped his image.

—Revelation 16:2

judgments to destroy those who would destroy the world.

While the vial judgments generally parallel the trumpet judgments in nature if not in scope, this particular judgment could not occur in the first half of the Tribulation, because the "mark of the beast" is not internationally enforced until the last half. Whether the sores mentioned in this verse will be a physically induced reaction from taking the "mark" or a supernatural divine judgment is not certain. Terry Cook, in his book *Mark of the New World Order,* makes the following observations on pages 299–300:

> The English word mark (*Strong's Exhaustive Concordance of the Bible,* No. 5480) is from the Greek word *charagma* (pronounced Khar'-ag-mah). *Charagma* is connected by the *Expanded Vine's Expository Dictionary of New Testament* words to *stigma, Strong's* No. 4742, in which *Strong's* references *stigma* back to the Greek word *stizo,* then defines *stizo* as follows: "**. . . to prick, stick, incise, or punch for recognition of ownership. . . .** Scar of service: **a mark**" [emphasis added].
>
> This is perhaps the best definition of HOW the Mark of the Beast will be given to everyone. I think it is a clear picture of the identifier being placed into and under the skin . . . and for now, the technology that fills the bill is the biochip RFID transponder.
>
> The secular American College Dictionary defines *mark* as: ". . . an impression upon anything, such as a line, cut, dent, stain, bruise, brand, . . . an affixed or impressed device . . . a sign or token . . . a distinguishing feature . . . to put a *mark on for identification. . . .*"
>
> It also defines *stigma* as: "A mark of disgrace or infamy; a stain or mark of reproach; a mark or sign of defect or degeneration; a mark on the skin; a *mark made* by a branding iron *on the skin of a criminal or slave*" [emphasis added].
>
> Another secular reference, *Rodale's Synonym Finder,* lists the following synonyms for *mark*: ". . . cut, gash, scratch, slash, scar, pock, notch, chip, nick, pit, dent, impressions, bruise, sign, symbol, indication, *brand, identification; marking, token . . .*" [emphasis added].
>
> By this time it ought to be obvious to anyone with an open, unbiased mind that the Mark of the Beast of the Antichrist will be used to *identify* those who are owned by him during the seven-year period known as the Great Tribulation. Without his mark of ownership in the skin of the right hand or forehead, no one on earth will be permitted to buy or sell anything. Remember, the Greek word *stizo* indicates that the Mark will be *"pricked, stuck, incised, or punched"* into the skin "as recognition of ownership." Doesn't this sound incredibly close to having an ID microchip/biochip transponder the size of a grain of rice injected with a twelve-gauge hypodermic needle through and under the skin? Could this be merely a scientific coincidence

. . . or could it be an exact fulfillment of "end times" scriptures, such as Revelation 13:16–18?

It is common practice today to put computer chips in horses, cows, and family pets for identification purposes. With the increase in world terrorism, personal identification is becoming an increasing national and international problem. A small computer chip, possibly in the hand or in the forehead, would solve a lot of problems. Those who are already getting their own personal computer chip implanted in their body are called "Chipsons." A reaction to such an implanted device could cause sores, or as we have noted, the sores could be a divine-sent judgment. We should remember that the Tribulation period will not be "business as usual." There will be angelic activity, 144,000 sealed Israelites running around, two supernatural witnesses, etc.

Sores and blisters all over the faces of those who have taken the "mark of the beast" should cause the readers to make sure of their salvation by faith in Jesus Christ to miss this awesome judgment at the pouring out of the first vial of the wrath of God.

The judgment of the second vial of God's wrath corresponds to the judgment of the second trumpet (Rev. 8:9). The exception is that the judgment of the second trumpet only affects one-third of the seas and oceans; the second vial judgment kills every living thing in the seas and oceans, seemingly all forms of the millions of marine life and those in the remaining ships. We would assume by "sea" the text means all major seas and oceans; although there is a possibility that only the Great Sea, or the Mediterranean Sea, is referenced. It is not conceivable that sufficient amounts of poisons could be poured into the seas and oceans to cause such a condition. As noted in our comments on Revelation 8:9, the death of the earth's larger bodies of waters could be caused by oceanic nuclear war in attempting to destroy ships and submarines with atomic capabilities. The oceans become "as" the blood of a dead man. It is the red blood cells that carry oxygen to the body parts, without which the flesh dies. Plankton in the seas and oceans produce a great amount of the earth's oxygen, and if all marine life dies, the sea is in reality like the blood of a dead man. The deadly contamination of the seas and oceans, regardless of the cause, may be the reason we read in Revelation 21:1: "And I saw a new heaven and a new earth: for the first heaven and the first earth were passed away; **and there was no more sea."**

And the second angel poured out his vial upon the sea; and it became as the blood of a dead man: and every living soul died in the sea.

—Revelation 16:3

The judgment that follows the pouring out of God's wrath in the third vial corresponds somewhat to the judgment that followed the sound of the third trumpet (Rev. 8:10–11). The difference is that in this vial judgment it seems that all the rivers and fresh water sources become blood, or at least the remaining uncontaminated rivers and fresh waters.

And the third angel poured out his vial upon the rivers and fountains of waters; and they became blood. And I heard the angel of the waters say, Thou art righteous, O Lord, which art, and wast, and shalt be, because thou hast judged thus.

—Revelation 16:4–5

For they have shed the blood of saints and prophets, and thou hast given them blood to drink; for they are worthy. And I heard another out of the altar say, Even so, Lord God Almighty, true and righteous are thy judgments.

—Revelation 16:6-7

We read in Revelation 11:6 that the two witnesses have power to change water to blood. It is possible that the two witnesses may be involved in the judgment of turning water into blood in the first half of the Tribulation, but not in the second half as the length of their ministry will be only three and one-half years. The oceans become "as" the blood of a dead man, but the rivers and fresh water sources, we read, "become blood." The army of Genghis Kahn, when low on food, would cut the veins in their horses' necks and drink the blood as they rode along. We would assume that the blood of human beings would probably not taste worse than horses' blood. In China, serving congealed pigs' blood is considered a delicacy. Nevertheless, to have to drink blood to keep from dying from thirst would certainly be a loathsome experience.

Jesus prophesied that just as the blood of Zecharias was shed between the temple and the altar, so would the blood of the priesthood which killed Him be shed in the same place. Josephus confirms that when the priests begged Titus for their lives, Titus replied that since there was no temple, there was no need for priests. Their throats were cut on the remains of the temple steps and their blood ran down to the altar of burning. The saints and prophets slain mentioned in verse six of Revelation 16 will doubtless be those who will die by beheading for refusing to take the "mark of the beast." We can imagine the millions of gallons of blood resulting from the beheading of millions of people in cities around the world. Therefore, in retribution God turns all the fresh water to blood.

This will be a horrible judgment, and some may protest that a God of love could not do such a thing. But the third angel of vials of God's wrath, declares, "O Lord, this is a righteous judgment." In other words, it is the right thing to do. And another angel from the altar, the second witness, affirms, "Even so, Lord God Almighty, true and righteous are thy judgments." In the closing days of the age of grace, God was silent as 6 million Jews, including 1.5 million children, were burned in the furnaces of Nazi Germany. But in the Tribulation, God will not be silent. This will be a time of justice when God balances the scales.

And the fourth angel poured out his vial upon the sun; and power was given unto him to scorch men with fire. And men were scorched with great heat, and blasphemed the name of God, which hath power over these plagues: and they repented not to give him glory.

—Revelation 16:8-9

The pouring out of the fourth vial of God's wrath corresponds with the judgment of the sounding of the fourth trumpet (Rev. 8:12). We can only assume that there will be fluctuating solar activity throughout the Tribulation period. On the Day of Pentecost when the disciples spoke in other languages to the Jews from other countries who were in Jerusalem, Peter observed, "But this is that which was spoken by the prophet Joel . . . And I will shew wonders in heaven above, and signs in the earth beneath; blood, and fire, and vapour of smoke: The sun shall be turned into darkness, and the moon into blood, before that great and notable day of the Lord come" (Acts 2:16,19–20).

The speaking in other languages with the coming of the Holy Spirit was a sign to Israel that God would, upon evidence of a national repentance, send Jesus back at that time (Acts 3:19–21). But Israel did not repent and only a partial fulfillment of Joel's prophecy took place. The solar activity in the last half of the Tribulation will not only be a judgment against an Antichrist world government and a Christ-rejecting world, it will also be a sign to Israel that their deliverance is near: "Moreover the light of the moon shall be as the light of the sun, and the light of the sun shall be sevenfold, as the light of seven days, in the day that the LORD bindeth up the breach of his people, and healeth the stroke of their wound" (Isa. 30:26). Jesus (Matt. 24:29), Malachi (Mal. 4:1), and at least a dozen other prophets prophesied that the sun would become brighter and then dark in the Tribulation and many would be burned up. But what about the remnant of Israel in a secret hiding place awaiting the coming of Messiah? If the remnant of Israel is in Petra, as we believe, then that is a place of caves. They will be able to escape the direct heat from the sun.

Dr. Henry Morris offers an interesting thought and references several scriptures to bolster his conclusion that when the sun becomes seven times hotter in the Tribulation, the ice and snow that are frozen at the North Pole and South Pole will melt. We know that God will not destroy the world again by water, but this may add to mankind's general tribulations. The ninth chapter of Amos foretells the regathering of Israel into the land after the Tribulation and certain other prophetic events that will occur at that time:

> And the Lord GOD of hosts is he that toucheth the land, and it shall melt, and all that dwell therein shall mourn: and it shall rise up wholly like a flood; and shall be drowned, as by the flood of Egypt. . . . In that day will I raise up the tabernacle of David that is fallen, and close up the breaches thereof; and I will raise up his ruins, and I will build it as in the days of old.
>
> —Amos 9:5,11

When Adam and Eve sinned, God cursed the earth and increased their sorrows and troubles to bring them back to Him in repentance. The judgments of the Tribulation are to bring His earthly people, Israel, back to Him in repentance and offer a suffering world that has brought judgment upon itself His eternal salvation. But we read in verse nine of Revelation 16 that even when the Lord demonstrates His presence and power in the heavens, men will still not repent and cry out to God to save them.

As I have already noted in several places in this study of the Revelation, the prophecies relating to the solar activity during the Tribulation concern the sun becoming exceedingly bright and hot, and then becoming dark.

And the fifth angel poured out his vial upon the seat of the beast; and his kingdom was full of darkness; and they gnawed their tongues for pain, And blasphemed the God of heaven because of their pains and their sores, and repented not of their deeds.

—Revelation 16:10-11

Also, as noted, the scriptures give an accurate scientific forecast of our sun entering a nova stage, wherein the atoms are stripped of their shells and the entire mass shrinks into a small ball perhaps no more than fifteen miles across. A teaspoon of matter would weigh thousands of tons, and gravity would be so intense that even light could not escape, even though the core would be immeasurably hot. Some believe this is what hell will be like—a lake of fire where there is no light. At this time in the Tribulation the Antichrist will have control over all the world (Rev. 13:7–8); and if the sun becomes dark, it follows that all the world will be dark.

We read that during the ten plagues upon Egypt, it was so dark the darkness could be felt. This occurred about the time that Thera (Santorini) blew up in a great volcanic explosion. Thera is north of Cairo, Egypt, approximately 350 miles, and some think the darkness was caused by the thick volcanic ash, and this is why it could be felt.

It is scientifically obvious, without God's divine intervention, the earth could not continue in darkness for more than a day or two. Without a heat source, the earth would become a frozen ball with no light. Even the oceans would freeze solid. But for a few hours at least, those who have taken the "mark of the beast" will suffer a different dimension of pain and suffering from their burns and sores as they sit in complete cold and darkness wondering what will happen next. We are not told how God will restore light. Perhaps after the dark stage of the nova, the sun will emerge as a ring-nova.

And the sixth angel poured out his vial upon the great river Euphrates; and the water thereof was dried up, that the way of the kings of the east might be prepared.

—Revelation 16:12

Unless God would miraculously restore light and heat to the world, there would be no reason for further judgments or angelic activity. However, the parade of the angelic messengers with the seven vials of God's wrath continues. The sixth angel pours out his vial upon the river Euphrates.

We read in Genesis 2:11–14 that in the Garden of Eden there were four rivers. One of the rivers is the Euphrates. It is also fairly easy to identify another river, the Hiddekel, because we read this river went "toward the east of Assyria." This river is the Tigris. The Tigris flowed on the eastern side of Nineveh, present-day Mosul, the capital of the Assyrian Empire. History verifies that the Tigris was called Indigna by the Persians and Dijlah by the Assyrians. We have crossed the Tigris at both Mosul and Baghdad. It is a wide, deep, clear river. It is also full of fish. That leaves two rivers to identify, the Pison and the Gihon. The Gihon is associated with Ethiopia (Heb. —Cush), and Josephus indicated that it is the Nile, and that the Pison is the Ganges. The Tigris is formed by melting ice and snow on the east side of Mount Ararat, and the Euphrates is formed by melting snow and ice flowing down the west side of Mount Ararat. At one time, the Tigris and Euphrates joined together in what is now the Persian Gulf. The Nile and Ganges are now separated by two thousand miles. However, we have to remember that at the time of the Tower of Babel (built on the Euphrates River), in the days of Peleg (Gen. 10:25), the earth was divided. This is why Nimrod built the Tower of Babel. The solid world land mass was being broken apart into continents and islands, so the people were afraid, ". . . Lest we be scattered abroad upon the face of the whole earth" (Gen. 11:4). NASA through satellite photography has discerned the dry bed of a huge river that once flowed from west to east across the Sahara Desert. So it is possible that the Nile and the Ganges were the other two rivers that once flowed through Eden. But the Euphrates River was the eastern boundary of the Roman Empire, and the eastern boundary of the land God gave Israel. It is also generally recognized as a boundary between the oriental and occidental worlds.

We read in Revelation 9:14–21 that four angels (demons) are bound in the River Euphrates, and once loosed, an army of 200 million will march across the river to Armageddon. Genghis Kahn led an army of 150,000 Mongols across the Euphrates, but it was not time for the Antichrist to appear, so Genghis did not become the Antichrist. As far as drying up the Euphrates for such an army to cross on a dry riverbed would be no great feat today. There are now at least a dozen dams across the Euphrates in Turkey, Syria, and Iraq. The largest of these dams is across the Euphrates near the rebuilt tourist site of old Babylon. Even though the construction of a pontoon bridge across the Euphrates by an army corps of engineers would be no problem, it would be much easier and much quicker for such a huge army with all its equipment to cross over on dry ground.

As we write this commentary, the Euphrates River is being mentioned hundreds of times every day on world radio and television, and appearing hundreds of times in world newspapers, because the U.S. Army is busy along the Euphrates from the Persian Gulf to the Syrian border conquering Iraq, the land of old Babylon. This may indicate that the fulfillment of Revelation 16:12 may be nearer than we think.

And I saw three unclean spirits like frogs come out of the mouth of the dragon, and out of the mouth of the beast, and out of the mouth of the false prophet. For they are the spirits of devils, working miracles, which go forth unto the kings of the earth and of the whole world, to gather them to the battle of that great day of God Almighty. Behold, I come as a thief. Blessed is he that watcheth, and keepeth his garments, lest he walk naked, and they see his shame. And he gathered them together into a place called in the Hebrew tongue Armageddon.

—Revelation 16:13–16

With the drying up of the Euphrates we are introduced to three "unclean spirits" like frogs. These are frog-like croaking spirits that come from Satan, the Antichrist, and the False Prophet. We know that Satan is a liar from the beginning; the Antichrist is given a big mouth spouting great words against God and anything that is of God; the False Prophet is going to be a big blabbermouth in order to convince the world to worship the Antichrist as their god.

There once was a girl walking along the road who stopped to look at a frog in a mud puddle. The frog spoke to the girl, and said, "If you will kiss me, I will turn into a handsome prince. I will marry you and take you to my father's kingdom where you will have anything you desire and be happy ever after." The girl put the frog in her purse and told it that she would think about it and get back to him. Several days later the frog became impatient and croaked, "You have had time to think about my offer. What do you say?" The girl replied, "You're offer was indeed most generous, but I have decided that I had rather have a talking frog"!

Likewise, the unsaved world today would rather listen to talking frogs than the Word of God and be born again a child of God and live with the Lord in heavenly places. Every time I hear some liberal preacher, evolutionist, or one-world politician talking on radio or television about what we have to do to have a better world, I think of a frog mouthing the promises of Satan, the Antichrist, or the False Prophet.

It appears that the devil knows his time is short (Rev. 12:12). The Antichrist and the False Prophet operate by the power of Satan (Rev. 13:2; 13:12). Through these two, all nations are convinced that they must send their armies to Jerusalem to prevent their world from being invaded by an army from outer space. In the mindset of the unregenerate and remaining world population, Jerusalem is the heart of the problem, so the roots of Zionism must be destroyed (Zech. 14:1–3).

It is difficult to determine at this time all the motivations for the armies from North America, South America, Europe, and the Orient to come to either the aid, or to battle, the Antichrist and his forces. The drying up of the Euphrates doubtless has something to do with Daniel 11:44–45:

> But tidings out of the east and out of the north shall trouble him: therefore he shall go forth with great fury to destroy, and utterly to make away many. And he shall plant the tabernacles of his palace between the seas in the glorious holy mountain; yet he shall come to his end, and none shall help him.

Armageddon (Heb.—*Har Magedon*) means "Mount of Slaughter," so named because of the site of many battles that have taken place there. As noted, some historians say that more blood has been shed on this spot than any other place on earth. I have stood many times on Megiddo and looked up and down the Valley of Jezreel where the armies of the world will one day meet for deployment. At the western end of the valley is an Israeli army airfield, which is overlooked by Mount Carmel where Elijah fought the prophets of Baal. But regardless of the motivations for this coming battle that will rage for two hundred miles to the south, God will allow it to ultimately destroy those who would destroy the earth.

Between verse fourteen concerning the gathering of the armies of the nations and verse sixteen of Revelation 16, is a somewhat mysterious reminder: "Behold, I come as a thief. Blessed is he that watcheth, and keepeth his garments, lest he walk naked, and they see his shame." A large book could be written on this one verse. Dr. Seiss does not commit himself on the object of this admonition; Dr. Hindson makes no comment at all; Dr. Morris seems to favor the interpretation that this verse is directed to the few believers in the Tribulation who have escaped, to that time, the execution squads of the Antichrist. Dr. Walvoord seemed to have believed that the admonition is generally directed to Christians today.

Jesus used the example of the thief in the night to teach the imminency of His return, "Therefore be ye also ready: for in such an hour as ye think not the Son of man cometh" (Matt. 24:44). Paul wrote to the Christians at Thessalonica that they knew beyond doubt that Jesus would return ". . . as a thief in the night" (1 Thess. 5:2). Paul continued, however, to tell the Christians at Thessalonica that they would have no excuse for allowing that day to ". . . overtake you as a thief." To the dead and sleeping Sardis church, Jesus wrote, ". . . If therefore thou shalt not watch, I will come on thee as a thief, and thou shalt not know what hour I will come upon thee . . ." (Rev. 3:3). John admonished Christians in general: "And now, little children, abide in him; that, when he shall appear, we may have confidence, and not be ashamed before him at his coming" (1 John 2:28). Peter wrote of the coming of the signs of the last days, "Wherefore, beloved, seeing that ye look for such things, be diligent that ye may be found of him in peace, without spot, and blameless" (2 Pet. 3:14).

The warning admonition in Revelation 16:15 is consistent with others of a similar meaning throughout scripture; and specifically within the Revelation 16 context. Christians and non-Christians alike are not to wait until they see the armies of all nations gathering on the plain of Jezreel to get ready for the Lord's return. We should always be watching and waiting for His coming with imminent expectations.

Chronology Check

Before proceeding in the commentary on the pouring out of the seventh vial of God's wrath, perhaps we need to again orient the Tribulation order of events. The Tribulation judgments are determined by:

1. Opening of the six seals of the seven sealed books.
2. Opening of the seventh seal reveals six trumpet judgments.
3. The sounding of the first six trumpets.
4. The seventh trumpet signals seven vials of wrath.
5. The pouring out of the seventh vial finishes (completes) all the judgments required.

Required for what?

1. To destroy those who are destroying the earth.

And the seventh angel poured out his vial into the air; and there came a great voice out of the temple of heaven, from the throne, saying, It is done. And there were voices, and thunders, and lightnings; and there was a great earthquake, such as was not since men were upon the earth, so mighty an earthquake, and so great. And the great city was divided into three parts, and the cities of the nations fell: and great Babylon came in remembrance before God, to give unto her the cup of the wine of the fierceness of his wrath. And every island fled away, and the mountains were not found.

—Revelation 16:17-20

And there fell upon men a great hail out of heaven, every stone about the weight of a talent: and men blasphemed God because of the plague of the hail; for the plague thereof was exceeding great.
—Revelation 16:21

2. To put down all power and authority on earth in rebellion against God's plan and purpose.
3. To establish the Kingdom of Jesus Christ on earth.
4. Jesus Christ to claim His prepared bride.
5. Israel to finally acknowledge Jesus Christ as Messiah.
6. To restore nature to its Edenic perfection.
7. To bind Satan in the bottomless pit for one thousand years.

Judgments of the Seventh Vial

The term "it is done," or "it is finished" is found in many scriptures. The personality of the phrase depends upon the context. Jesus prayed to the Father that the "cup" He was to drink on the cross be passed, but there was no other way. When He had paid the ultimate price for our sin, He said, "It is finished" (John 19:30). Matthew indicated Jesus proclaimed this declaration in a "loud voice," like a marathon runner finishing first in the race, a cry of victory. However, when the angel of the seventh vial informed John "it is done," the meaning would be like finishing the last row of hoeing forty acres of grassy cotton. Although the vast majority of readers do not know the real meaning of this statement, believe me, if they had hoed forty acres of grassy cotton, they would. In other words, the judgments of the Tribulation were difficult and unpleasant, but they had to be done. The last phrase, "it is done," is also found in Revelation 21:6. There is a New Heaven and a New Earth; a New Jerusalem; no more sin; no more pain; no more sorrow; no more death; God will have forever His redeemed family (Rev. 21:7), who will praise Him and love Him for all eternity—**not because they had to, but because they chose to.** This will be to God's eternal love and glory. HALLELUJAH!

But before this happens, the judgments of the seventh vial of God's wrath must occur. The first judgment that takes place is a great earthquake, an earthquake so great that it can't even be measured on the Richter scale. As a result of this earthquake, the islands will be no more and the mountains will be leveled. All the deserts will be done away with. All the geological changes due to man's rebellion against God will be corrected, "For we know that the whole creation groaneth and travaileth in pain together until now" (Rom. 8:22). The four curses that God put on this present creation because of sin will be erased in this tremendous earthquake, and all the land area will be back together in one piece again. How is this going to happen? I don't know. But God knows what to do, and He has the power to do it.

We read that in the course of the final Tribulation judgments released by the pouring out of the seventh vial of God's wrath, there will be storms that will drop hailstones as huge as one hundred pounds each. Here in Oklahoma during the spring and summer we often have hail that accompanies thunderstorms or tornadoes. I remember one storm that dropped hailstones that weighed one pound each. All the leaves on the trees were knocked off; thousands of birds were killed; even cats and dogs caught in the storm were killed. But think what it would be like to suffer hail that weighed one hundred times this weight. Even steel buildings could not protect people nor animals. "Hast thou entered into the treasures of the snow? or hast thou seen the treasures of the hail, Which I have reserved against the time of trouble, against the day of battle and war?" (Job 38:22–23).

It is interesting to take a concordance and see just how many times God has used hail as an instrument of judgment. But according to Job, God has reserved the greatest hailstorm for one of His final judgments of the Tribulation.

We also note that in the final vial judgments, God remembers "great" Babylon. In Revelation 14 where the judgments of the last half of the Tribulation are previewed, we are informed that Babylon will fall. But why would God remember a nation that has lain dormant in the dust of history for two thousand years, and only being revived as Iraq in these last days? "Make bright the arrows; gather the shields: the LORD hath raised up the spirit of the kings of the Medes: for his device is against Babylon, to destroy it; because it is the vengeance of the LORD, the vengeance of his temple" (Jer. 51:11).

Paul used the destruction of the temple by Babylon to encourage Christians to not defile their bodies: "If any man defile the temple of God, him shall God destroy . . ." (1 Cor. 3:17). As we may have noted before, Rome and Babylon destroyed the temple. The destruction of Herod's Temple by Rome occurred after Paul wrote his epistles to the churches. However, both Babylon and Rome yet must be destroyed as the temples were destroyed. Regardless what happens in Babylon (Iraq) after the Desert Storm War of 1991, or the U.S.—Iraqi war of 2003, both that nation and Rome will be decimated like Sodom and Gomorrah (Isa. 13:19).

Yet, we must declare with the angels of Heaven, *Righteous and just are thy judgments, O Lord, because without that blessed hope of your return, this present world would have no hope.*

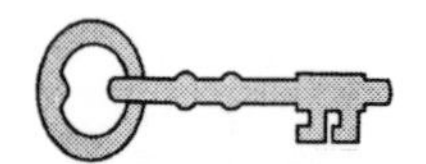

Key #25: City of Seven Hills

And there came one of the seven angels which had the seven vials, and talked with me, saying unto me, Come hither; I will shew unto thee the judgment of the great whore that sitteth upon many waters: With whom the kings of the earth have committed fornication, and the inhabitants of the earth have been made drunk with the wine of her fornication.

—Revelation 17:1-2

Chapter Seventeen

The Woman Who Rides the Beast

Chapters seventeen and eighteen of Revelation concern a Tribulation judgment that has already been determined and announced—the final destruction of Babylon. In Revelation 14:8 the angelic announcement is heard, "Babylon is fallen." In Revelation 16:19 the destruction of "great Babylon" is reported. In chapters seventeen and eighteen, John is given further details about the religious, economic, and political nature of the last Babylon.

In chapter thirteen of Revelation, we have the beast with seven heads and ten horns, and the same beast appears in chapter seventeen. In chapter thirteen, the national composition of the beast is given; in chapter seventeen, the satanic nature of the beast in the color of scarlet is emphasized. In chapter thirteen, the Antichrist, the beast that comes up out of the bottomless pit is also evident in chapter seventeen. So everything and every personality in chapter thirteen are present in chapter seventeen, except one —the "great whore." And why is not the "great whore" in chapter thirteen? It appears that God wants to give us a clear focus on the characters of the two main personalities in the Tribulation in chapter thirteen. To introduce the "great whore" in chapter thirteen would detract our attention from the main subject. However, in chapters seventeen and eighteen, the activity of the "great whore" in relation to other things occurring in the Tribulation is given. And even so, there is a wide variance of opinions among Bible scholars as to just who the "great whore" is and what part she plays in this drama of the end time scenario.

Dr. J. A. Seiss wrote in 1870:

> The subject itself is one of great prominence in the Apocalypse, as in all the prophecies; but it has proven about as difficult as it is conspicuous.

> On none of the current methods of treating this Book is it possible to come to any clear, consistent, and satisfying conclusions with regard to it. The body of preterist expositors have found themselves necessitated to take Great Babylon as meaning the city, the church, or the ecclesiastical system of Rome, not so much because the features of the record call for it, or really admit of it, when fairly dealt with, but because unable on their theory to do any better. That Rome and the Romish system are involved, may readily be admitted; but that this is all, and that the sudden fall of Great Babylon is simply the fall of Romanism, or the utter destruction of the city of Rome, must be emphatically denied, if the inspired portraiture is to stand as it is written. If we cannot find more solid ground than that on which the Rome theory rests we must consign the whole subject to the department of doubt and uncertainty, and let all these tremendous foreshowings pass for nothing.

I would disagree with Dr. Seiss in that the woman of Revelation 12 is the church; however, he did seem to believe that Mystery Babylon was a religious system rather than just a city of revived Babylon. Babylon in 1870 was still under drifting sand.

Dr. John Morris and Dr. John Walvoord both propose that the Babylon of chapters seventeen and eighteen of Revelation are the same Babylon represented by the head of gold in the image of Daniel 2, so does Mark Hitchcock in his book *The Second Coming of Babylon*. Dr. Ed Hindson in his commentary on Revelation takes aggressive exception with those who interpret Mystery Babylon to be the Babylon on the Euphrates for the following reasons:

1. The early church unanimously viewed "Babylon" as Rome. None of the early church fathers held that Babylon was to be taken literally. They all viewed it as symbolic of the Roman Empire in general and the city of Rome in particular.
2. The reformers and puritans were also unanimous in taking "Babylon" as a symbol of Rome. The only difference was that they extended it to refer to papal Rome as the apostate church of the last days.
3. There is no valid reason today to assume that ancient Babylon will literally be rebuilt and rise to power overnight as the dominant world city and capital of the Antichrist.

Dr. Hindson protests further that "Mystery Babylon" cannot be the Babylon on the Euphrates:

> A basic survey of the revelator's description of Babylon quickly reveals that it cannot be ancient Babylon in modern Iraq. Remember, it is portrayed as the city of the Antichrist, who rules the whole world. It is a center of

commerce, enterprise, and trade. And it is the city that shed the blood of the "witnesses of Jesus." Babylon does not qualify in any of these regards. Notice also the characteristics of the ***apocalyptic "Babylon"***:

1. Rich and prosperous (17:4)
2. Immoral and drunken (17:2,6)
3. Associated with Satan and the beast (17:7–8)
4. City that sits on seven mountains (17:9)
5. Leader of a ten-nation confederacy with Roman (European) roots (17:12–13)
6. City that reigns over many nations (17:15–18)
7. Center of commercial enterprise (18:3,11–13)
8. Sailors cross the sea to get there (18:17–18)
9. An entertainment capital (18:22–23)
10. Burns up in one hour (18:9–10,17–19)

Of course, the Babylon on the Euphrates we know. However, this does not mean we know Mystery Babylon. Dr. Hindson has put forth some sound reasons why the Babylon of Revelation 17 and 18 will not be the nation of Iraq or the rebuilt city of Babylon.

I was in Babylon in 1978 and visited this ancient city as it was being restored by Saddam Hussein as a world tourist attraction. In defense of Dr. Morris' and Dr. Walvoord's positions on the Babylon of the Tribulation, the Desert Storm War of 1990–91 is clearly prophesied in the first nine verses of Isaiah 13 and also certain prophecies in Jeremiah 50–51. This was the unfinished war, and the American/British invasion of Iraq in April 2003 finished that war. The son of President Bush of 1991, George W. Bush, finished the job his father started. And what do we read in prophecy about this war: **"The day of the LORD is at hand . . . the day of the LORD cometh . . ."** (Isa. 13:6,9).

Against Babylon, Isaiah prophesied, "Behold, I will stir up the Medes [Afghanistan] . . . Babylon . . . shall be as when God overthrew Sodom and Gomorrah." This is to happen in the Day of the Lord, the Tribulation. There are some who are predicting that as a result of the elimination of Saddam Hussein's government, Iraq (Babylon) will once more become the most important political and economic center of the Middle East, and possibly the entire world. If this should be the correct interpretation of Iraq's future in light of Revelation 17, then the Tribulation period would be at least ten to twenty years in the future, and possibly longer.

The historic understanding of Mystery Babylon of Revelation 17 is that it is the city of Rome. For example Tertullian in A.D. 197 said, "Babylon, in the writing of our own John, is a figure of the city of Rome. For she is equally great and proud of her sway."

We could continue and quote Hippolytus, Victorinus, and others. The general agreement of church leaders in the first few centuries after Christ was that John's Babylon meant Rome. When Emperor Constantine, after A.D. 300, prostituted Christianity and made it a state religion, that identified Mystery Babylon with Rome even more. After the breakup of the Roman Empire in A.D. 450, and the invention of the Holy Roman Empire concept, the kings of Europe were anointed and crowned by the pope. Without this holy (or unholy) benediction upon the crown heads of Europe, kings did not become kings. Once blessed by the pope, and the king pledged his loyalty to the pope and the church, then the king received the Divine Right of Kings. In other words, the king could do no wrong. The king could rob whom he wanted; enslave whom he wanted; kill whom he wanted; and he was covered by the sovereignty of God because he was God's servant. Finally, the pope refused to grant Henry VIII a special dispensation to continue killing wives in order to remarry, but this was a rare exception. This relationship between the kings of Europe, the church, and the pope does express the communications the kings have with the "great whore" as set forth in Revelation 17:2.

The word for "whore" in Revelation 17 is *porne,* meaning "fornicatress." The word is also used in conjunction with adultery. The kings of Europe committed political and spiritual fornication in their submission to the will of the Vatican and the pope for permission to sin in their royal responsibilities. Dave Hunt in his books, tapes, and videos also makes a strong case for Mystery Babylon being the Roman Catholic church. Terry Alexander in his book *Characters of Revelation* has the following to say about the "great whore":

> Where on earth will we find such a religious system? We only need to look in the *Catholic Encyclopedia* to find our answer. We read: "It is within the city of Rome, called the city of Seven Hills, that the entire area of Vatican State proper is now confined." In Vatican City, we have all the ingredients necessary to make up this MYSTERY BABYLON THE GREAT. We should note here that there are many churches that are headquartered in a city, but Vatican City *is* the church. The words Vatican and Rome are used worldwide *as one word.*
>
> Also, Revelation 17:4 tells us that this woman used two colors in her array: purple and scarlet. The same *Catholic Encyclopedia* tells us that Catholic bishops wear *purple,* cardinals wear *scarlet,* and the pope wears *rose* and *scarlet* (red).
>
> Then we notice the golden cup in her hand in verse four. This golden cup (chalice) is the most important vessel in the Roman Catholic church.

Also, verse four reveals great wealth was attributed to this woman. It is common knowledge that most of the wealth of the Roman church has been acquired by the *sale of salvation*: you are required to pay your way *in* on earth, and then someone has to pay your way *out* of purgatory. No doubt, many millions have been deceived into paying for a mythical salvation that Jesus Christ has already provided *free of charge*. It is common knowledge that the Roman church is the wealthiest organization on earth.

And finally we note verse eighteen: "And the *woman* which thou sawest is that great *city*, which reigneth over the kings of the earth."

Where on earth is there a city that is a church, with which every nation has connections? Only one: *Vatican City*. Every major nation on earth *exchanges ambassadors* with Rome. It is very hard for me to imagine that nations would exchange ambassadors with a church, but, that is exactly what happens with Rome. Truly, the pope is earth's most powerful ruler in existence today. Also, down through the centuries, it is undisputed that popes have reigned over kings. It is no different today. Only one city fits the description of Revelation 17:18, and that city is Vatican City (Rome). Vatican City is totally one of a kind in the earth today; none like it.

I realize that our remarks and supporting commentaries by other theologians on the first two verses of Revelation 17 have been overly exhaustive. Nevertheless, this is one of the most controversial chapters of the Bible, and what makes this chapter exceedingly so is its contemporary associations. Mystery Babylon could be the Babylon on the Euphrates; it could be Rome and the Roman Catholic church; it could be the United States. Although there may be other candidates, these are the primary ones. Developments in the next five years relating to any or all of these entities could sway the evidence one way or another.

In Revelation we have four women:

1. Jezebel—the false queen, the harlot church
2. The Woman with Twelve Stars—Israel
3. The Great Whore—Mystery Babylon
4. The Bride of Christ—the true church

Jezebel represents evil theocracy; the Great Whore represents evil religion; the Woman with Twelve Stars represents God's earthly people, Israel; and the Bride of the Lamb, of course, represents the blood-bought and glorified church in Heaven.

The scarlet-colored beast is probably the Revived Roman Empire, the kingdom that produces the Antichrist. It is to be noted that the woman is riding the beast, not leading it or walking beside it. It is the Antichrist that blasphemes the Name of God and anything that is of God. That the

So he carried me away in the spirit into the wilderness: and I saw a woman sit upon a scarlet coloured beast, full of names of blasphemy, having seven heads and ten horns. And the woman was arrayed in purple and scarlet colour, and decked with gold and precious stones and pearls, having a golden cup in her hand full of abominations and filthiness of her fornication: And upon her forehead was a name written, MYSTERY, BABYLON THE GREAT, THE MOTHER OF HARLOTS AND ABOMINATIONS OF THE EARTH. And I saw the woman drunken with the blood of the saints, and with the blood of the martyrs of Jesus: and when I saw her, I wondered with great admiration.

—Revelation 17:3-6

woman represents a false and filthy religious system, regardless what else she may represent, should be beyond controversy. Her apparel of purple signified that she is kept by kings; her supportive color of scarlet indicates she is indeed of Satan. Next, we notice that the woman is decked with gold, precious stones, and pearls. She is very, very rich.

I had always heard the expression "Holy Toledo." I always thought this was a reference in some way to Toledo, Ohio. Perhaps the Holy Roller movement had started in Toledo, or perhaps Toledo has an unusual number of churches. But in 1982 on a Bible tour that included Spain and Portugal, we made a side trip to Toledo from Madrid. I did not even know until then that there was a Toledo, Spain. Toledo, evidently, served as the Roman Catholic capital of Spain, dating back to before the Spanish Inquisition. I was amazed and awe-struck; perhaps more than John was when he saw the Great Whore in a vision. The town had a wall around it that looked to be about one hundred feet high and the Catholic Cathedral of Toledo was something to behold. Inside were golden idols weighing hundreds of pounds, along with jewelry and artifacts of gold, silver, diamonds, and other precious gems beyond description. At last I learned that Holy Toledo was not Toledo, Ohio. However, I questioned that Holy Toledo was really ever holy. I thought, while wealth like this is lying around in Roman Catholic churches and institutions, the pope is on television bemoaning the hunger of the downtrodden masses.

The wealth of the so-called Church of Latter Day Saints (Mormons) doubtless runs into the billions of dollars, including ownership and investments in hotel chains, supermarkets, and real estate. Protestant and non-Catholic churches also have holdings and properties in the hundreds of millions of dollars from the investment of annuity and retirement funds. But none can compare with the wealth of the Roman Catholic church. While we have no current statistics on the net worth of the Catholic church, we submit this ten-year-old report by Avro Manhattan listed on the website of Chick Publications:

> The Vatican has large investments with the Rothschild's of Britain, France, and America, with the Hambros Bank, with the Credit Suisse in London and Zurich. In the United States it has large investments with the Morgan Bank, the Chase-Manhattan Bank, the First National Bank of New York, the Bankers Trust Company, and others. The Vatican has billons of shares in the most powerful international corporations such as Gulf Oil, Shell, General Motors, Bethlehem Steel, General Electric, International Business Machines, T.W.A., etc. At a conservative estimate, these amount to more than 500 million dollars in the U.S.A. alone.
>
> In a statement published in connection with a bond prospectus, the

> Boston archdiocese listed its assets at Six Hundred and Thirty-five Million dollars ($635,891,004), which is 9.9 times its liabilities. This leaves a net worth of Five Hundred and Seventy-one million dollars ($571,704,953). It is not difficult to discover the truly astonishing wealth of the church, once we add the riches of the twenty-eight archdioceses and 122 dioceses of the U.S.A., some of which are even wealthier than that of Boston.
>
> Some idea of the real estate and other forms of wealth controlled by the Catholic church may be gathered by the remark of a member of the New York Catholic Conference, namely "that his church probably ranks second only to the United States Government in total annual purchase." Another statement, made by a nationally syndicated Catholic priest, perhaps is even more telling. "The Catholic church," he said, "must be the biggest corporation in the United States. We have a branch office in every neighborhood. Our assets and real estate holdings must exceed those of Standard Oil, A.T.&T., and U.S. Steel combined. And our roster of dues-paying members must be second only to the tax rolls of the United States Government."
>
> The Catholic church, once all her assets have been put together, is the most formidable stockbroker in the world. The Vatican, independently of each successive pope, has been increasingly orientated towards the U.S. The Wall Street Journal said that the Vatican's financial deals in the U.S. alone were so big that very often it sold or bought gold in lots of a million or more dollars at one time.
>
> The Vatican's treasure of solid gold has been estimated by the United Nations World Magazine to amount to several billion dollars. A large bulk of this is stored in gold ingots with the U.S. Federal Reserve Bank, while banks in England and Switzerland hold the rest. But this is just a small portion of the wealth of the Vatican, which in the U.S. alone, is greater than that of the five wealthiest giant corporations of the country. When to that is added all the real estate, property, stocks and shares abroad, then the staggering accumulation of the wealth of the Catholic church becomes so formidable as to defy any rational assessment.
>
> The Catholic church is the biggest financial power, wealth accumulator and property owner in existence. She is a greater possessor of material riches than any other single institution, corporation, bank, giant trust, government or state of the whole globe. The pope, as the visible ruler of this immense amassment of wealth, is consequently the richest individual of the twentieth century. No one can realistically assess how much he is worth in terms of billions of dollars.

To even list the assets of the Roman Catholic church and its business relationships, legal and perhaps illegal, would require encyclopedia sets that would fill the Library of Congress. For example, the following report comes from Americans United for Separation of Church and State, dated July/August 2002:

> Five U.S. state insurance commissions are suing the Vatican, charging that high-ranking officials in the Roman Catholic church helped an American financier engage in insurance fraud.
>
> According to a Wall Street Journal report, Frankel sought to use the Vatican as a front for a foundation that he would secretly control. He allegedly offered to transfer $55 million to a Vatican account, allowing the church to keep $5 million. Frankel is accused of using the other $50 million, which he claimed was Vatican money, to buy insurance companies, which he later bilked for more than $200 million.

The next thing we notice about this woman of the night who has a questionable reputation is that she has a gold cup in her hand. When the "cup" is used symbolically in the Bible, it can refer to riches, suffering, death, salvation, etc. The reader may at this time exercise his only research ability and check the biblical references to "cup." But a similar passage to Revelation 17:4 is found in Jeremiah 51:7, "Babylon hath been a golden cup in the LORD's hand, that made all the earth drunken: the nations have drunken of her wine; therefore the nations are mad."

The question is, was Jeremiah referencing the Babylon of his day, a Babylon of the last days, or Mystery Babylon? When the prophets spoke about Israel's future as led by the Holy Spirit, it is obvious that not all they prophesied applied to the Israel of A.D. 70. Much of what they prophesied applied to Israel in the last days, some in the Tribulation, and some in the Millennium. It seems obvious this prolonged prophecy rule also could have applied to Babylon. If the entire seventeenth chapter of Revelation applies only to the Babylon on the Euphrates, past, present, or future, then we are in the wrong pew. We might as well shut up and get on to the next chapter.

The next thing we notice about this rich but wicked woman of the night is that her existence is filled with abominations and filthy fornications.

Martin Luther, a young, pious Catholic monk, in 1511, looked forward to his pilgrimage to Rome and the Vatican. He returned to Germany bitterly disillusioned, and wrote:

> Rome is a harlot. I would not take a thousand gulden not to have seen it, for I never would have believed the true state of affairs from what other people told me had I not seen it myself. The Italians mocked us for being pious monks, for they hold Christians fools. They say six or seven masses in the time it takes me to say one, for they take money for it and I do not.

> The only crime in Italy is poverty. They still punish homicide and theft a little, for they have to, but no other sin is too gross for them. . . . So great and bold is Roman impiety that neither God nor man, neither sin nor shame, is feared. All good men who have seen Rome bear witness to this; all bad ones come back worse than before.

Later, Luther wrote to Pope Leo X about the Babylonian connection in the Roman Catholic church:

> Of your person, excellent Leo, I have heard only what is honorable and good . . . but of the Roman See, as you and all men must know, it is more scandalous and shameful than any Sodom or Babylon, and, as far as I can see, its wickedness is beyond all counsel and help, having become desperate and abysmal. It made me sick at heart to see that under your name and that of the Roman Church, the poor people in all the world are cheated and injured, against which thing I have set myself and will set myself as long as I have life, not that I hope to reform that horrible Roman Sodom, but that I know I am the debtor and servant of all Christians, and that it is my duty to counsel and warn them.

Four hundred and eighty years after Luther wrote the preceding letter to Pope Leo X, the Roman Catholic church has been rocked with sex abuse cases. According to an article in the *Washington Post* quoting Michael Winters, a Catholic writer, ". . . everybody knows today that half our clergy are gay. . . ." A homosexual is a male who practices sex with another male. When a homosexual quits this abomination, he is no longer a homosexual. According to FADICA and other sources, 90 percent of the sex abuse cases against the Roman Catholic church involve Catholic priests taking advantage of young boys. Another report by Foundations and Donors in Catholic Activities dated April 24, 2003, stated that 80 percent of Catholics have changed their contribution amounts to the church because of sexual abuse cases. The settlement of sex abuse cases out of court from 1990 to 2003 by the Roman Catholic church has run into the hundreds of millions of dollars. Although in Europe homosexual abuse of boys is considered as a lesser judicial concern, the Catholic church is having to spend more millions to support children of priests born out of wedlock.

Those who need further verification of the depths of sexual abuse within the Catholic church may consult the website of the National Institute for the Renewal of the Priesthood, from a transcript of an NBC-TV "Meet the Press" discussion between Father Donald Cozens and Stephen Rossetti. The source of sexual abominations in the Catholic church is rejecting God's Word:

> Now the Spirit speaketh expressly, that in the latter times some shall depart from the faith, giving heed to seducing spirits, and doctrines of devils; Speaking lies in hypocrisy; having their conscience seared with a hot iron; Forbidding to marry, and commanding to abstain from meats, which God hath created to be received with thanksgiving of them which believe and know the truth.
>
> —1 Timothy 4:1–3

Saints and Martyrs of Jesus

Most who have written commentaries on Revelation scamper past verse six of Revelation 17. It just isn't politically or religiously correct anymore to talk or write about those responsible for killing God's people, past, present, or future. We might hurt someone's feelings.

First we notice that the Great Whore is drunk with the blood of two groups of God's people: "the blood of the saints" and "the blood of the martyrs of Jesus." If the verse had read, "drunken with the blood of saints and martyrs of Jesus" we might assume this was just one group. However, John seems to indicate there are the saints of God and Christians. Of course, Christians are saints, but the saints of the Old Testament would not be classified as Christians. There were the faithful of Israel who were killed in the time of the Babylonian captivity, although these may not be the "saints" referenced here. The martyrs of Jesus could well be those who have died for their faith in Jesus Christ during the Church age. In the messages to the churches, church members or Christians are not referenced as saints. The saved of the Tribulation period are referenced as "saints" twelve times from Revelation 5:8 to 19:8, and one time in the Millennium (Rev. 20:9).

Inclusively, if the blood of those murdered for their faith is both those of the Church age and the Tribulation, then the identification of the Great Whore would be made easier. Under the law, disobedience could result in physical death. But mercy, grace, and truth came by Jesus Christ. Jesus came first to confirm the promises made to Israel, and secondly to offer Himself in death and satisfy the penalty of the law. Consequently, Jesus repeatedly stressed that He came not to take men's lives, but give life more abundantly (John 10:10).

On Bible or mission tours, I always lead devotionals and give Bible studies, even on the buses. In Guilin, China, on one tour, my local guide kept heckling me to read out of Mao's *Little Red Book,* contending that Mao was greater than Jesus. Finally, I said in front of our group to him, "Well, Mao is given credit for killing at least 80 million people, but Jesus never killed anyone. So, on that basis, I guess you could say that Mao was greater than Jesus." The guide never bothered me again.

There is no basis whatsoever for a representative church authority, or any ecclesiastical body, to condemn anyone to death. The New Testament itself makes a definitive separation between church and state. Only the state has the authority and responsibility for administering the death penalty for crimes committed (Rom. 13). Yet in the Dark Ages and Middle Ages, the Roman Catholic hierarchy issued death decrees for millions of Christians for no other reason, in some cases, than for not baptizing their infants into Catholic church membership.

John Hus of Bohemia was burned at the stake in 1415, accused of being a disciple of the late John Wickliffe. Pope Martin V in 1429 sent the following decree to the king of Poland:

> Know that the interests of the Holy See, and those of your crown, make it a duty to exterminate the Hussites. Remember that these impious persons dare proclaim principles of equality; they maintain that all Christians are brethren, and that God has not given to privileged men the right of ruling the nations; they hold that Christ came on earth to abolish slavery; they call the people to liberty, that is to the annihilation of kings and priests.
>
> While there is still time, then, turn your forces against Bohemia; burn, massacre, make deserts everywhere, for nothing could be more agreeable to God, or more useful to the cause of kings, than the extermination of the Hussites.

For the complete story of the execution of the millions who dared to defy the will of the Catholic church we suggest the following books: *Foxe's Book of Martyrs; The Woman Rides the Beast* by Dave Hunt; and *Martyrs Mirror,* a Mennonite publication by Braught. *Martyrs Mirror* is a double-size book, 1,153 pages, containing documented records of those hanged, beheaded, or burned at the stake, including names, places, and dates.

In the wake of the Protestant Reformation movement by Luther, independent Baptist groups were also strengthened. In the late 1600s the Roman Catholic church began to lose its authority and will to determine who lived and who died at the stake. However, we are warned in the Revelation that during the Tribulation religious oppression will exceed anything of like nature that occurred during the Dark Ages.

I am not so closed minded as to contend that the Roman Catholic church is the Great Whore of Revelation 17. However, I would be grossly negligent if I did not at least point the reader to obvious parallels. We must also consider the Islamic scourge that swept over the Middle East, Asia Minor, Spain, and the Balkans from the seventh to the sixteenth centuries, claiming the lives of additional millions of Christians. Fanatic Islam today is still persecuting Christians, even unto death, in nations like Sudan and Indonesia. And, of course, we must take into account the millions of Christians who were martyred in the Soviet Union between 1917 and 1990, as well as the millions who lost their lives in China between 1965 and 1975 in the so-called Cultural Revelation. In the Revelation, the apostle John is assured that Christians who have given their lives for their faith in Jesus Christ are remembered before the throne of God day and night. In the Revelation, those who are persecuted for Christ's sake are also comforted in that justice belongs to the Lord; He will repay.

If we interpret verse seven of Revelation 17 to be a reference to the Roman Catholic church, then its organizational structure, doctrines, and various organizations, and overall influence over many nations is something to be wondered at. The same could be said of the Roman Empire, how it existed in a broken form for over fifteen hundred years, and now at the end of the age is reforming. This too is something to wonder about.

The beast that comes up out of the bottomless pit once more described in verse eight is the Antichrist and his kingdom as also set forth in Daniel 7 and Revelation 13. The only new thought we have to add on this section of Revelation 17 is to wonder if the beast kingdom is viewed historically from A.D. 96 or from a contemporary Tribulation stage. The seven hills have also been interpreted as being seven world empires that have or will precede the Revived Roman Empire. Daniel was mainly concerned with the ten horns on the beast because they represented ten kings within the Revived Roman Empire who would be in power when the Messiah comes and fulfills the covenants made with Israel. But from a Tribulation viewpoint, at the time of John, Rome was still one empire. In about A.D. 450 Rome broke up into seven empires as foretold in Daniel 2: England, Germany, France, Belgium, Netherlands, Spain, and Portugal. Denmark was outside the Roman Empire, and Italy would have been the eighth empire except it simply remained a dormant state. The other nations that broke off Rome attained empire status through territorial expansions. These seven nations did in effect tread down the whole world as we have noted previously. This interpretation could satisfy the prophecy: the Great Whore, Rome, existing in these seven nations. Of course, England partially dropped out when Henry VIII established his own church. However, the ten kings could come from these nations.

After Rome broke up into national entities, there was no central commercial control. To bridge the gap between raw materials and productions, "common fairs" were held annually near Paris. After World War II when these European powers lost their colonies, there was an even more severe need for economic cooperation. A commercial trade arrangement called the "Common Market" was arranged between six European nations. That commercial union grew to ten nations and then became the European Union with a common parliament representing fifteen nations. At the writing of

And the angel said unto me, Wherefore didst thou marvel? I will tell thee the mystery of the woman, and of the beast that carrieth her, which hath the seven heads and ten horns. The beast that thou sawest was, and is not; and shall ascend out of the bottomless pit, and go into perdition: and they that dwell on the earth shall wonder, whose names were not written in the book of life from the foundation of the world, when they behold the beast that was, and is not, and yet is. And here is the mind which hath wisdom. The seven heads are seven mountains, on which the woman sitteth. And there are seven kings: five are fallen, and one is, and the other is not yet come; and when he cometh, he must continue a short space. And the beast that was, and is not, even he is the eighth, and is of the seven, and goeth into perdition. And the ten horns which thou sawest are ten kings, which have received no kingdom as yet; but receive power as kings one hour with the beast. These have one mind, and shall give their power and strength unto the beast. These shall make war with the Lamb, and the Lamb shall overcome them: for he is Lord of lords, and King of kings: and they that are with him are called, and chosen, and faithful.

—Revelation 17:7-14

this commentary, the European Union has grown to twenty-five nations with a common currency, the euro. To set forth just a few items concerning the reforming of the Humpty Dumpty Roman Empire, we reference a few sentences from a communication we received from Alan Franklin, English newspaper editor and author of the book *EU: Final World Empire,* dated April 3, 2003:

1. With ten new members from the Communist bloc, this will bring EU up to 450 million population. The ten have had a brief moment of freedom from Communism; now they can't wait to give it away.
2. Britain soon cannot join the U.S.A. in further unilateral action.
3. Tony Blair has called for a president of the EU.
4. All EU countries will shortly vacate their foreign embassies to allow re-staffing with EU representatives.
5. The criminalizing of all criticism against the EU.
6. Rising anti-Americanism and anti-Israelism. There is now a far more serious problem from the U.S. than Iraq and the Middle East.
7. EU rules now force churches to employ atheists.
8. The completion of a rapid-moving 60,000 swift strike force capable of defeating most modern armies.

It will be interesting to see how fast the European Union expands and develops to fulfill its role in Bible prophecy. With the rapid growth of the EU, there are internal concerns that it will become another UN debating club. Therefore, it has been suggested that voting powers on political and military decisions be vested in the original ten members. Should this occur, it would set the stage for ten kings to receive power with the Antichrist for a short time. According to verse thirteen of Revelation 17, the ultimate control of the Revived Roman Empire will be given to the Antichrist, the Little Horn of Daniel 7.

In verse fourteen of Revelation 17 we are informed that this conspiracy will fight to prevent the Lord Jesus Christ establishing His throne on Mt. Zion in Jerusalem. However, it is nice to know the outcome in advance —THEY LOSE!

And he saith unto me, The waters which thou sawest, where the whore sitteth, are peoples, and multitudes, and nations, and tongues. And the ten horns which thou sawest upon the beast, these shall hate the whore, and shall make her desolate and naked, and shall eat her flesh, and burn her with fire.

—Revelation 17:15-16

The angel explains that the waters upon which the Great Whore sits means nations, races, and languages. This would certainly seem to favor the Roman Catholic church, or perhaps even Islam, as the best candidate instead of Old Babylon or Iraq.

We also have to remember the tremendous wealth of the Roman Catholic church as one reason why the ten kings turn against this system, eat her flesh, and burn her with fire. The eating of the flesh probably refers to taking her gold, gems, properties, and other riches, and may include not only the burning of her edifices, but also the ecclesiastics who support her blasphemy. We must point out again that both political Rome and ecclesiastical Rome burned thousands of faithful Christians at the stake. The fate of the Great Whore is perhaps typified in the following jingle:

There was a woman from Niger,
Who went riding on the back of a Tiger.
They returned from the ride,
With the woman inside,
And a smile on the face of the Tiger.

Although the Great Whore engages in political fornication in promoting the Antichrist as God, few men respect a prostitute, even when they get what they pay for. Neither will the Antichrist share his evil power with anyone else. The Great Whore is dumped so that only the Antichrist is worshipped by those who have the "mark of the beast."

An interesting NewsMax item, dated June 9, 2000, deserves our attention:

EUROPEAN UNION REPLACE GOD!

Brussels: The European Union needs to be seen "to do more for itself" on the world stage in order to check a US tendency for unilateral action, according to EU External Affairs Commissioner Chris Patten. . . . "In the past, people asked God to deliver them from evil. Today they look to international institutions—and in Europe, that means the European Union," he said.

So this EU representatives states that the European Union should replace God in taking care of the world's population, that religious institutions are too self-centered to care for people, even those within their own folks. So the reason for destroying the Tribulation world church is well stated, if not well intended. There are few cities in the world that qualify as headquarters for world religious systems. We leave the answer to the intelligence of the individual reader.

For God hath put in their hearts to fulfil his will, and to agree, and give their kingdom unto the beast, until the words of God shall be fulfilled. And the woman which thou sawest is that great city, which reigneth over the kings of the earth.

—Revelation 17:17-18

Key #26: Babylon Baloney

And after these things I saw another angel come down from heaven, having great power; and the earth was lightened with his glory. And he cried mightily with a strong voice, saying, Babylon the great is fallen, is fallen, and is become the habitation of devils, and the hold of every foul spirit, and a cage of every unclean and hateful bird. For all nations have drunk of the wine of the wrath of her fornication, and the kings of the earth have committed fornication with her, and the merchants of the earth are waxed rich through the abundance of her delicacies.

—Revelation 18:1-3

Chapter Eighteen

Everybody Loves a Mystery?

The cliché that "everyone loves a mystery" is not exactly true, especially not to me as I try to unravel the mystery of "Great Babylon" and "Mystery Babylon" that John describes to us in Revelation chapters seventeen and eighteen.

Why was John not more specific about names, dates, places, etc.? The scriptures, and especially prophecy, have actually been protected by a certain amount of ambiguity in wording. What if John had related the activities of Mystery Babylon in its contemporary setting today? The Revelation would have been discarded as the work of an insane person. Even so, some of the early church theologians were not in favor of including it in the Bible as it is.

In observing what others say about Babylon in chapters seventeen and eighteen, I found the following:

1. Some believe Great Babylon and Mystery Babylon are the Babylon on the Euphrates that will again become the religious and commercial metropolis of the world.
2. Some believe both Babylons are the Revived Roman Empire embraced in traditional Roman Catholicism.
3. Some believe there will be two destructions of Babylon: chapter seventeen refers to the destruction of ecclesiastical Babylon; chapter eighteen refers to the destruction of commercial Babylon.
4. Some believe in two different end-time Babylons:
   a. The Babylon on the Euphrates and Rome.
   b. The Babylon on the Euphrates and U.S.A.
5. Some unite both Babylons in the coming one-world governmental system of Antichrist.

The preceding variety of opinions are found in current books by prominent prophetic scholars and authors. If we scramble together all these ideas, what we have is Babylon Baloney. One possible consideration as to the identity of Mystery Babylon that I pursued in my book *U.S. in Prophecy* is that New York is a credible candidate. The reader is probably thinking, "Surely you can't be serious?" Well, let's take a look:

1. New York City is known as the "Babylon on the Hudson."
2. Across the bay and opposite the Statue of Liberty from New York City is Babylon on Long Island, a city with a population of 12,600.
3. God warns, ". . . Come out of her, my people . . ." (Rev. 18:4). Israel is referenced in many scriptures as God's earthly people. In 1968 Saddam Hussein either killed or deported every Jew in Iraq. The only Jews in Babylon, or the entire nation of Iraq today, would be Jews in the United States Army. However, New York City has a larger Jewish population than all of Israel.
4. Babel was a multiracial city, and so was Babylon. New York City, as well as the entire U.S.A., has a multiracial population.
5. Mystery Babylon appears to be a large seaport and commercial city. New York City is the busiest harbor city in the world.
6. In Latin, Semiramis, Nimrod's queen, is Mea Domina. In English it is interpreted as Madonna (*Babylon* by John Oates). Madonna is an American entertainer and vulgar sex symbol. She was invited to be the "Queen of the Ball" of Babylon by the Iraqi official in charge who said, "Madonna lives here with the Iraqi people" (*LA Times*, January 16, 1987).
7. Semiramis had a son named Tammuz long after Nimrod died (Ezek. 8:14). According to tradition, Semiramis then built the first obelisk as a phallus symbol to honor Nimrod. The largest obelisk in the world is in our nation's capitol, Washington, D.C.—the Washington Monument to honor the father of the United States.
8. Babylon was a world empire, and the United Nations Headquarters Building is located in New York City.
9. All people from all nations had to bow before the image of Nebuchadnezzar, king of Babylon. The Statue of Liberty on Ellis Island in New York Harbor is the same size as Nebuchadnezzar's image, and it welcomes people from all over the world to the United States.
10. Babylon is described as a cup of gold filled with abominations. In 1945 the United States owned 70 percent of the world's gold supply. At the UN's insistence, in order to form a world economy, we gave away our gold. In 1967 we wrote, "You'll wonder where the yellow went, when you open the vaults at the Fort Knox Mint." The media and entertainment industry have used the riches God blessed the nation with to

spread pornographic filth throughout the world.

11. Babel, which became Babylon, was famous for its high tower. New York City not only had the highest tower in the world, it had two high towers.
12. Babylon will be destroyed in one hour (Rev. 18:19). On September 11, 2001, in one hour the Twin Trade Towers were destroyed and the Pentagon partially destroyed.

Could the United States actually be the Mystery Babylon of Revelation 17 and 18? Our nation is probably like Nineveh was—on probation. God has indeed blessed this nation above all nations, but we have taken God out of our schools and our courts. As a consequence, the United States is in a moral freefall plunge to oblivion. Of those whom God blesses much, He expects much. We will give our own humble opinion, for what it is worth, as to the identity of Babylon and Mystery Babylon at the conclusion of this chapter.

I agree with Dr. Walvoord and Dr. Seiss in that the first three verses of chapter eighteen refer to the destruction of ecclesiastical Babylon as we read ". . . is become the habitation of devils, and the hold of every foul spirit, and a cage of every unclean and hateful bird." As evil and abominable as the Great Whore system is, when it is destroyed, it is taken over by those who are even more evil and abominable.

The angel that announces the destruction of ecclesiastical Babylon is described as "another angel," meaning one different from the angel of chapter seventeen. This is probably the same angel that announces the fall of Babylon in chapter fourteen. The fact that this angel is described as having great power indicates the importance of the mission in bringing an end to this evil and wicked system.

And I heard another voice from heaven, saying, Come out of her, my people, that ye be not partakers of her sins, and that ye receive not of her plagues. For her sins have reached unto heaven, and God hath remembered her iniquities. Reward her even as she rewarded you, and double unto her double according to her works: in the cup which she hath filled fill to her double.

—Revelation 18:4–6

Revelation 18:4 is almost a repeat of Jeremiah 51:45, and as noted before, some of the prophecies concerning Babylon in Jeremiah 50–51 refer to the Babylon of Jeremiah's day and some to the Babylon of the last days. Jesus even quoted Jeremiah concerning Israel's rejection of Him as the Messiah. The word "people" appears in the Old Testament approximately two thousand times, and the word appears in the New Testament approximately two hundred times. In the Old Testament, God often refers to Israel as "my people," meaning that He has made special covenants and promises to the people of Israel. In the Desert Storm conflict of 1990–91, there were many foreign workers from other countries in Iraq. In November and December of 1990, thousands were trying to get out of Iraq to return to their own countries before hostilities began. We thought at the time that perhaps this was a sign the church would soon be out of here and the Tribulation would begin. It was not the time, but it was clearly a warning from God that the

Tribulation was not too far off. In the war of March/April 2003, there was no mass exodus from Iraq because few foreign workers had returned.

The judgmental emphasis in Revelation 18:4–8 still seems to be against ecclesiastical Babylon, because the Great Whore boasts that she is no widow. The members of Christ's true church have already been called out to be made ready to become the eternal bride of Jesus Christ. The members of the world church, which will include the millions of unsaved in apostate churches, will be as a widow, left behind. The religious harlot becomes the prostitute of Antichrist who then allows his kings to ravage her. One day the leaders of this abominable religious system will be living in luxury, and the following day their properties will be confiscated and they themselves will be fleeing for their lives.

How much she hath glorified herself, and lived deliciously, so much torment and sorrow give her: for she saith in her heart, I sit a queen, and am no widow, and shall see no sorrow. Therefore shall her plagues come in one day, death, and mourning, and famine; and she shall be utterly burned with fire: for strong is the Lord God who judgeth her.

—Revelation 18:7–8

John would have been quite familiar with the lifestyle of Roman citizens in A.D. 96. Not only did all roads lead to Rome, but so did much of the ocean merchant ship traffic. Rome governed the civilized and known world of the first century. Goods, spices, food grains, and even fruits, came from all parts of the kingdom, even as far as China, India, and Africa. Personal accounts of the parties the rich and famous of the day threw are replete in historical accounts. Guests were invited to not only enjoy the food, but also the choice of women present as well. They would eat until they could eat no more, and then feathers were provided that they could push down their throats and vomit. Then they would return to eat more. Such opulence and gluttony would not have been common in Babylon that was on the Euphrates in A.D. 96. While still a fairly large city, it had declined in population and importance. The main commercial exchange city of the time was Petra in what is now southern Jordan. There was no Suez Canal in A.D. 96, so goods were brought up the Red Sea and taken to Petra, a Roman city, and taken by camel caravan to Caesarea or Alexandria for transshipment to Rome. Millions of dollars in taxes were also taken by Rome from commercial transactions in Petra. One thing that got Mark Antony in hot water with the Roman senate was that he gave Petra to Cleopatra for a birthday present. Goods of all kind also poured into Rome from the roads the Caesars built that covered much of the European continent.

And the kings of the earth, who have committed fornication and lived deliciously with her, shall bewail her, and lament for her, when they shall see the smoke of her burning, Standing afar off for the fear of her torment, saying, Alas, alas that great city Babylon, that mighty city! for in one hour is thy judgment come. And the merchants of the earth shall weep and mourn over her; for no man buyeth their merchandise any more: The merchandise of gold, and silver, and precious stones, and of pearls, and fine linen, and purple, and silk, and scarlet, and all thyine wood, and all manner vessels of ivory, and all manner vessels of most precious wood, and of brass, and iron, and marble, And cinnamon, and odours, and ointments, and frankincense, and wine, and oil, and fine flour, and wheat, and beasts, and sheep, and horses, and chariots, and slaves, and souls of men. And the fruits that thy soul lusted after are departed from thee, and all things which were dainty and goodly are departed from thee, and thou shalt find them no more at all.

—Revelation 18:9–14

However, John was not referencing the greed and wealthy extravagance of Rome or Babylon in his day. He was shown what was going to happen in the last days of the Tribulation Babylon. The twenty-eight categories of foods and merchandise listed by John will cover all items of international trade and commerce today. Dr. Henry Morris in his comments on one particular item of commerce—slaves—wrote that the Greek word for slaves indicates captive women for sexual purposes. This problem is a matter of great concern today for international law enforcement agencies. We notice another item of interest—chariots—which could refer to automobiles and other types of motorized vehicles. We find an interesting prophecy relating to chariots in the last days in Nahum 2:3–4,13:

> The shield of his mighty men is made red, the valiant men are in scarlet: the chariots shall be with flaming torches in the day of his preparation, and the fir trees shall be terribly shaken. The chariots shall rage in the streets, they shall justle one against another in the broad ways: they shall seem like torches, they shall run like the lightnings. . . . Behold, I am against thee, saith the LORD of hosts, and I will burn her chariots in the smoke, and the sword shall devour thy young lions: and I will cut off thy prey from the earth, and the voice of thy messengers shall no more be heard.

The prophecy of Nahum was initially against the city of Nineveh in the prophet's day. However, it seems evident it had a dual meaning as Nineveh today is Mosul, Iraq, and Nahum's description of the flashing chariots raging in the streets quite accurately applies to the modern automobiles. The "day of his preparation" is a direct reference to the Tribulation period. There are other items of interest in the list of Babylon's international commerce that we cannot consider for lack of time and space.

We should keep an open mind concerning the chronology of the Tribulation in relation to the destruction of the Babylonish system, because according to verse eleven of Revelation 18, economic panic will follow on a world basis. This would mean that the judgment of the "Great Whore" will occur some time before the battle of Armageddon.

The revelation to John describing the destruction of Babylon is graphic and in much detail. I have been to the island of Patmos several times. It is a lonely, wind-swept, semi-desolate place that served Rome as a penal colony. It was the Alcatraz of the Roman Empire. Being shown the destruction of the delicious fruits and delicious foods in Babylon was probably painful to John, as he lived on mostly dried grains.

The most understandable presentation on the destruction of Babylon in all its ecclesiastical, commercial, and economic reverberations is to consider what happened in the aftermath of the tragedy of the Twin Trade Towers. I had the pleasure of enjoying dinner twice on the top story of one of the towers. It was a fantastic sight to be immersed in a panoramic view of the billions of lights from Connecticut, New York City, and down the coast of New Jersey. Hundreds of corporations with financial and economic tentacles reaching around the world had offices in the two towers. In one hour, all these offices, along with three thousand employees, were gone. The smoke from the towers' destruction could be seen for miles at sea. For several days scenes from around the world were shown on TV where masses of people mourned for the loss of life and the destruction of these two prominent

The merchants of these things, which were made rich by her, shall stand afar off for the fear of her torment, weeping and wailing, And saying, Alas, alas, that great city, that was clothed in fine linen, and purple, and scarlet, and decked with gold, and precious stones, and pearls! For in one hour so great riches is come to nought. And every shipmaster, and all the company in ships, and sailors, and as many as trade by sea, stood afar off, And cried when they saw the smoke of her burning, saying, What city is like unto this great city! And they cast dust on their heads, and cried, weeping and wailing, saying, Alas, alas, that great city, wherein were made rich all that had ships in the sea by reason of her costliness! for in one hour is she made desolate.

—Revelation 18:15–19

world business icons. There was a considerable economic shock to our nation, and to a lesser degree in the economic world, in the wake of the Twin Towers' destruction. At the writing of this commentary over two years later, the economy in the United States has not yet fully recovered. The airline industry has been seriously affected and the lives of millions of Americans who travel have been complicated. All this is the result of the destruction of just two buildings. What if all of New York City had been destroyed? We can begin now to understand why there will be great sorrow and mourning when the great commercial metropolis identified as Babylon in Revelation will meet its doom.

Seven times in Revelation 17–18 the ultimate and final destruction of Babylon is announced by the angels. We are informed that the martyred apostles and prophets are to rejoice at the destruction of the city and system. Babylon could be guilty of killing some of the prophets and the Roman Empire for killing some the apostles. However, it appears the entire Babylonish system, which would include the Holy Roman Empire (Catholicism), is involved.

Rejoice over her, thou heaven, and ye holy apostles and prophets; for God hath avenged you on her. And a mighty angel took up a stone like a great millstone, and cast it into the sea, saying, Thus with violence shall that great city Babylon be thrown down, and shall be found no more at all. And the voice of harpers, and musicians, and of pipers, and trumpeters, shall be heard no more at all in thee; and no craftsman, of whatsoever craft he be, shall be found any more in thee; and the sound of a millstone shall be heard no more at all in thee; And the light of a candle shall shine no more at all in thee; and the voice of the bridegroom and of the bride shall be heard no more at all in thee: for thy merchants were the great men of the earth; for by thy sorceries were all nations deceived. And in her was found the blood of prophets, and of saints, and of all that were slain upon the earth.

—Revelation 18:20–24

Another reference is made that Babylon has deceived the nations by sorceries. The word in the Greek is *pharmakeia,* meaning drugs like opium and heroin. Drug addiction is one of mankind's most serious problems in these last days, and a large percentage of the drugs come from the Middle East—Afghanistan and Turkey. Terrorist organizations also engage in international drug traffic. Another puzzling reference is made to the merchants of Babylon being the great men of the earth. This reference would stress that Babylon is indeed a large commercial entity with a world business outreach.

Where Is Babylon?

Dr. J. A. Seiss wrote, even when the ruins of Babylon were lying covered with sand, that something would happen to cause the rebuilding of the city into another gigantic area of international importance. This could happen now that the United States has ended the cruel and corrupt regime of Saddam Hussein and the billions of dollars from oil used to build up the nation. The city of Babylon has been restored to some extent already as a tourist attraction. That the Babylon on the Euphrates will be destroyed in what I believe will be a nuclear desolation is beyond question. Babylon is one of the nations that destroyed the temple, so it must be destroyed as Sodom and Gomorrah. This has not happened yet, but it will (Jer. 50:28; Isa. 13:19). In 1980 when I went to Shanghai, China, it was the filthiest, most dilapidated, ugly, depressive city I had ever seen. Twenty years later, in 2000, when I visited Shanghai it was colorful, beautiful, sparkling, with elevated highways, skyscrapers of one hundred stories or more, and bustling traffic. Likewise, Babylon on the Euphrates could be rebuilt in just two or three years, but there is no way I can see or understand how it will fulfill all the prophecies describing the future destruction of Babylon. There must be another major city called "Mystery Babylon" that must also be destroyed.

The only other nation or empire that destroyed the temple was the Roman Empire. As already brought out in this study, the Roman Empire is being revived in the form of the European Union. The European Union has grown in size at the writing of this commentary to twenty-five nations. Its political and economic prowess on a world basis is sure to increase. The aim of the European Union is to dethrone the United States as the major world power. The historic association of the Roman Catholic church with the nations within the European Union increases the odds that Rome, with its Vatican City, will be the Mystery Babylon that will also be destroyed in one hour like Sodom and Gomorrah.

London, England, also has a history, location, world influence, and economy that could make it a possible candidate for Mystery Babylon. I have also presented several reasons why New York City is a serious possibility to be Mystery Babylon. Although England did kill some Christians, especially during the reign of Queen Mary, the nation's association with the Roman Catholic church was ruptured during the reign of Henry VIII. Also, in the eighteenth and nineteenth centuries, England produced many great Christian pastors and theologians, and sent missionaries to many nations. I question if London could be considered a likely candidate for Mystery Babylon. And although there are many similarities between Mystery Babylon and the United States, the United States has befriended the Jew and has in many ways been a friend to Israel. Also, except in a few rare incidents in this nation's early history, has the government persecuted Christians or killed anyone because they were a Christian. There is no blood of the prophets or apostles on our history books, at least not yet.

In my book, *U.S. in Prophecy,* I have provided many reasons why I believe that Isaiah 18 is a prophecy about the United States. If I am correct, and I believe that I am, then our nation will be one that will go into the Millennium and send representatives to worship the Lord Jesus Christ when He reigns in Jerusalem (Isa. 18:7).

Chapter Nineteen

The Woman and the Bride

In verse one of chapter nineteen, John records that after the ultimate destruction of Babylon, he hears the voices of many people in Heaven. These are not the voices of angels; they are real people, probably those who have been martyred by the Babylonish system.

Now what are these "much people" saying, or shouting, as the case may be? They are shouting ALLELUIA; *alleluia* in the Greek is the same as *hallelujah* in Hebrew: *hallal* means praise and *Yah* is an abbreviation for Jehovah. It is usually interpreted, "Praise ye the Lord" in the King James Version. In Revelation we find ten "alleluias." In Revelation 19 we find four, but there should be five, because in verse five the English is used, "Praise our God."

The last five psalms are hallelujah (alleluia) songs of praise unto God, and the five alleluias of Revelation 19 correspond with the last five psalms. The last five psalms are songs of the coming messianic Kingdom when Jesus Christ truly reigns on David's throne. Out of concern that the reader may have only the New Testament, or too lazy to read the last five psalms, I will briefly explain:

Alleluia #1. The multitude of martyrs in Heaven praise God for their salvation and the glory, honor, and power which is theirs in being joint-heirs with Jesus Christ. The martyrs also give praise to God for judging the "great whore" that has corrupted the earth with sin and killed the saints.

> Praise ye the LORD. Praise the LORD, O my soul. . . . Happy is he that hath the God of Jacob for his help, whose hope is in the LORD his God . . . Which executeth judgment for the oppressed: which giveth food to the hungry.

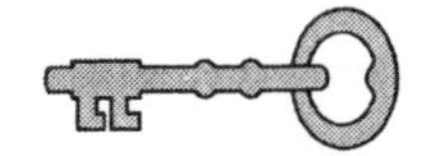

Key #27: The Wedding

And after these things I heard a great voice of much people in heaven, saying, Alleluia; Salvation, and glory, and honour, and power, unto the Lord our God: For true and righteous are his judgments: for he hath judged the great whore, which did corrupt the earth with her fornication, and hath avenged the blood of his servants at her hand. And again they said, Alleluia. And her smoke rose up for ever and ever. And the four and twenty elders and the four beasts fell down and worshipped God that sat on the throne, saying, Amen; Alleluia. And a voice came out of the throne, saying, Praise our God, all ye his servants, and ye that fear him, both small and great. And I heard as it were the voice of a great multitude, and as the voice of many waters, and as the voice of mighty thunderings, saying, Alleluia: for the Lord God omnipotent reigneth.

—Revelation 19:1-6

> The LORD looseth the prisoners: . . . The LORD shall reign for ever, even thy God, O Zion, unto all generations. Praise ye the LORD.
>
> —Psalm 146:1,5,7,10

Alleluia #2. The second "alleluia" of chapter nineteen is found in verse three when the same congregation of martyrs in Heaven praise God, not only for judging the "Great Whore," but the consignment of all who have taken part in this abomination of abominations to an eternal hell.

> Praise ye the LORD. Sing unto the LORD a new song, and his praise in the congregation of saints. . . . For the LORD taketh pleasure in his people: he will beautify the meek with salvation. . . . Let the high praises of God be in their mouth, and a twoedged sword in their hand; To execute vengeance upon the heathen, and punishments upon the people; To bind their kings with chains, and their nobles with fetters of iron; To execute upon them the judgment written: this honour have all his saints. Praise ye the LORD.
>
> —Psalm 149:1,4,6–9

Alleluia #3. The third "alleluia" in chapter nineteen is found in verse four, where the twenty-four elders and the four beasts shout "alleluia" and "amen." The word *amen* in both the Hebrew and Greek means, "It is so!" The heavenly senate of twenty-four elders and the four angelic watchers over the creation verify by acclamation that the judgments of God against Babylon in all their religious, economic, and political roots, both temporal and eternal, are righteous. They agree that Babylon deserves destruction and its adherents eternal punishment. We read in Deuteronomy 32:35 that God will take vengeance on those who persecute Israel, and Paul wrote in Romans 12:19, "Dearly beloved, avenge not yourselves, but rather give place unto wrath: for it is written, Vengeance is mine; I will repay, saith the Lord."

> Praise ye the LORD. Praise ye the LORD from the heavens: praise him in the heights. Praise ye him, all his angels: praise ye him, all his hosts. . . . Let them praise the name of the LORD: for his name alone is excellent; his glory is above the earth and heaven. He also exalteth the horn of his people, the praise of all his saints; even of the children of Israel, a people near unto him. Praise ye the LORD.
>
> —Psalm 148:1–2,13–14

Alleluia #4. The fourth "alleluia" is found in verse four and interpreted in the King James Version, "Praise our God." The identity of the speaker is not noted, but it comes from the throne of God. The speaker, or speakers, could be the seven angels with the seven trumpets and the seven angels with the seven vials of wrath. Or it could be seven angels in charge of the seven unspeakable thunder judgments. In chapter nineteen of Revelation God is declaring His justice for Israel and His love for the church. The church in this chapter is already in Heaven awaiting the marriage supper; the remnant of Israel is looking forward to the Millennium and justice for over two thousand years of persecution.

> Praise ye the LORD: for it is good to sing praises unto our God; for it is pleasant; and praise is comely. The LORD doth build up Jerusalem: he gathereth together the outcasts of Israel. He healeth the broken in heart, and bindeth up their wounds. . . . He sheweth his word unto Jacob, his statutes and his judgments unto Israel. He hath not dealt so with any nation: and as for his judgments, they have not known them. Praise ye the LORD.
>
> —Psalm 147:1–3,19–20

Alleluia #5. The fifth "alleluia" in chapter nineteen roars over John like a mighty flood as every redeemed soul in Heaven and every member of the angelic host thunder the command to praise the Lord God because He now reigns "omnipotent." There is no soul on earth or in Heaven, there is no spirit being in the universe, more powerful than the Lord God. As the apostle Paul by inspiration of God wrote in 1 Corinthians 15:24–25: "Then cometh the end, when he shall have delivered up the kingdom to God, even the Father; when he shall have put down all rule and all authority and power. For he must reign, till he hath put all enemies under his feet."

> Praise ye the LORD. Praise God in his sanctuary: praise him in the firmament of his power. Praise him for his mighty acts: praise him according to his excellent greatness. . . . Let every thing that hath breath praise the LORD. Praise ye the LORD.
>
> —Psalm 150:1–2,6

Here Comes the Bride

While my ministry responsibilities at Southwest Radio Church Ministries preclude normal pastoral duties, I have been privileged over the years to unite several couples in the bonds of matrimony, for better or for worse. There is nothing in the spectrum of emotional experiences like the appearance of the bride, dressed in radiant white, followed by her attendants, and the entire congregation standing with excited joy for her. As for the bride, this is her one moment in time. When the organist sounds the first chord, it is a time for everyone in the bride's presence to be "glad and rejoice."

So magnificent and rapturous is the moment of the bride's appearance

Let us be glad and rejoice, and give honour to him: for the marriage of the Lamb is come, and his wife hath made herself ready. And to her was granted that she should be arrayed in fine linen, clean and white: for the fine linen is the righteousness of saints. And he saith unto me, Write, Blessed are they which are called unto the marriage supper of the Lamb. And he saith unto me, These are the true sayings of God.

—Revelation 19:7–9

And I fell at his feet to worship him. And he said unto me, See thou do it not: I am thy fellowservant, and of thy brethren that have the testimony of Jesus: worship God: for the testimony of Jesus is the spirit of prophecy.

—Revelation 19:10

that this example is used, not only in Scripture, but in contemporary advertising, for comparative illustrations. The appearance of the New Jerusalem will be like a bride adorned for her husband (Rev. 21:9). The joy of a bride on her wedding day is compared to the joy of our salvation: "I will greatly rejoice in the LORD, my soul shall be joyful in my God; for he hath clothed me with the garments of salvation . . . as a bride adorneth herself with her jewels" (Isa. 61:10).

The traditional biblical wedding had four separate and distinct parts:

1. Parents of the boy and the girl to be united in marriage would sign a contract when both the bride and the bridegroom were quite young, often at age twelve, the age of accountability. The boy's parents would agree to a dowry arrangement with the girl's parents.
2. Until the time the official wedding took place, the girl would be considered the espoused wife of the boy. If the girl was found to be unfaithful during this time, the boy would not have to complete the marriage agreement. Especially was this true in the case of a boy in the lineage of Aaron. A priest was forbidden to marry a woman who was not a virgin (Lev. 21:13–14; Deut. 22). Mary was espoused to Joseph as his wife, but when she was found to be pregnant, he was determined to put her away from him until God revealed to him that Mary had not done anything contrary to the law.
3. From the time of the initial marriage contract to the time the bridegroom claims his bride, the husband's father assists his son in preparing a home for his wife. Jesus said in John 14:2–3, "In my Father's house are many mansions: if it were not so, I would have told you. I go to prepare a place for you. And if I go and prepare a place for you, I will come again, and receive you unto myself; that where I am, there ye may be also."
4. The bridegroom accompanied by friends and/or relatives goes to the home of the bride, and after proper ceremony, takes his bride to her new home. A marriage supper where friends come by invitation subsequently takes place. God willing, they live happily together ever after.

Now, the sixty-four dollar question: Who is the Lamb's wife?

In the Old Testament, Israel by covenant is put in a position of a wife with God. But when the Son of God came to claim His wife, she had not only been unfaithful as set forth in Hosea, but Israel said, ". . . We will not have this man to reign over us" (Luke 19:14). We read in John 1:11, "He came unto his own, and his own received him not."

We read in Hebrews 5:1-5 that Jesus Christ is our High Priest, and a high priest could not have an unfaithful wife, even in type. Even though a few who have written commentaries on Revelation see Israel as the bride of Revelation 19, I think it is highly improbable. We read in Jeremiah

31:31–32, "Behold, the days come, saith the LORD, that I will make a new covenant with the house of Israel, and with the house of Judah: Not according to the covenant that I made with their fathers in the day that I took them by the hand to bring them out of the land of Egypt; which my covenant they brake, although I was an husband unto them, saith the LORD." Although Israel will not be in a spiritual position as the bride of the Lamb, the saved of the nation will inherit what God has promised them in the Abrahamic covenant. We read in Romans 11:1–2: "I say then, Hath God cast away his people? God forbid. For I also am an Israelite, of the seed of Abraham. . . . God hath not cast away his people which he foreknew. . . ."

The example of the relationship of the church to Jesus Christ as the bride, we should keep in mind, is spiritually symbolic. This relationship could be explained in other dimensions, but this is the best way that the Holy Spirit explains it to us. Eve, the first woman, was made from a rib, part of Adam's flesh. God gave her to Adam as his wife, a helpmate. Paul explained the Christian's relationship to Jesus Christ thusly: "For we are members of his body, of his flesh, and of his bones. For this cause shall a man leave his father and mother, and shall be joined unto his wife, and they two shall be one flesh. This is a great mystery: but I speak concerning Christ and the church" (Eph. 5:30–32).

Paul also explained the relationship of the entire body of Christians, the one and only true church, to Jesus Christ this way: "Husbands, love your wives, even as Christ also loved the church, and gave himself for it; that he might sanctify and cleanse it with the washing of water by the word, That he might present it to himself a glorious church, not having spot, or wrinkle, or any such thing; but that it should be holy and without blemish" (Eph. 5:25–27).

Paul referred to another traditional wedding example in 2 Corinthians 11:2, "For I am jealous over you with godly jealously: for I have espoused you to one husband, that I may present you as a chaste virgin to Christ."

Just as Adam gave up a part of himself for Eve, Jesus Christ gave Himself for the church. The church, that body composed of the universal membership of all who have placed their faith in Jesus Christ, are espoused to Him. Jesus Christ will come for His church at the Rapture, and we will go with Him to His Father's throne in Heaven. He will claim the church in an eternal helpmate relationship. It will be a sanctified and holy church, because He will have cleansed it with His own blood and imputed His own righteousness into every member (Rom. 4:20–24; 10:6–10).

What will we do as the helpmate of our Lord for all eternity? Helpmates in the home are always busy, so I would assume that we are not just going to float around on clouds and play harps. According to Ephesians 1:15–23, we will reign and serve Jesus Christ, "Far above all principality, and power, and might, and dominion, and every name that is named, not only in this world, but also in that which is to come" (Eph. 1:21). There are billions upon billions of miles in space containing billions and billions of stars and planets. I believe we will indeed go where no man has gone before.

The Scriptures tell us that we will know each other in Heaven, but as far as personal relationships are concerned, we will be as the angels of God. While there will be no sexual relationships in Heaven, what God will replace it with will be a million times better. The Mormons teach that the wives in Heaven will give birth to babies (I suppose every nine months) for all eternity. While this may sound like Paradise to the Mormon men, it sounds more like the opposite for the Mormon women.

While some may believe that Israel will be the Lamb's wife, I think the volume of evidence indicates the bride is the church. In fact, that the bride is that of the Lamb speaks to us of the church. Israel today is looking for their Messiah King, not the Messiah Lamb. Jesus Christ will be Israel's King, but Israel will not be the bride.

In Revelation 19:9 we read that there will be invited guests at the marriage supper of the Lamb. We are not told just whom the invited guests will be, but we can assume that the guests will be the saved of Israel, the Old Testament saints, and perhaps the Tribulation martyrs who died for their faith. And, we are not told if the marriage supper will be held in Heaven or on earth. If on earth, then the leaders of the nations that go into the Millennium may be invited. You fathers who have marriageable daughters should be glad you don't have to pay for this marriage supper, because I believe it is going to be a real extravaganza. According to the parable of the ten virgins, only those who have the Holy Spirit in that day will be invited to the marriage supper.

After the marriage of the Lamb and the marriage supper is revealed to John by the mighty angel, he falls down and worships the angel. The angel commands John that all worship is to be directed to Jesus Christ, that an angel is simply a messenger or servant of that Lord whom we should serve. John is also reminded that Jesus is the Spirit and testimony of prophecy. In other words, all prophecy in one way or another is to reveal Jesus Christ as Lord and Savior, and His coming again as Lord of Lords and King of Kings. Without this great light at the end of the tunnel of time, there would be no need or excuse for prophecy. All prophetic teachings should be used to glorify Jesus Christ, the only Name under Heaven whereby men and women must be saved.

The King Is Coming

It appears that immediately after the marriage of the Lamb takes place in Heaven, Heaven opens and John sees the Lord Jesus Christ descending to earth. While the One on the white horse is not identified as the Lord, He is given one of the three names by which He is mentioned in this chapter, other than the Lamb. But He is not coming back as the Lamb slain from the foundation of the world; He is returning as King of Kings and Lord of Lords on a mission of war. According to James 4:1–2, the cause of war between men and nations is lust. It is often argued that there is no just or right cause for war, but the war that Jesus Christ wages at His return is just and right, because this is the final act to destroy those who would destroy the earth.

One of the three names by which Jesus is known is Faithful and True. Jesus Christ is a gentleman; He keeps His Word. He said that He would return, and here in chapter nineteen of Revelation we see that He will keep His Word. His mission at the Rapture is to take His church to Heaven; His mission at His Second Coming to earth is war against Antichrist and his armies.

In the Bible we read that Jesus Christ is known by many names: Wonderful, Counselor, the Mighty God, the Everlasting Father, the Prince of Peace (Isa. 9:6), and many more. But we also read in Judges 13:18 that He has a name that is secret. As John looks upon the rider on the white horse, he notices that his eyes are like a flame of fire, indicating that He is coming back in judgment. Also, John notices that on His head are many crowns. The Greek for crowns in this verse is *diadems,* meaning crowns of kings over nations. When Jesus comes back, He will be wearing the crown of every nation in the world, because He will rule over every nation.

John uses in this verse a name for Jesus Christ that he used in the first verse of his gospel: "In the beginning was the Word, and the Word was with God, and the Word was God" (John 1:1). We also read that ". . . the Word was made flesh, and dwelt among us . . ." (John 1:14). Jesus Christ is the living Word of God. He was born in swaddling clothes. At His trial and subsequent crucifixion, His robe was soaked in His own blood. At His Second Coming, His clothes will be wet with the blood of those who have conspired to put Antichrist on the throne of this world (Isa. 63:1–6).

The word for "horse" in the Greek text is *hippos,* which means literally a four-legged animal that men ride and we call horse in English. Isaiah describes the second coming a little differently: "For, behold, the LORD will come with fire, and with his chariots like a whirlwind, to render his anger with fury, and his rebuke with flames of fire. For by fire and by his sword will the LORD plead with all flesh: and the slain of the LORD shall be many" (Isa. 66:15–16).

Chariots, whirling like whirlwinds, could be interpreted to be almost any kind of celestial, flying vehicles. In other places, Jesus is seen coming with the clouds of Heaven. We read in Revelation 1:7, "Behold, he cometh

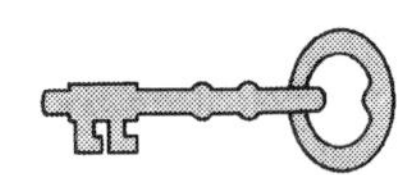

Key #28: Why So Many Crowns?

And I saw heaven opened, and behold a white horse; and he that sat upon him was called Faithful and True, and in righteousness he doth judge and make war.

—Revelation 19:11

His eyes were as a flame of fire, and on his head were many crowns; and he had a name written, that no man knew, but he himself.

—Revelation 19:12

And he was clothed with a vesture dipped in blood: and his name is called The Word of God.

—Revleation 19:13

And the armies which were in heaven followed him upon white horses, clothed in fine linen, white and clean.

—Revelation 19:14

with clouds; and every eye shall see him. . . ." The Greek word for clouds in this verse is *nephele,* meaning a small, thin cloud. So when John sees horses, he does not necessarily mean that there are horses in Heaven. Sorry to disappoint you, horse lovers, but I interpret the horses of Revelation 19 to be symbolic of another mode of heavenly transportation.

And out of his mouth goeth a sharp sword, that with it he should smite the nations: and he shall rule them with a rod of iron: and he treadeth the winepress of the fierceness and wrath of Almighty God.

—Revelation 19:15

The rider of the white horse of Revelation 6:2, whom we have previously identified as the Antichrist, had one crown on his head. Jesus Christ returns with many crowns on His head. The first rider had a bow. Both Isaiah and John describes Jesus Christ as returning with a sword. All prophecies relating to the battle of Armageddon describes the action as the Lord treading a giant winepress. This is the closest thing to that which the prophets and John could visualize to describe what is actually going to happen. The dispensation of God's mercy and grace has ended. The dispensation of the law and justice has returned, and Jesus Christ as King of all nations will rule over them for a thousand years with an unbending and unwavering rule of divine law. No more world courts, no more United Nations.

And he hath on his vesture and on his thigh a name written, KING OF KINGS, AND LORD OF LORDS.

—Revelation 19:16

We read in the accounts of Jesus' crucifixion by Matthew and Luke that the soldiers mockingly put a crown of thorns on His head, and over His head on the cross a board was nailed with words in Hebrew, Greek, and Latin, the three main languages of that time, "THIS IS JESUS THE KING OF THE JEWS." When Jesus Christ returns, the name King of Kings and Lord of Lords will be written on his uniform, and anyone who tries to prove that He is not King of Kings and Lord of Lords will die at the battle of Armageddon or be judged by Him in the Millennium.

And I saw an angel standing in the sun; and he cried with a loud voice, saying to all the fowls that fly in the midst of heaven, Come and gather yourselves together unto the supper of the great God; That ye may eat the flesh of kings, and the flesh of captains, and the flesh of mighty men, and the flesh of horses, and of them that sit on them, and the flesh of all men, both free and bond, both small and great.

—Revelation 19:17-18

For centuries there were no vultures, or any other birds, in Israel. The reason was that the Romans, Crusaders, and then the Turks, denuded the land of all the trees. The goats even pulled up the grass by the roots. Mark Twain in visiting Israel in 1865 said that it was the most desolate country on the face of the earth. But when Israel began to return after 1865, trees were planted and the land began once more to blossom as a rose. With the return of forests and vegetation, birds and animals began to return also. Today in Israel, vultures are again nesting. Many other kinds of birds are also multiplying by the millions. The natural migration land bridge for birds between Asia and Africa has been restored. During the two annual migrating seasons, billions of birds fly over Israel, and the battle of Armageddon could occur either in early spring at Passover, or in the fall at Roshashana. According to related prophecies to both the battle of Gog and Magog, and Armageddon, there will be millions of birds to eat the flesh of those killed. This will certainly be possible now that birds of all kinds, including vultures, are back in Israel, another sign of the soon return of Jesus Christ.

. . . thus saith the Lord GOD; Speak unto every feathered fowl, and to every

> beast of the field, Assemble yourselves, and come; gather yourselves on every side to my sacrifice that I do sacrifice for you, even a great sacrifice upon the mountains of Israel, that ye may eat flesh, and drink blood. Ye shall eat the flesh of the mighty, and drink the blood of the princes of the earth, of rams, of lambs, and of goats, of bullocks, all of them fatlings of Bashan.
>
> —Ezekiel 39:17–18

> Come near, ye nations, to hear; and hearken, ye people: let the earth hear, and all that is therein: the world, and all things that come forth of it. For the indignation of the LORD is upon all nations, and his fury upon all their armies: he hath utterly destroyed them, he hath delivered them to the slaughter. Their slain also shall be cast out, and their stink shall come up out of their carcases, and the mountains shall be melted with their blood. . . . For it is the day of the LORD's vengeance, and the year of recompences for the controversy of Zion. . . . There shall the great owl make her nest, and lay, and hatch, and gather under her shadow: there shall the vultures also be gathered, every one with her mate.
>
> —Isaiah 34:1–3,8,15

As we have already learned from the books of Daniel and Revelation, the ten kings (nations) comprising the Revived Roman Empire submit all their authority to Antichrist, the new president of Planet Earth. In Revelation 13 we are informed that Antichrist will have complete authority over all nations, races, and languages. The only nation in the world to be released from Antichrist's power will be Jordan (Dan. 11:41). At the middle of the Tribulation period, an army from Europe, probably aided by forces from surrounding Islamic nations, will invade defenseless Israel. Jews who do not escape to Petra will be killed. Then the Antichrist ascends the Temple Mount and declares himself to be God. After the catastrophic judgments of the seven vials of the wrath of God, Antichrist gathers the armies of the world into Israel to challenge the return of Jesus Christ and the armies of Heaven. An army of 200 million marches in from the East, and the battle of Armageddon takes place, raging from Megiddo to Bozrah near Petra. The scriptures are not clear as to just who is fighting whom in this battle, but the intents and purposes of Antichrist's army is to prevent the Second Coming of Jesus Christ to establish His own Kingdom from Heaven over this world. In the Bible, there are many accounts of the coming battle of Armageddon, including the books of Ezekiel, Jeremiah, Joel, Daniel, and others. It is impossible to reference all these accounts, so we submit only Isaiah 34:1–6,8:

And I saw the beast, and the kings of the earth, and their armies, gathered together to make war against him that sat on the horse, and against his army. And the beast was taken, and with him the false prophet that wrought miracles before him, with which he deceived them that had received the mark of the beast, and them that worshipped his image. These both were cast alive into a lake of fire burning with brimstone.

—Revelation 19:19–20

> Come near, ye nations, to hear; and hearken, ye people: let the earth hear, and all that is therein; the world, and all things that come forth of it. For the indignation of the LORD is upon all nations, and his fury upon all their armies: he hath utterly destroyed them, he hath delivered them to the slaughter. Their slain also shall be cast out, and their stink shall come up out of their carcases, and the mountains shall be melted with their blood. And all the host of heaven shall be dissolved, and the heavens shall be rolled together as a scroll: and all their host shall fall down, as the leaf falleth off from the vine, and as a falling fig from the fig tree. For my sword shall be bathed in heaven: behold, it shall come down upon Idumea, and upon the people of my curse, to judgment. The sword of the LORD is filled with blood, it is made fat with fatness, and with the blood of lambs and goats, with the fat of the kidneys of rams: for the LORD hath a sacrifice in Bozrah, and a great slaughter in the land of Idumea. . . . For it is the day of the LORD's vengeance, and the year of recompences for the controversy of Zion.

At the victorious conclusion of the battle of Armageddon, the Antichrist and the False Prophet will be captured, and both will be consigned to the lake of fire. This is most unusual in that they do not stand before the Great White Throne Judgment; their eternal punishment has already been determined. Also, it could be that (as inferred in chapter thirteen) both of these super-demonic individuals may have come up out of perdition; therefore, they are returned to their place of eternal punishment.

And the remnant were slain with the sword of him that sat upon the horse, which sword proceeded out of his mouth: and all the fowls were filled with their flesh.

—Revelation 19:21

We are informed that Jesus Christ will put down all of man's institutions and authority. This judgmental process will be in progress during the Tribulation. The terminating act is when the remainder of Antichrist's army and world leaders who supported him are killed. As General Douglas McArthur stated in World War II, there is no substitute for victory. Compromising with evil only delays the ultimate solution.

With the destruction of the armies of Antichrist and the nations of the world, Jesus Christ brings the faithful Jewish remnant from Petra to establish His government and reign upon the throne of David for a thousand years. We know that the army from Heaven will include the warrior angels, but what about the church, meaning individual Christians that have been caught up before the Tribulation begins? The scriptures are somewhat ambiguous on this possibility. We are told that we will reign and rule with Jesus Christ, so we would assume that Christians in their glorified bodies will come back with Him. As far as fighting at the battle of Armageddon, in deference to conscientious objectors to capital punishment or military service, I defer to render an opinion. It seems that God has left this matter up to our own imagination and conclusions.

Chapter Twenty

The Millennium: "This Is the Day Which the Lord Hath Made"

> The LORD hath chastened me sore: but he hath not given me over unto death. Open to me the gates of righteousness: I will go into them, and I will praise the LORD: This gate of the LORD, into which the righteous shall enter. I will praise thee: for thou hast heard me, and art become my salvation. The stone which the builders refused is become the head stone of the corner. This is the LORD'S doing; it is marvellous in our eyes. This is the day which the LORD hath made; we will rejoice and be glad in it. Save now, I beseech thee, O LORD: O LORD, I beseech thee, send now prosperity. Blessed be he that cometh in the name of the LORD: we have blessed you out of the house of the LORD.
>
> —Psalm 118:18–26

One day with God is as a thousand years (Ps. 90; 2 Peter 3). Six times in this chapter of Revelation we are informed that Jesus Christ will reign with the saints on earth for one thousand years. This is that day referred to in Psalm 118. The Lord has chastened Israel now for almost two thousand years, because Israel at His first coming did not say, **". . . Blessed is he that cometh in the name of the Lord"** (Matt. 23:39).

Jeremiah prophesied that at the Lord's first coming Israel would be cast down because the nation would not know the time of the Messiah's visitation (Jer. 8:12; 10:15; 11; 23:12). However, Jeremiah wrote of the second coming of the Lord:

> Behold, the days come, saith the LORD, that I will raise unto David a righteous Branch, and a King shall reign and prosper, and shall execute

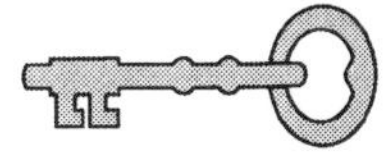

Key #29: How Long the Devil's Chain?

And I saw an angel come down from heaven, having the key of the bottomless pit and a great chain in his hand. And he laid hold on the dragon, that old serpent, which is the Devil, and Satan, and bound him a thousand years, And cast him into the bottomless pit, and shut him up, and set a seal upon him, that he should deceive the nations no more, till the thousand years should be fulfilled: and after that he must be loosed a little season.

—Revelation 20:1-3

> judgment and justice in the earth. In his days Judah shall be saved, and Israel shall dwell safely: and this is his name whereby he shall be called, THE LORD OUR RIGHTEOUSNESS.
>
> —Jeremiah 23:5–6

Even after two thousand years since the Messiah was born in Bethlehem, Judah is not saved and Israel certainly is not dwelling in their land safely. But that **day** for Israel must come when the people can be glad and rejoice. If it is not coming as some theologians protest, then we might as well delete two-thirds of the Old Testament. If that day is not coming, then God is a liar, and we know that God cannot lie (Heb. 6:18).

The contemporary, doctrinal views regarding the Millennium are:

1. **Premillennial.** World conditions will get worse and worse as Jesus and the prophets foretold. Jesus will return then at the end of the Tribulation to save the earth from those who are destroying it (Rev. 11), and establish His Kingdom on earth and rule from Jerusalem for one thousand years. Those Christians and/or churches that so understand eschatology are divided into five groups concerning the Rapture or Translation of the church:
   A. The church will be taken out of the world before the Tribulation begins (pre-Trib).
   B. Only those who are spiritually prepared will be raptured before the Tribulation begins (partial Rapture).
   C. The church will go through the first half of the Tribulation and then be raptured (mid-Trib).
   D. The church will be raptured just before the vials of God's wrath is poured out upon the earth (pre-Wrath).
   E. The entire church must go through the Tribulation (post-Trib).
2. **A-millennial.** Until Augustine (about A.D. 375), early church leaders without exception were premillennial in doctrine. With the Romanization of the church and Israel being nonexistent for over three hundred years with no evidence of ever returning to a national status, St. Augustine concluded the church had inherited all the promises of God and the Millennium actually began with the birth of Jesus Christ. There would be no future Millennium as the early church leaders understood. Most Protestant churches retain this interpretation of the Millennium, even though the first thousand years after the birth of Jesus has long ago expired, and even though Israel is once again a nation.
3. **Postmillennial.** This understanding of the Millennium is an adaptation of A-millennialism—not that we are really in the Millennium, but that the church must work to bring it into reality. This position on

the Millennium excludes Israel and the need for the Second Coming. Many of the postmillennial proponents today are "Dominion Now" expositors.

The reader needs to keep in mind that before A.D. 300, church leaders were premillennial in doctrine. It was Augustine and the Roman Catholic church after A.D. 300 that changed Christian understanding about the biblical position on the Second Coming. This was to exalt the pope and the theocratic state rather than Jesus Christ.

Eusebius (A.D. 120) said, ". . . there will be a millennium after the resurrection from the dead, when the personal reign of Christ will be established on the earth."

Justin Martyr (A.D. 160) said: "I and others who are right-minded Christians on all points are assured that there will be a resurrection of the dead, and a thousand years in Jerusalem, which will then be built. . . . For Isaiah spoke in this manner concerning this record of a thousand years."

Hippolytus (A.D. 205) said: "The Sabbath is the type and symbol of the future kingdom of the saints when they shall reign with Christ after He comes from heaven, as John says in his Revelation. For 'a day with the Lord is as a thousand years.'"

In a *Dictionary of Early Christian Beliefs* published by Hendrickson, there is an extensive section on the Millennium and the Second Coming, which references many other early Christian leaders on this subject. This 700-page book can be ordered from Southwest Radio Church, P.O. Box 100, Bethany, OK. 73008—$25.00 plus $5 shipping and handling.

Binding of Satan

After the battle of Armageddon and the casting of Antichrist and the False Prophet into the lake of fire, John sees an angel coming down from heaven with a key to the bottomless pit and a "great chain" in his hand. The angel binds Satan with the chain and casts him into the bottomless pit for a thousand years. Six things that happen to Satan:

1. The angel grabs Satan.
2. The angel binds Satan.
3. The angel casts Satan into the bottomless pit.
4. The angel shuts the door to the bottomless pit.
5. A thousand-year time lock is placed on the door.
6. After one thousand years the chain and lock will be removed.

The A-millennial people say that we are in the Millennium now and that Satan is bound. If so, then he must be on a very long chain. We are not told which angel binds Satan, but it could be Michael, as we read this archangel fights the devil (Rev. 12:7; Jude 9).

Before the Millennium begins, the devil is bound in the bottomless pit. Why? We read in Genesis 2:8 that before Adam and Eve sinned, God would communicate with them and the first man and woman would talk and walk with God. But after Adam and Eve sinned, they could only approach God through a Mediator. In the Millennium, it seems that God's relationship to men and women will be much the same as it was with Adam and Eve in the garden of Eden before the devil entered. Men and women will still have the capability to sin, but Satan and his demons will not be present to present temptations or accuse them before God. It will be a much more peaceful world; a world in which there is no war, or prisons. Man will not have the excuse, "The devil made me do it".

And I saw thrones, and they sat upon them, and judgment was given unto them: and I saw the souls of them that were beheaded for the witness of Jesus, and for the word of God, and which had not worshipped the beast, neither his image, neither had received his mark upon their foreheads, or in their hands; and they lived and reigned with Christ a thousand years.

—Revelation 20:4

Millennium Governance

We read in Daniel 12:11 that from the time the Antichrist commits the "abomination of desolation" until the Jews are regathered into the land will be 1,290 days. We are told in many other scriptures that from the time the Antichrist commits the abomination of desolation to the end of the Tribulation will be forty-two and one-half months, or 1,260 days, three and one-half Jewish years. Why the extra thirty days, or one Jewish month? Then, we read in verse twelve of Daniel 12: "Blessed is he that waiteth, and come to the thousand three hundred and five and thirty days."

The context of Daniel 12 does indicate the extra thirty days will be needed to get the Jews out of Petra and back into Israel, and perhaps to even move the Jews still alive in other nations to Israel. "For I will take you from among the heathen, and gather you out of all countries, and will bring you into your own land" (Ezek. 36:24).

Although we are not told exactly that this is why the thirty extra days are needed, it is implied. But about the other forty-five days? We simply are not told, but again it would seem reasonable that this time may be needed to establish the Kingdom government. Thrones, or positions of judicial and governmental authority, will be established. There are at present 192 nations in the world. Inasmuch as the Antichrist, the False Prophet, and their kings and rulers will be gone, there will be many positions to be filled.

The mother of James and John asked Jesus to give her two sons the favored positions in Christ's coming Kingdom, but Jesus deferred. However, He did promise the twelve apostles that they would sit upon twelve thrones in His Kingdom (Matt. 19:28). We also read in Daniel 7:22 that the "saints of the most High" will be given judgment in the Kingdom.

The resurrection of the Old Testament is associated with the coming of a Redeemer. Job declared:

> For I know that my redeemer liveth, and that he shall stand at the latter day upon the earth: And though after my skin worms destroy this body, yet in my flesh shall I see God: Whom I shall see for myself, and mine eyes shall behold, and not another. . . .
>
> —Job 19:25–27

Daniel placed the time of Israel's resurrection when ". . . there shall be a time of trouble, such as never was since there was a nation. . . ." Then the prophet said: ". . . many of them that sleep in the dust of the earth shall awake, some to everlasting life, and some to shame and everlasting contempt" (Dan. 12:1–2).

The resurrection of Israel is also placed at the last days when the Messiah would come in Isaiah 26 and Ezekiel 37. The lot of the Old Testament saints in resurrection is earthly. The lot of the church in resurrection is heavenly places or worlds in outer space. It has been suggested that when the number of the church reaches the number of angels who followed Satan and left their heavenly places, then the Rapture will occur. It is difficult to find a millennial, earthly promise to the church; however, Revelation 20:6 seems to include the church: "Blessed and holy is he that hath part in the first resurrection: on such the second death hath no power, but they shall be priests of God and of Christ, and shall reign with him a thousand years."

It is evident beyond dispute that the first resurrection includes first, Jesus Christ, then the church of the dispensation of grace, then the saved of the Tribulation period, then the Old Testament saints, and in that order. All the others who have lived and died since Adam will not be raised until the end of the Millennium. These are the lost dead. We read in Revelation 20:5, "But the rest of the dead lived not again until the thousand years were finished. . . ."

The Chief Judge of all nations during the Millennium will be Jesus Christ. We read in two scriptures in Revelation that Jesus Christ will rule all nations with a rod of iron (Rev. 12:5; Rev. 19:15). In Revelation 2:27, it is promised that overcomers will likewise rule the nations with a rod of iron, even as Jesus received this authority from God the Father. The overcomers apparently will be those during the Tribulation who were beheaded for claiming the blood of Jesus Christ for salvation and refusing to take the mark of the beast or worship the Antichrist as God. These will likewise rule with Jesus for the entire one thousand years. Beheading was a method of execution adopted by the ancients because it was terminal, and it was believed that beheading would separate soul and body forever, and there would be no resurrection. Revelation 20:4 proves this heathenish belief to be an error. Rome used two methods of execution: crucifixion for non-Romans, and beheading for Roman citizens. Jesus was crucified, but Paul, being a Roman citizen, was beheaded. Beheading remained the customary method of execution for nations which broke off the Roman Empire. The *Encyclopaedia Britannica* gives the records of crude machines with a weighted blade which dropped down upon the necks of prisoners severing heads from bodies. One of the oldest machines was called the "maiden" in Scotland. King Henry VIII liked to behead his wives to get rid of them. Beheading was used as a method of capital punishment in Germany, Italy, and other European countries.

On December 1, 1789, Dr. Guillotine, a member of the French Assembly, sponsored legislation that: ". . . in all cases of capital punishment it shall be same kind—that is, decapitation—and it shall be executed by means of a machine." This is how the beheading machine became known as the guillotine. Inasmuch as the empire of the Antichrist will be the Revived Roman Empire, it follows that beheading will be the method of execution. However, those who will be beheaded during the Tribulation will be raised in an immortal body and reign with Jesus Christ.

It is ironic that the guillotine was developed as an instrument of mercy, yet it will be used as an inhuman method of killing millions during the Tribulation.

Judgment of the Nations

We read the introduction to the prophetic discourse on the coming judgment of the nations in Matthew 25:31–33:

> When the Son of man shall come in his glory, and all the holy angels with him, then shall he sit upon the throne of his glory: And before him shall be gathered all nations: and he shall separate them one from another, as a shepherd divideth his sheep from the goats: And he shall set the sheep on his right hand, but the goats on the left.

All commentaries by scholars I have ever read put this event immediately after the battle of Armageddon. I think this interpretation is bad chronology. We read that when Jesus Christ returns He will sit, or rule, upon the throne of His glory. This will be the throne of David which the angels said He would sit upon at His birth. He will rule all nations with a rod of iron. The rules will be that the kings of nations come up to Jerusalem to worship Him. If there is disobedience, or if Egypt does not come up, upon those nations will no rain fall until they learn obedience. If any curse the Jews rather than bless them, these nations will be accursed. The rules for national obedience in the Millennium will be the beatitudes of Matthew 5. Those nations which are accounted righteous under the thousand-year reign of Jesus Christ will go into the New Heaven and the New Earth and, as we read in Matthew 25:46, receive "life eternal." The goat nations will appear at the Great White Throne Judgment.

During the Church age dispensation, nations or people that have pursued anti-Jewish programs and persecutions have suffered already. This will be even more specific in the Millennium when Israel truly becomes God's earthly people. To be granted "life eternal" on the basis of being kind to someone else, even the Jews, is not God's message to mankind for this age (Matt. 25:46), or a basis for judgment either at the Second Coming.

Citizens of the Kingdom

But the rest of the dead lived not again until the thousand years were finished. This is the first resurrection. Blessed and holy is he that hath part in the first resurrection: on such the second death hath no power, but they shall be priests of God and of Christ, and shall reign with him a thousand years.

—Revelation 20:5–6

Forty-two hundred years after the flood (A.D. 1830), earth's population had grown to one billion souls. Yet, from A.D. 1987 to A.D. 2000 (just thirteen years), earth's population increased by one billion, from five billion to six billion. This increase came in spite of all the contraceptive devices, abortions, and birth control programs. The more people on earth, the less time it takes to produce one billion human beings. Soon the increase will be one billion a year, then one billion a month, then one billion a day, then one billion every hour. The population exponential curve indicates this could happen within the next hundred years. In just my lifetime, earth's population has tripled.

If the Lord does not come in the next twenty years (by 2023), then there could be ten billion or more humans on earth. During the Tribulation, two-thirds to three-fourths of earth's population will not endure until the end. However, we read that the nations will go into the Millennium because Jesus Christ must rule over all nations. Those human beings who live through the Tribulation and go into the Millennium may live up to one thousand years. God told Adam that the day he ate of the tree of knowledge of good and evil, he would die. It can be said that Adam in suffering separation from God because of sin, died spiritually. Adam's sin also brought progressive physical death; and inasmuch as one day is with God as a thousand years, no man, even before the flood, lived a thousand years.

> But be ye glad and rejoice for ever in that which I create: for, behold, I create Jerusalem a rejoicing, and her people a joy. And I will rejoice in Jerusalem, and joy in my people: and the voice of weeping shall be no more heard in her, nor the voice of crying. There shall be no more thence an infant of days, nor an old man that hath not filled his days: for the child shall die an hundred years old; but the sinner being an hundred years old shall be accursed. And they shall build houses, and inhabit them; and they shall plant vineyards, and eat the fruit of them. They shall not build, and another inhabit; they shall not plant, and another eat: for as the days of a tree are the days of my people, and mine elect shall long enjoy the work

> of their hands. They shall not labour in vain, nor bring forth for trouble; for they are the seed of the blessed of the LORD, and their offspring with them. And it shall come to pass, that before they call, I will answer; and while they are yet speaking, I will hear. The wolf and the lamb shall feed together, and the lion shall eat straw like the bullock: and dust shall be the serpent's meat. They shall not hurt nor destroy in all my holy mountain, saith the LORD.
>
> —Isaiah 65:18–25

God cursed His original creation on earth because of sin:

1. When Adam and Eve sinned.
2. When Cain killed Abel.
3. At the time of the flood.
4. Divided the earth at Babel.

In the Millennium, the first three curses will be removed as the ecology and environment return to pre-flood conditions. This could be the result of the changed in the relation of the sun and moon to the earth that will occur in the Tribulation. In any event, as Peter said, if God promised it, then He knows how to do it (2 Pet. 2:9).

With the completion of the first resurrection at the beginning of the Millennium, the curse of sin on the creation on earth will be removed. Sin in the Millennium will be severely judged and limited. Capital punishment will be enforced according to the law (Ten Commandments).

> For I reckon that the sufferings of this present time are not worthy to be compared with the glory which shall be revealed in us. For the earnest expectation of the creature waiteth for the manifestation of the sons of God. For the creature was made subject to vanity, not willingly, but by reason of him who hath subjected the same in hope, Because the creature itself also shall be delivered from the bondage of corruption into the glorious liberty of the children of God. For we know that the whole creation groaneth and travaileth in pain together until now. And not only they, but ourselves also, which have the firstfruits of the Spirit, even we ourselves groan within ourselves, waiting for the adoption, to wit, the redemption of our body.
>
> —Romans 8:18–23

We are plainly informed by John that all who have part in the "first resurrection" will reign and rule with Jesus Christ for one thousand years. If the reader is a Christian, then that is YOU! The first resurrection includes Jesus

Christ; all Christians saved during the dispensation of grace; saved Israel; and Old Testament saints, which includes Job, Adam and Eve, etc.

The probability of people in the Millennium living next door to the saints in spiritual bodies raises some interesting questions. I am interested even in communicating with some of the Old Testament patriarchs or apostles.

> "Hey Abe! How about you and I beaming over to Pebble Beach for eighteen holes today?"
>
> "Sorry Noah. Sarah wants me to mow the lawn and dig a new well today."

Next I would go to Peter's house.

> "Hey Pete! How about you and I flying up to Vancouver today? I hear the salmon are running."
>
> "Sorry Noah. I've got to fix the hole in my mother-in-law's roof today."

Some who have written commentaries on Revelation believe that Christians in their resurrected bodies will be in the New Jerusalem which will be like a satellite above the earth. This opinion is difficult to prove. Nevertheless, I personally can hardly wait to find out what I will be doing in the Millennium. Whatever it will be, I am sure it will be exciting.

The account by John regarding the termination of the thousand-year reign of Jesus Christ encompasses the release of Satan from the bottomless pit for a little season. The Tribulation is referred to in Revelation 6:11 as a little season, so Satan is allowed only a few years at most to do his dirty work. Even after a thousand years of peace, plenty, and perfect government, man fails again for the second time. As the armies of the nations come to destroy Jerusalem and the camp of the saints, fire comes down from Heaven and destroys them all. Whether all the people on earth, not including the resurrected saints, are destroyed is not clear. From the account of the judgments of the nations in Matthew 25, it appears that only the goat nations will be annihilated, because the sheep nations are promised eternal life.

During the Millennium, according to Ezekiel 40–48, the tribes of Israel will again be divided and inhabit the land given them by God. There will be a huge Millennial Temple, which according to Zechariah 6, Jesus Christ Himself will build. The waters of the Dead Sea will become alive with fish from the Mediterranean Sea. According to Isaiah 35 and 65, anyone at the age of one hundred will be considered to be a youth and all illnesses, disease, and physical disabilities will be healed. But the lie of Satan is that God is just not giving man everything that he deserves, so when Satan is set free

And when the thousand years are expired, Satan shall be loosed out of his prison, And shall go out to deceive the nations which are in the four quarters of the earth, Gog and Magog, to gather them together to battle: the number of whom is as the sand of the sea. And they went up on the breadth of the earth, and compassed the camp of the saints about, and the beloved city: and fire came down from God out of heaven, and devoured them. And the devil that deceived them was cast into the lake of fire and brimstone, where the beast and the false prophet are, and shall be tormented day and night for ever and ever.

—Revelation 20:7-10

for a few months to test once more the free will of men, the human race makes the wrong choice once more.

Some Bible scholars link Gog and Magog of Revelation 20:8 with the same conspiracy in Ezekiel 38–39, but it cannot be the same event. After the battle of Ezekiel 38, Israel spends seven years cleaning the land. After the battle of Revelation 20:8, the earth is burned up. After the battle of Ezekiel 38, a remnant of the invading army is left. After the battle of Revelation 20:8, none are left. Gog and Magog have a limited number of allies in the battle of Ezekiel 38; in the battle of Revelation 20:8, Gog and Magog are joined by all nations. The center of Satan's rebellion is located in the race of Gog and Magog, and this seems to be the reason for the greatest anti-God conspiracy the world has ever experienced, which occurred within the Soviet Union in the last century.

Will man ever be satisfied with his own estate in life? Not in this present earth and social order. Nevertheless, beyond the Millennium lies another chance for mankind to live at peace with himself and with God.

The Great White Throne Judgment

And I saw a great white throne, and him that sat on it, from whose face the earth and the heaven fled away; and there was found no place for them. And I saw the dead, small and great, stand before God; and the books were opened: and another book was opened, which is the book of life: and the dead were judged out of those things which were written in the books, according to their works. And the sea gave up the dead which were in it; and death and hell delivered up the dead which were in them: and they were judged every man according to their works. And death and hell were cast into the lake of fire. This is the second death. And whosoever was not found written in the book of life was cast into the lake of fire.

—Revelation 20:11-15

With the final rebellion of mankind against God at the end of the Millennium, the earth and the heaven (meaning the first heaven, the atmosphere) disappeared. This event will not be simply a renovation of this present earth. The Scripture states without qualification that this earth will have served its purpose; it will not be in evidence. War against God, which is sin against God, contaminates. Rather than curse creation again, God makes a new planet, like the world was when Adam and Eve were first created.

Of God's everlasting covenant with Israel, Isaiah prophesied: "For as the new heavens and the new earth, which I will make, shall remain before me, saith the LORD, so shall your seed and your name remain" (Isa. 66:22).

The apostle Peter wrote of the destruction of this earth:

> But the day of the Lord will come as a thief in the night; in the which [in the thousand years] the heavens shall pass away with a great noise, and the elements shall melt with fervent heat, the earth also and the works that are therein shall be burned up. . . . Nevertheless we [the saved], according to his promise, look for new heavens and a new earth, wherein dwelleth righteousness.
>
> —2 Peter 3:10,13

How will this happen? We have to remember that Paul said the things which appear are made out of things which do not appear (Heb. 11:3). Scientists now say that everything in the universe came into being in an instant —from something, possibly no bigger than a basketball, in an instant. But the Bible says that all matter appeared as God spoke. God can also speak and everything will disappear. Atoms are seen only by their activity. If the shells were stripped from atoms, a million people could dance on the head of a pin.

A great white throne is set, called to order, and the earth and heavens fly away—disappear. Why? Because only that which is righteous can stand before this mighty, holy throne. Certainly, this earth is not clean from sin, and the heavens which have been defiled by the ungodly activity of Satan are not clean (Job 15:15).

All who were not raised in the first resurrection will be raised in the second resurrection to stand at the Great White Throne Judgment. I do not believe that anyone saved during the Millennium will stand at this judgment. Only sinners who have died during the thousand years will be raised to appear at this judgment. All the saved—the righteous of the Millennium—will be taken over this judgment into the New Heavens and the New Earth. So all those resurrected to stand in judgment at the Great White Throne will be the lost dead from Cain to the last rebellion. Christians will stand before the Judgment Seat (Bema) of Jesus Christ to receive a reward for their works, deeds, or service (1 Cor. 3; 2 Cor. 5:10). But nothing is said about any believer appearing before the Judgment Seat of Christ being cast into hell or the lake of fire. The opposite is true; though a Christian receives no reward, or loses his reward, he will be saved. That is the plain truth of Scripture. On the other hand, nothing is said about any appearing before the Great White Throne Judgment being saved—all are condemned.

The identity of the Great Judge at the White Throne is, of course, Jesus Christ as Daniel and John saw Him: awesome, powerful, omnipotent, holy. Only such a judge would be worthy to send a man to an eternal hell. We read in John 5:22 that God the Father judges no man, but He has committed all judgment to His Son.

Jesus said that if He was lifted up that He would draw all men unto Him. Daniel described the Great White Throne Judgment scene in these words:

> I beheld till the thrones were cast down, and the Ancient of days did sit, whose garment was white as snow, and the hair of his head like the pure wool: his throne was like the fiery flame, and his wheels as burning fire. A fiery stream issued and came forth from before him: thousand thousands ministered unto him, and ten thousand times ten thousand stood before him: the judgment was set, and the books were opened.
>
> —Daniel 7:9–10

We are informed in verse fifteen of Revelation 20 that the resurrected dead standing at the Great White Throne will be cast into the lake of fire because their names are not written in the Book of Life. So we must examine this Book of Life with the light of Scripture.

1. Some theologians believe that at conception, the name, or identity, of every person is written in the Book of Life. David wrote in Psalm 139:16 that in God's book, all his body members were written. Then, if that person dies without accepting God's way of salvation, his name is blotted out of the Book of Life. Moses pleaded with God in Exodus 32:31–33: "And Moses returned unto the LORD, and said, Oh, this people have sinned a great sin, and have made them gods of gold. Yet now, if thou wilt forgive their sin—; and if not, blot me, I pray thee, out of thy book which thou has written. And the LORD said unto Moses, Whosoever hath sinned against me, him will I blot out of my book." We know from Romans 3:23, ". . . all have sinned, and come short of the glory of God." From the Old Testament position, it would appear that all who die in their sins will be blotted out of the Book of Life.
2. From the New Testament doctrinal position of the church, the security of the believer, it appears that the Christian's name is irreversibly written in the Book of Life: "And I intreat thee also, true yokefellow, help those women which laboured with me in the gospel, with Clement also, and with other my fellowlabourers, whose names are in the book of life" (Phil. 4:3). "He that overcometh . . . I will not blot out his name out of the book of life . . ." (Rev. 3:5). According to the gospel, Christians have overcome the world through faith in Jesus Christ.
3. In the book of Revelation, we read of those whose names are not written in the Book of Life. "And all that dwell upon the earth shall worship him, whose names are not written in the book of life of the Lamb slain from the foundation of the world" (Rev. 13:8). ". . . And they that dwell on the earth shall wonder, whose names were not written in the book of life from the foundation of the world, when they behold the beast that was, and is not, and yet is" (Rev. 17:8).

It is also made clear from Revelation 21:27 that only those whose names are written in the Lamb's Book of Life will be allowed to inhabit the New Heavens or the New Earth. All others, the resurrected lost dead, will be suffering eternal agony in the lake of fire.

To reconcile the overall biblical teachings about the Book of Life is most difficult. There are some truths about the mysteries of God that will not be fully understood until Christians are given the answers in Heaven. As far as those mentioned in Revelation whose names were never written in the Book of Life, these are referred to as those who will worship the Antichrist as the true Christ. When the Lamb was slain for sin from the foundation of the world, these names were not even entered in His book. The foreknowledge of God is absolute, because He lives in eternity. Just as Christians are preordained from the foundation of the world to live eternally with Jesus Christ (Rom. 8:29–30), it appears that those who take the mark of the beast have been preordained to spend eternity with him in the lake of fire. This does not mean they are not included in "whosoever will," but it does mean these people will consciously, and of their own choice, worship Antichrist instead of Jesus Christ, and God knew from the foundation of the world that they would make this decision.

At the Great White Throne Judgment, there will be two sets of books. It could be that in the first set, the name of every person conceived is written, and the Great Judge checks the name in the first book and then checks to see if the name appears in the second book, the Book of Life. It is also possible that the first set of books contains a record of every sin committed by those standing before this final bar of judgment, because we read, ". . . the dead were judged out of those things which were written in the books, according to their works" (Rev. 20:12). How many sins does the average person commit in the average life span? A thousand, a million, a billion? How long will the lost suffer in the lake of fire for each sin committed? A thousand years, a million years, a billion years? All we know is that the torment will be eternal. And, will there be degrees of punishment in the lake of fire, just as there will be degrees of rewards in Heaven? The wording of Revelation 20:11–15 does seem to indicate such to be true.

Jesus said in Matthew 25:41 that hell was prepared for the devil and his angels, and in other scriptures it is revealed that hell was enlarged to receive men and women who would die in their sins. Hell is a confining place of torment until the Great White Throne Judgment. In Revelation 20:13, we read that at the last judgment, hell will deliver up the souls of the dead, and then, both death and hell will be cast into the lake of fire.

Paul wrote in 1 Corinthians 15:24–26: "Then cometh the end, when he shall have delivered up the kingdom to God, even the Father; when he shall have put down all rule and all authority and power. For he must reign, till he hath put all enemies under his feet. The last enemy that shall be destroyed is death."

There is a saying that death kills more people than anything else. But at the end of the Millennium at the Great White Throne Judgment, death will be destroyed by Jesus Christ. No person will ever have to worry about, or face, death anymore. The last enemy will be destroyed. In these days of high-pressure multimedia politics, the candidate promises everything possible—better housing, better schools, better jobs, better environment, better health, and even longer life. But one thing they cannot promise—no death.

Jesus Christ is the only One in the universe who can promise you that.

Beyond the Great White Throne Judgment lies an eternal, never-ending lake of fire. Is such a thing scientifically possible? Scientists now tell us that in the process of the law of entropy, stars nova, meaning that they exhaust the supply of hydrogen and the fusion atomic process goes out of control. The star (and our sun is a medium-sized star) gets hot and bright for seven to fourteen days, the atoms are stripped of their shells, and the entire mass is compressed into a small area where the gravity is so intense no light can escape. Isaiah, John, Jesus, and Joel described such an event for our sun. Astronomers call novas black holes. They are black; the hottest place in the universe, bottomless, and the semi-solid atomic pile could be classified as a lake. If our sun were to nova, all nine planets of our solar system, including the earth, would be sucked into its vortex. Whether such a black hole will be the lake of fire may be questionable; nevertheless, there will be an eternal lake of fire where the devil, the fallen angels, and all who die in their sins will be forever separated from God in eternal torment.

The only way to escape is to have their names written in the Lamb's Book of Life with the blood of Jesus Christ that can never be blotted out.

Chapter Twenty-One

The New Jerusalem

The roll of those who have received eternal life in the first resurrection is as follows:

1. The saved before the flood:
   a. Adam and Eve (probably)
   b. Righteous Abel
   c. The righteous of the lineage of Seth (Enoch for sure)
   d. Noah, and probably his wife, three sons, and their wives
2. The faithful of the patriarchal age:
   a. Job
   b. Abraham, Isaac, and probably Sarah and Rebekah
   c. Melchizedek, Jabez, and others of that time who acknowledged the God of Abraham
3. The saved of Israel:
   a. Jacob, his sons, and their descendants who lived and died in the promise of the coming Messiah
   b. The converts of John the Baptist who believed in Jesus Christ, the Messiah who had come
   c. The converts of the seventy disciples that Jesus sent preaching the gospel of the Kingdom
   d. The twelve apostles who were all Israelites (except Judas)
   e. Those who heard Jesus personally and received Him as the Messiah
4. The millions or billions in the Church age (dispensation of grace) who put their faith in Jesus Christ as God's only begotten Son who died for their sins
5. The saved of the Tribulation period:
   a. The 144,000 sealed Israelites
   b. The martyrs who refuse the mark of the beast and put their faith in Jesus Christ

And I saw a new heaven and a new earth: for the first heaven and the first earth were passed away; and there was no more sea. And I John saw the holy city, new Jerusalem, coming down from God out of heaven, prepared as a bride adorned for her husband. And I heard a great voice out of heaven saying, Behold, the tabernacle of God is with men, and he will dwell with them, and they shall be his people, and God himself shall be with them, and be their God. And God shall wipe away all tears from their eyes; and there shall be no more death, neither sorrow, nor crying, neither shall there be any more pain: for the former things are passed away. And he that sat upon the throne said, Behold, I make all things new. And he said unto me, Write: for these words are true and faithful.

—Revelation 21:1-5

Besides these of the first resurrection, there will also be the nations and peoples that are not deceived by Satan at the end of the Millennium (Matt. 25:31–34; Rev. 21:24). God's plan and purpose for mankind will be fulfilled. He will have His great and righteous assembly who will love and serve Him for eternity—not because they had to, but because they chose to of their own free will. This will be the crowning glory and honor of the Almighty Creator.

But where will God put all these billions of redeemed souls? In the New Heaven and the New Earth, of course. The Greek word for "new" in Revelation 21:1 is *kainos,* meaning "fresh, and newly made" (*Youngs*). Jesus said that in His Father's house were many mansions and that He had gone to prepare a place for us (the saved). This will be like moving into a new house, especially designed for the saved who will by then have new spiritual bodies. There will be no need for the sea in this new planet. Dr. Henry Morris in his book on Revelation believes that because we will have bodies that will not have blood we won't need water.

In many ways our earth is a beautiful place, but it has been marred by war, man's greed, and sin. The new heaven around the earth, and the earth, will be made new and perfect: "For as the new heavens and the new earth, which I will make, shall remain before me, saith the LORD, so shall your seed and your name remain" (Isa. 66:22). "And all the host of heaven shall be dissolved, and the heavens shall be rolled together as a scroll . . ." (Isa. 34:4).

I was interested recently in an article on the collapse of the universe that appeared in the *Dallas Morning News:*

> SEATTLE—By now most people have learned to ignore signs that say "the end is near."
>
> For one thing, such signs have been around forever, and the world still seems to be here. Besides, whenever the doomsayers are silly enough to forecast a specific date, it comes and goes with no noticeable devastation. Prophets of universal termination therefore have little credibility.
>
> Even among astronomers, the fear of an impending end of the whole universe has faded. Many used to think that the expanding universe was slowing down and would someday reverse direction and collapse on itself, ending all of existence in a big crunch. But the latest data from space show that the universe grows bigger at a faster and faster rate. It seems destined to expand forever.
>
> So everybody may freeze to death as the universe's energy dissipates, but the universe itself would remain in existence, cold, harsh and lifeless—not all that much different from the way things are today.
>
> It turns out, however, that such a view of the fate of the universe may

be too optimistic.

Whether the universe will really expand forever depends on what is making the expansion accelerate today, notes the Russian cosmologist Andrei Linde of Stanford University. All that scientists know for sure (well, they're pretty sure) is that a mysterious "dark energy" pervades space, exerting a repulsive force blowing space apart. Nobody knows exactly what that dark energy is.

It might be a rather simple form of energy that Einstein once suggested, permeating space with a constant strength everywhere and at all times. Such a "cosmological constant" would probably guarantee expansion forever.

But perhaps the dark energy is not so constant, or maybe the constant energy is accompanied by some other variety that alters the astronomical calculations.

Dr. Linde and his favorite collaborator, Renata Kallosh, have explored various theories of dark energy and reach a startling conclusion: In most plausible scenarios, the universe does *not* expand forever.

"In most of the cases, the universe is collapsing," Dr. Linde reported this month in Seattle at a meeting of the American Astronomical Society.

In fact, the universe might collapse any day now.

We live in the so-called scientific age. For the past one hundred years, man's knowledge has been doubling every two and one-half years. Scientists admit the universe and all living things demonstrate an "intelligent design," but they will not call it God. They can observe the powers of the universe and they call them the dark force and the light force, but they will not call the force God. They admit the incomprehensible complications of life, yet they call it evolution and not God. Considering the extremely difficult formulations that make even the life of a one-celled microbe possible, if there was only one blade of living grass in the universe it would be an unfathomable miracle. All the scientific minds in the world today have not been able to produce even a one-celled microbe. Why? Because Jesus said that He was the way, the truth and the LIFE. All things were created by Him and for Him.

As John observes the New Earth, he sees the New Jerusalem coming through the heavens. It appears the New Jerusalem will be a satellite around the New Earth. The New Jerusalem is called the bride because that is where the bride of Christ will live eternally. We call the church building the church, but the building is not the church; it is the Christians who go to that building to assemble and worship who are the church.

The New Jerusalem is also called the "tabernacle of God" and He will be like an eternal Father to all who inherit the New Earth in which there will be no one who suffers pain, sorrow, or death. This is the twenty-first time, or three times seven, that John hears a voice commanding him to

And he said unto me, It is done. I am Alpha and Omega, the beginning and the end. I will give unto him that is athirst of the fountain of the water of life freely. He that overcometh shall inherit all things; and I will be his God, and he shall be my son. But the fearful, and unbelieving, and the abominable, and murderers, and whoremongers, and sorcerers, and idolaters, and all liars, shall have their part in the lake which burneth with fire and brimstone: which is the second death.

—Revelation 21:6-8

write. The voice in effect says, "John, this may be difficult to believe, but go ahead and write it down anyway, because it is the truth. I will create a new heaven and earth where my eternal family will live without death, sorrow, and pain."

Some scientists say this universe is expanding and this earth will last forever; others say it could collapse at any time. Man simply cannot know, but we who are saved believe God. It will happen just as the infallible Word of God has foretold.

Once again in Revelation 21:6 Jesus identifies Himself as the first and last. What the Creator purposed in the beginning of the creation of the earth He has now finished. In making the Lord's reference to the "water of life" more meaningful to the reader, please pardon another personal example. If the reader, like myself, had been picking cotton on a very long row in one hundred-degree temperature and could not get water until reaching the end of the row, the relief provided by a cool drink is almost ecstatic. I remember also landing on New Caladonia in the South Pacific in World War II, and my unit had to march twenty-five miles, with full pack, in unbearable heat, limited to one canteen pint of water. The thirst we experienced was almost torturous. The woman of Samaria that Jesus met at the well was suffering from another kind of thirst, spiritual thirst. Most of us suffer from temptations of sin, guilt, worry, and fear. The spiritual waters that Jesus will give us in eternity will fill us with such glorious life that we will never again thirst for those things that depreciate or defeat us.

In verse seven the overcomers in the New Heaven and New Earth, all who have overcome sin and death through faith in Jesus Christ, will inherit all things as a member of God's family:

1. ". . . heir of the world . . . through the righteousness of faith" (Rom. 4:13).
2. ". . . we are the children of God: And if children, then heirs; heirs of God, and joint-heirs with Christ . . ." (Rom. 8:16–17).
3. "And if ye be Christ's, then are ye Abraham's seed, and heirs according to the promise" (Gal. 3:29).
4. "That being justified by his grace, we should be made heirs according to the hope of eternal life" (Titus 3:7).
5. ". . . Hath not God chosen the poor of this world rich in faith, and heirs of the kingdom which he hath promised to them that love him?" (Jam. 2:5).
6. "Are they [angels] not all ministering spirits, sent forth to minister for them who shall be heirs of salvation?" (Heb. 1:14).
7. ". . . being heirs together of the grace of life; that your prayers be not hindered" (1 Pet. 3:7).

In verse eight Jesus tells John that in the New Heaven and New Earth there are not going to be any ungodly people around, ever, because they will all be in hell. No one in the New Heaven or New Earth will ever lie to you, cheat you, defame you, assault you, insult you, or try to kill you. You can walk the streets of the New Jerusalem for a million years-plus without a worry or even a red traffic light.

The City of God

In another vision John is taken to the very top of a high mountain where he saw the New Jerusalem descending from Heaven. We are not told which high mountain. It could be Mount Moriah, Mount Everest, or another planet in our solar system. The New Jerusalem is again referred to as the Lamb's bride because that is to be the place He has prepared for her.

Some commentaries take these verses back into the Millennium and see the New Jerusalem as a satellite of the earth during the Lord's thousand-year reign on earth. While we cannot be dogmatic, the chronology to me indicates the New Jerusalem will be an eternal satellite of the New Earth. An alternate explanation is that the New Jerusalem could be present in the Millennium and then continue on until the earth is created new.

The New Jerusalem will be a cube city, 12,000 furlongs on each side. One furlong at the time of the writing of the Revelation was between 600 feet and 607 feet, making each side approximately 1,380 miles. Most commentaries round the size off at 1,500 miles horizontal and perpendicular. John describes the city as having twelve foundations (sections), with about one hundred miles between each section. One level would be approximately one million square miles; twelve levels would be about 12,000 million square miles. One section will be about one-half the size of the United States.

Nebuchadnezzar attempted to make Babylon a counterfeit Jerusalem. Babylon was only fifteen miles square, and the hanging gardens barely got off the ground, only a few hundred feet.

If we estimate that the New Jerusalem will be populated at the rate of one thousand per square mile, there will be room for twelve billion. Cities today have a greater rate of population per square mile. But even if we cut the population rate down to one hundred per square miles there would still be a total of 1.2 billion residents, about the present population of China in 2003. The earth's population in 2003 is six billion, but how many people have lived and died since the flood? I do not have time to try to figure this one out, but if a reader would like to take a stab at it, let me know.

We read in John's account of the New Jerusalem that each of the twelve levels will be made out of a different precious gem. The gems that were on the high priest's breastplate were:

And there came unto me one of the seven angels which had the seven vials full of the seven last plagues, and talked with me, saying, Come hither, I will shew thee the bride, the Lamb's wife. And he carried me away in the spirit to a great and high mountain, and shewed me that great city, the holy Jerusalem, descending out of heaven from God, Having the glory of God: and her light was like unto a stone most precious, even like a jasper stone, clear as crystal; And had a wall great and high, and had twelve gates, and at the gates twelve angels, and names written thereon, which are the names of the twelve tribes of the children of Israel: On the east three gates; on the north three gates; on the south three gates; and on the west three gates. And the wall of the city had twelve foundations, and in them the names of the twelve apostles of the Lamb. And he that talked with me had a golden reed to measure the city, and the gates thereof, and the wall thereof. And the city lieth foursquare, and the length is as large as the breadth: and he measured the city with the reed, twelve thousand furlongs. The length and the breadth and the height of it are equal. And he measured the wall thereof, an hundred and forty and four cubits, according to the measure of a man, that is, of the angel. And the building of the wall of it was of jasper: and the city was pure gold, like unto clear glass. And the foundations of the wall of the city were garnished with all manner of precious stones. The first foundation was jasper; the second, sapphire; the third, a chalcedony; the fourth, an emerald.

—Revelation 21:9-19

The fifth, sardonyx; the sixth, sardius; the seventh, chrysolite; the eighth, beryl; the ninth, a topaz; the tenth, a chrysoprasus; the eleventh, a jacinth; the twelfth, an amethyst. And the twelve gates were twelve pearls; every several gate was of one pearl: and the street of the city was pure gold, as it were transparent glass.

—Revelation 21:20–21

Sardius	Ligure	Topaz
Agate	Carbuncle	Amethyst
Emerald	Beryl	Sapphire
Onyx	Diamond	Jasper

The precious gems that make the foundations of the New Jerusalem are:

Jasper	Chrysolite	Sapphire
Beryl	Chalcedony	Topaz
Emerald	Chrysoprasus	Sardonyx
Jacinth	Sardius	Amethyst

If the reader will check, he or she will discover that five of the precious stones on the high priest's breastplate are not a foundational stone in the New Jerusalem. However, some of the stones in the Hebrew are the same stones in the Greek by a different name. Ladies' diamonds by any other name would be just as valuable. For example, we read of the "agate" that its name is also "chalcedony."

The one stone that was on the high priest's breastplate that I had difficulty finding as a New Jerusalem foundation stone is the diamond. If the reader will check an encyclopedia, or a jeweler's book on precious stones, he or she will discover that the diamond is a metal, the hardest metal found in the universe. It is 100 percent carbon. Light entering a diamond is broken up into its various rainbow colors and reflected upward. A good Ph.D. dissertation would be a presentation on the foundation stones of the New Jerusalem. Israel is perhaps the chief owner and market of diamonds. I could say that perhaps the reason that diamonds are absent in the composition of the twelve levels of the New Jerusalem is that the Jews are going to try to keep them—but I wouldn't say that, so I won't.

On the subject of precious stones, it is also interesting to compare birthstones to the stones on the breastplate and the foundation stones in the New Jerusalem:

January	Garnet
February	Amethyst
March	Blood Stone
April	Diamond
May	Emerald
June	Pearl or Alexandrite
July	Ruby
August	Peridot
September	Sapphire

October	Opal
November	Topaz
December	Turquoise

Most of these stones are the same stones in both categories. One interpretation of the Book of Life is that every person's name is written in this book when born, but the names of the lost will be blotted out. Someone has suggested, probably me, that the saved who will live in the New Jerusalem will be assigned to a level that corresponds with their birthstone. But again, I would not say this, so I won't.

There will be twelve gates to the New Jerusalem, three gates on each side. Whether there will be twelve gates at each level, or only the bottom level is not clear. But the names on the gates will be the twelve sons of Jacob: Reuben, Judah, Levi, Joseph, Benjamin, Dan, Simeon, Issachar, Zebulon, Gad, Asher, and Nephtali (Ezek. 48:31–34).

Ezekiel gives the size of the New Jerusalem as 4,500 measures on each side, or a total of 18,000 measures. There were many kinds of biblical linear measurements: stadia, furlong, etc. Another measurement was the distance, or land surface, a team of oxen could plow in a day. I have plowed with horses and mules, but no oxen. Therefore, my estimate of Ezekiel's 18,000 measures would be only a guess, but based on the actual size of the New Jerusalem, a measure would be 1,666 feet.

The gates to the city will be pearl. The obvious question would be, where is the oyster that produced the pearl? But with God, nothing is impossible.

The names of the twelve apostles will be on the twelve foundations. It is obvious that Judas' name will not be on the foundation. We would assume that the twelfth apostle will be Matthias (Acts 1:26), or the apostle Paul.

I have been to Jerusalem some forty-five times, and each time I find my visit to this place where Jesus ministered and died more exciting. Regardless how many times I go or how long I stay, I am always looking forward to returning. This longing will be forever satisfied when we take up permanent residence in the most beautiful, exciting, glorious city in the universe. The most exciting blessing about going to the New Jerusalem is that the Lord Jesus Christ will be there, ". . . and so shall we ever be with the Lord" (1 Thess. 4:17).

Being a Jew, John would have obviously looked for a temple in the New Jerusalem, but there was no temple. God—Father, Son, and Holy Spirit—were there; therefore, there was no temple. The temple was a physical icon which portrayed God. The candlestick manifested the glory of God that would light the New Jerusalem for eternity. The table of shewbread spoke of the bread of life that would come down from Heaven with eternal life.

And I saw no temple therein: for the Lord God Almighty and the Lamb are the temple of it. And the city had no need of the sun, neither of the moon, to shine in it: for the glory of God did lighten it, and the Lamb is the light thereof.

—Revelation 21:22-23

And the nations of them which are saved shall walk in the light of it: and the kings of the earth do bring their glory and honour into it. And the gates of it shall not be shut at all by day: for there shall be no night there. And they shall bring the glory and honour of the nations into it. And there shall in no wise enter into it any thing that defileth, neither whatsoever worketh abomination, or maketh a lie: but they which are written in the Lamb's book of life.

—Revelation 21:24-27

The laver of cleansing spoke of the washing away of our own sins in the blood of God's Son. The altar of sacrifice looked forward to the sacrifice for sin to be offered by Jesus Christ.

We live in a time when every homeowner, almost without exception, locks their doors in the daytime as well as night. This is a manifestation of sin and terrorism in the world. In the New Jerusalem the gates will never be shut because there will be no one there who will lie, cheat, steal, rob, or murder.

The riches of this world will be so common in the New Jerusalem there will be no reason to steal. Besides the foundations being made of precious gems, the streets will be pure gold. Quoting from the *Encyclopaedia Britannica:*

> In the finely divided state the color of gold is variable, depending upon the size of the particles. The usual color of precipitated gold is brown, but black, purple, blue, and pink shades are known. In a very thin sheet or leaf, gold is translucent and transmits a greenish light. When pure, it is the most malleable and ductile of all metals; it can be beaten to not more than 0.00001 mm. in thickness, and a single gram has been drawn into a wire two miles long.

I have been to Bangkok several times. One-third of Bangkok is Buddhist temples. Every temple is plated with gold leaf and has to be refurbished every fifty years. But the New Jerusalem will never have to be refurbished; the pure gold will last forever. Only pure gold is translucent and the glory of God will shine right through it.

We read in Revelation 21:24 that the "nations of them which are saved shall walk in the light of it." There will be a New Heaven, a New Earth, and a New Jerusalem. Will there be nations on earth? Will the nations that remain faithful to God in the Millennium inherit the New Earth?

The Book of Revelation reveals to us the things we need to know concerning the future. It does not necessarily reveal everything we want to know. But the unrevealed mystery of the future is what makes life more interesting, and as the hymn goes, "we will understand it better by and by."

Chapter Twenty-Two

It Is Finished

And he shewed me a pure river of water of life, clear as crystal, proceeding out of the throne of God and of the Lamb. In the midst of the street of it, and on either side of the river, was there the tree of life, which bare twelve manner of fruits, and yielded her fruit every month: and the leaves of the tree were for the healing of the nations.

—Revelation 22:1-2

Jesus Christ said of sinful, suffering humanity in John 10:10,28, " . . . I am come that they might have life, and that they might have it more abundantly. . . . I give unto them eternal life; and they shall never perish, neither shall any man pluck them out of my hand."

On the cross, when Jesus Christ took the place of every sinner who would place his or her sins on Him by faith, past, present, or future, He cried, ". . . It is finished . . ." (John 19:30). The apostle who recorded these final three words of Jesus gives us in this final chapter in the Bible the abundant life that Jesus Christ made possible to everyone who accepts God's grace through faith in Him. On the cross, Jesus finished the redemption for man that He was sent to accomplish. When we believed on Jesus Christ and were born again into God's family, we possessed the abundance of salvation. However, only when we stand on the streets of the New Jerusalem and behold the beautiful river flowing from the throne of God will we understand the abundance of the abundant life He promised. In the New Jerusalem in the New Heaven and New Earth the abundance of life is emphasized: the river of life and the tree of life will be there.

I will not attempt to describe the river that will flow from the throne of God, or try to explain if this will be H_2O water or spiritual waters. There are some heavenly truths that are impossible to approach with earthly language. The pronoun "it" in Revelation 22:2 refers back to the New Jerusalem at the end of Revelation 21.

On either side of the river of life John sees the "tree of life." Adam and Eve were banned from the garden of Eden because of God's concerns that they would eat of it in their sinful condition and live forever. All who enter the New Jerusalem will have eternal life, so why the tree of life? I will answer that question when we get there, but I would assume it is a special blessing and one of the surprises that the Lord has in store for those who love Him.

It appears there will not be just one tree, but many because they are on both sides of the river of life. And, we may be somewhat puzzled by John's statement that the leaves will be for healing. Before the flood, man ate only vegetation and fruit. The evolutionists claim that every living thing evolved through a process of selection and survival. But why would an apple tree grow beautiful and delicious apples just to cover a few apple seeds? The same would be true of the orange, the peach, the tomato, and the watermelon. What about the banana? Why would a banana tree produce a banana when the banana itself has no reproduction function whatsoever? In the New Jerusalem, the trees of life will grow twelve different kinds of fruit in a year.

I remember when I was young back in the 1920s that when one of us kids would get sick, my mother would go out and dig up some roots or get some leaves off of bushes. She knew exactly what kind of herb or tree to go to for medicine. Recently, I began to have a problem with gout. Gout is extremely painful. At the office a co-worker checked on the Internet and the cure recommended was to eat black cherries. My wife Kim got several cans of black cherries, and I discovered that if I would eat a few cherries every few days, my gout would leave and not bother me anymore. At my annual checkup my doctor inquired about my health, and I told him about my gout; but I assured him it was no problem now that I was eating a few black cherries. He was surprised. He said he never heard of such a thing and wanted to prescribe for me an expensive drug. Aspirin and other medicines do come from herbs, trees, or forms of vegetation; but in recent years the medical profession has turned more to chemicals and biomedicines.

We read in Proverbs 3:18 that wisdom is a "tree of life" and in Proverbs 11:30 that righteousness is like a "tree of life." Whether the "tree of life" in Revelation 22 is symbolic, or whether it will be real fruit-bearing trees, I leave up to the reader. But confidentially, I opt for it being a real tree.

And there shall be no more curse: but the throne of God and of the Lamb shall be in it; and his servants shall serve him: And they shall see his face; and his name shall be in their foreheads. And there shall be no night there; and they need no candle, neither light of the sun; for the Lord God giveth them light: and they shall reign for ever and ever.

—Revelation 22:3–5

As noted previously in this study of Revelation, God brought a curse upon the earth four different times because of sin. But in the New Heaven and the New Earth there will be no curse upon the new creation because there will be no sin or sinner. The Greek word for servant is *doulos*, which is also interpreted as slave. One of the questions that most Christians have concerning going to Heaven is, what will we do there? Are we just going to sit around in the shade of a palm tree and play our harps? There is a huge universe with billions of miles of space and billions of solar systems. Service can either be work or a blessing. We will do whatever Jesus Christ tells us to do. It will indeed be service with a smile.

The apostle John wrote in his gospel, John 1:18, "No man hath seen God at any time; the only begotten Son, which is in the bosom of the Father, he hath declared him." Here in Revelation 22:4 we are informed that

God's servants shall see His face. There are many verses in Revelation where John goes back and references a point he made in his gospel. This is another reason why I believe that the same John wrote both books and the three epistles. No man born of Adam, a sinner, could look upon God without being burned up. But in the resurrection, we will indeed see God in all His glory. In service to God, we will be as a servant or slave, but in our relationship to the angels and the unlimited solar systems, we will be as kings and priests.

And he said unto me, These sayings are faithful and true: and the Lord God of the holy prophets sent his angel to shew unto his servants the things which must shortly be done. Behold, I come quickly: blessed is he that keepeth the sayings of the prophecy of this book. And I John saw these things, and heard them. And when I had heard and seen, I fell down to worship before the feet of the angel which shewed me these things. Then saith he unto me, See thou do it not: for I am thy fellowservant, and of thy brethren the prophets, and of them which keep the sayings of this book: worship God.

—Revelation 22:6–9

John was apparently overwhelmed by what he saw, but the angel assured him that what he saw was true, because the same God that revealed to Daniel, Ezekiel, Jeremiah, and the other prophets what would happen in the end of the age, is the same God who revealed to the apostle the Apocalypse. In the Revelation the total prophetic scope of eschatology revealed to the prophets in the Old Testament is simply put into one book in a comprehensive presentation. As Peter wrote in verse twenty-one of the first chapter of his second epistle, "For the prophecy came not in old time by the will of man: but holy men of God spake as they were moved by the Holy Ghost."

As noted in many scriptures in the Revelation, the warning is given, "Behold, I come quickly." The Greek wording means that when the events of Revelation begin to occur they will happen in quick succession. John again attempts to fall down and worship the angel, but the angel protests that he too is just a servant of the Lord like John, so direct worship to God. Paul warned in Colossians 2:18, "Let no man beguile you of your reward in a voluntary humility and worshipping of angels. . . ." In other words, Christians are not to humble themselves to angels nor worship angels. There are some false cults today disguised as Christians who teach that Jesus was an angel or that angels have power over Christians. Paul warned that to fall into such a deception could result in losing your reward.

And he saith unto me, Seal not the sayings of the prophecy of this book: for the time is at hand. He that is unjust, let him be unjust still: and he which is filthy, let him be filthy still: and he that is righteous, let him be righteous still: and he that is holy, let him be holy still. And, behold, I come quickly; and my reward is with me, to give every man according as his work shall be. I am Alpha and Omega, the beginning and the end, the first and the last.

—Revelation 22:10–13

Daniel was commanded to seal the prophecies of his book until the time of the end. The reason that Daniel was to be sealed is that the prophecies of that are to be understood progressively and historically. The book of Revelation is not to be understood historically, even though the preterists and some others have the prophecies of Revelation being fulfilled over the past two thousand years. In verse eleven there is a warning to repent and be saved by faith in Jesus Christ, because He will come quickly and those who are unholy and morally filthy will not have time to repent. The spiritual status of the world's millions at the time the Lord returns will determine their eternal destiny. He will separate the tares and the wheat, and His reward will either be a blessing or a curse. We read in Daniel 12:2, "And many of them that sleep in the dust of the earth shall awake, some to everlasting life, and some to shame and everlasting contempt."

Blessed are they that do his commandments, that they may have right to the tree of life, and may enter in through the gates into the city. For without are dogs, and sorcerers, and whoremongers, and murderers, and idolaters, and whosoever loveth and maketh a lie. I Jesus have sent mine angel to testify unto you these things in the churches. I am the root and the offspring of David, and the bright and morning star. And the Spirit and the bride say, Come. And let him that heareth say, Come. And let him that is athirst come. And whosoever will, let him take the water of life freely.

—Revelation 22:14-17

We now come to the seventh beatitude, or seventh blessing promised in this book:

1. "BLESSED is he that readeth, and they that hear the words of this prophecy, and keep those things which are written therein: for the time is at hand" (Rev. 1:3).
2. " . . . BLESSED are the dead which die in the Lord . . ." (Rev. 14:13).
3. ". . . BLESSED is he that watcheth, and keepeth his garments . . ." (Rev. 16:15).
4. ". . . BLESSED are they which are called unto the marriage supper of the Lamb . . ." (Rev. 19:9).
5. "BLESSED and holy is he that hath part in the first resurrection . . ." (Rev. 20:6).
6. ". . . BLESSED is he that keepeth the sayings of the prophecy of this book" (Rev. 22:7).
7. "BLESSED are they that do his commandments . . ." (Rev. 22:14).

Jesus admonished His disciples in the upper room, "If ye love me, keep my commandments" (John 14:15). Here again John references something the Lord said that he recorded in his gospel. Keeping the Lord's commandment is for Christians, not for the unsaved. As pointed out in verse fifteen, those who have died in their sins are outside the New Jerusalem. Keeping the Lord's commandments is a matter of rewards, not salvation. Keeping the Lord's commandments is a demonstration of continuing love for Jesus Christ. Keeping the Lord's commandments will result, among other things, in the role of the Christian and his or her position in the New Jerusalem. The greatest commandment is to love the Lord our God with all our mind, soul, and heart. The second greatest commandment is to love our neighbor as ourselves. If Christians can keep just these two commandments, they can fulfill the Ten Commandments in spirit.

Verses fourteen and fifteen of this closing chapter are to again assure the Christians that in the New Creation there will be no one who bring corruptions and disorder through sin. How would the reader like to live in a world where he or she could believe everything they read or were told; never have to lock their doors; never be concerned about someone entering and stealing or assaulting them? Finally, there will be a perfect world, but it will be Jesus Christ, not man, who will make it possible.

In verse sixteen, John is informed that the Revelation is to be taught in the churches. This is the first time the church has been mentioned in the Revelation since the twenty-second verse of chapter three. The Greek word for church is *ekklesia,* which means "that or those who are called out." We read in Acts 15:14–16,

> Simeon hath declared how God at the first did visit the Gentiles, to take out of them a people for his name. And to this agree the words of the prophets; as it is written, After this I will return, and will build again the tabernacle of David, which is fallen down; and I will build again the ruins thereof, and will set it up.

After chapter three of Revelation the church is not mentioned because it is called out of the world in chapter four. It is not in the world during the Tribulation. It is not evidenced in the world during the Millennium, although as the bride of Christ, it is assumed the church will reign and rule with the Lord. In verse sixteen of Revelation 22, Jesus is again referred to as the root of David, because after the Church age, Jesus will return and establish the throne of David once more.

The invitation to make your eternal home in the New Jerusalem that will be the capital city of the New Earth is given to every person alive on this present earth by the Holy Spirit and the bride, which we understand to be the church.

Many may doubt there is going to be a New Jerusalem where sinners who have been born again into God's family will live forever. But what if there really is a New Jerusalem that will come down from God out of Heaven?

I have been to the ziggurat of Ur. Nearby is the architecturally perfect tomb of an ancient queen who ruled from 2050 B.C., or before. She was buried with her chariots, servants, and jewels in the expectation of a future life. In ancient Egypt, the dead were buried in a fetal position, expecting a resurrection. The pyramids of Egypt were built by the pharaohs as gateways to the heavens in the life beyond. I have been to the Ming tombs and the Ching tombs in China, ornate and extensive tombs for the emperors and empresses of these dynasties. I have been to Karnak, the most extensive network of tombs in the world, then crossed over the Nile River to the unbelievable architectural wonder of the tomb of Hatshepsut, built by her lover. Around the mountain lies the Valley of the Kings, tombs of other Egyptian royalty where their mummies were laid to await the afterlife. I have seen the bodies of Lenin and Mao Tse-tung, lying in vacuum glass coffins; Flanders Field where the fallen of World War I were buried; and Arlington Cemetery, dotted with hundreds of thousands of crosses, and witnessed the amazing changing of the guards. I have been to Ephesus, Pergamos, Patmos, Petra, and dozens of other places familiar in ancient history, and viewed the thousands of sumptuous and decorative tombs prepared especially for the dead. I have stood upon the Mount of Olives and beheld the tombs of the prophets and the thousands of tombs and graves that cover the western slope, down through the Garden of Gethsemane, through the Kidron Valley, right up to the Golden Gate. Those in centuries past have buried their dead on Mount Olivet, because the Bible promises that the Messiah will one day stand upon this mountain and the dead will be brought up out of these graves and tombs in a resurrected body.

All these tombs and graves testify to the undeniable fact that as far back as the history of the human race can be traced, man has always believed that there was a life, a future, beyond death. There has been something in the nature, instinct, and mind of men and women that there is a resurrection.

It is the message of the church and the calling of the Holy Spirit to receive eternal life by faith in Jesus Christ.

For I testify unto every man that heareth the words of the prophecy of this book, If any man shall add unto these things, God shall add unto him the plagues that are written in this book: And if any man shall take away from the words of the book of this prophecy, God shall take away his part out of the book of life, and out of the holy city, and from the things which are written in this book. He which testifieth these things saith, Surely I come quickly. Amen. Even so, come, Lord Jesus. The grace of our Lord Jesus Christ be with you all. Amen.

—Revelation 22:18-21

As we consider the last few verses in the Revelation, the reader is again reminded that this is not the Revelation of John nor the Revelation of the Angels. This book is THE REVELATION OF JESUS CHRIST. Jesus Christ Himself issues the warning that not one of His words is to be deleted from this book; not a word is to be added. Not only is this true of Revelation, it is true of every book in the Bible. Moses by inspiration of God wrote: "Ye shall not add unto the word which I command you, neither shall ye diminish ought from it . . ." (Deut. 4:2).

Over and over Ezekiel wrote: "And the word of the LORD came unto me, saying" (Ezek. 38:1).

Paul wrote: "All scripture is given by inspiration of God . . ." (2 Tim. 3:16).

Every one of the sixty-six books in the Bible in some way claims to be a unique revelation from God. The Bible in all its comprehensive revelation has been proven to be the very Word of God. It has stood the test of time for two thousand years. The Authorized Version has been blessed of the Lord and stood as a proven witness of God's infallible Word since 1611. Yet today, so-called contemporary Bible publishers and translators have departed from the literal translation of the Textus Receptus and Masoretic texts to use dynamic equivalency, leaving out entire verses, converting masculine names and pronouns to gender-neutral words which change even some of the prophecies which relate to the last days. This too is the fulfillment of an end-time prophecy—men denying the Word of God and admiring teachers who will tickle their ears with vain repetitions.

In Revelation 22:20 Jesus warns, "Surely I come quickly." As we have noted before, we cannot know the day nor the hour, but as He said, we can know that His coming is near, EVEN AT THE DOORS (Matt. 24:33).

What are some of the signs of His soon coming:

1. The increase of knowledge—doubling every two and one-half years.
2. The increase of communications making possible the fulfillment of many prophecies noted in this study.

3. Israel a nation again as prophesied.
4. Miracle victories of Israel over overwhelming odds (Zech. 12).
5. The rise of world anti-Semitism (Zech. 14).
6. The rise of the Revived Roman Empire in the form of the European Union (Dan. 9).
7. Rise of pandemic epidemics like AIDS (Matt. 24).
8. Increase of earthquakes (Matt. 24).
9. Wars on a world scale (Matt. 24).
10. Rise of world terrorism—days of Noah (Matt. 24).
11. Rise of homosexuality—days of Lot (Matt. 24).
12. International significance of a forthcoming peace treaty with Israel (Dan. 9:27).
13. The prominence of the United States (Isa. 18).
14. The rise of Israel's ancient enemies: Egypt, Syria, Libya, Iraq (Babylon), Persia (Iran).
15. The wars of 1991 and 2003 against Iraq (Babylon) (Isa. 13:1–6).
16. Man's development of nuclear weapons (many biblical prophecies relating to Tribulation judgments and the Lord destroying those who would destroy the earth (Rev. 11).
17. Universal peace efforts, but no peace (1 Thess. 5:3).
18. The United Nations, world government (Rev. 13:7).
19. Great increase in population (Gen. 6:1). From the birth of Jesus Christ to A.D. 1830, world population increased to one billion. From 1987 to 2000, world population increased one billion (just thirteen years). Soon it will be one billion a year, one billion a month, etc.
20. At Babel there was a tower; in New York City there were two towers (Isa. 30:25; Zeph. 1:16).
21. The denial of the majority of pastors, ministers, and theologians that Jesus is coming back (2 Pet. 3:1–5).

EVEN SO—COME, LORD JESUS—SO BE IT!

Other Books by Dr. Noah Hutchings

Rapture and Resurrection
Dispensational overview of life after death

25 Messianic Signs in Israel Today
Contemporary fulfillment of prophecies about Israel

Daniel the Prophet
Verse-by-verse commentary on Daniel

The Great Pyramid: Prophecy in Stone
Mysteries about this ancient monument in Egypt

Petra in History and Prophecy
The cave city in Jordan where Israel will escape from the Antichrist

God the Master Mathematician
Mathematical designs in scripture and nature that prove a Creator

The New Creators
What the Bible says about genetic engineering and cloning

Romance of Romans
Verse-by-verse commentary on Romans

God Divided the Nations
Why God separated the human race into nations

The Persian Gulf Crisis
How Iraq fits into the end-time prophetic scenario

Where Leads the Road to Kosovo?
The disturbing precedent set by direct U.S. intervention

U.S. in Prophecy
Where and why the U.S. is referenced in prophecy

As It Is in the Days of Noah
An autobiography of the life and times of Noah Hutchings

Marginal Mysteries
Biblical information about such things as UFOs, the Bermuda Triangle, etc.

Why So Many Churches?
A dispensational appraisal of the Kingdom gospel verses the gospel of grace

About the Artist

Phan S'bong is the artist who drew the cover picture for this book, as well as many other books published by Southwest Radio Church and Hearthstone Publishing. Phan is a refugee from the Killing Fields in Cambodia. He came to the United States in 1981. He and his wife have four children and reside in their home in Oklahoma City. They attend church in Edmond, Oklahoma. Phan has no formal art training. His talents are a natural gift from God.